List of Drawings

WITH OUR BACKS TO
BERLIN

THE GERMAN ARMY IN RETREAT 1945

TONY LE TISSIER

SUTTON PUBLISHING

This book was first published in 2001 by
Sutton Publishing Limited · Phoenix Mill
Stroud · Gloucestershire · GL5 2BU

This paperback edition first published in 2005

British Library Cataloguing in Publication Data
A catalogue record for this book is available from the British
Library.

ISBN 0 7509 3751 3

Typeset in 10/12pt Iowan.
Typesetting and origination by
Sutton Publishing Limited.
Printed and bound in Great Britain by
J.H. Haynes & Co. Ltd, Sparkford.

Contents

Introduction

Leafing through the material I have accumulated from over twenty years of studying the Second World War Berlin battlefield scene, much of it 'feedback' from the German editions of my books, *The Battle of Berlin 1945* and *Zhukov at the Oder*, I came across so many interesting, hitherto unpublished pieces that I decided to bring some of them together here as a collection of short stories.

These heroic, often poignant accounts of the desperate, last-ditch defence of the Fatherland should not be taken in any way as an apology for the German cause. It is precisely because one so seldom hears their side of the story, that they deserve a wider readership. They are mainly told by former members of the Wehrmacht and even the dreaded Waffen-SS, some of them still surviving. Perhaps surprisingly, the stories are characterised by the same individual human warmth and soldiers' humour as you might normally expect from the 'good guys' – the GIs, British and Commonwealth infantry and armoured brigades, who had to contend with a surprising degree of resistance before ending the war in Europe. The lesson, I suppose, is that we are all pretty much alike, under the uniform.

With Allied forces – and, above all, the avenging Red Army of the Soviet Union – closing in on all sides; with their communications, fuel supplies and heavy industries under constant air attack, it is noteworthy that the German armed forces managed to maintain such an effective resistance. One has only to recall General Eisenhower's decision not to attack Berlin after his forces had reached the line of the River Elbe, because of the anticipated 100,000 further casualties this might cost him. Field kitchens still operated. Dispatch riders still got through. Transfer orders were carried out. Drill parades were still held, even under the Russian shellfire. Eventually, as in W.B. Yeats's famous line, 'Things fall apart, the centre cannot hold' . . . and the rout began. But the patriotic determination of the individual German soldier to defend his Fatherland with skill and discipline even at the cost of his life was never in question. Author Christabel Bielenberg summarised the situation neatly in *The Road Ahead*:

Germany had nothing to be proud of during Hitler's reign, but there were two outstanding exceptions. Firstly, the courage and tenacity of her soldiers when, inadequately equipped, they ultimately found themselves defending this country against the whole world. Secondly, the 20 July plot, when those who had taken part so nearly succeeded in ridding their country of a monster who had ruled over them for eleven years and who claimed their lives when they failed.

Only one of these stories covers the fighting on the Western front, where the US 94th Infantry Division had to breach the Siegfried Line in the severest of winter conditions, the infantry units suffering up to 500 per cent casualties. Despite bitter hand-to-hand combat, there was much mutual respect, as the stories about General Patton's handling of the surrender of 11th Panzer Division and the snatching of the famous Vienna Riding Academy's Lippizaner horses from under the noses of the Russians are included to show. (It is interesting to note that in the part of Germany that lies between the Moselle and Saar rivers, the Americans are still regarded as the 'Liberators' . . .)

In 'The Siege of Klessin', which I compiled mainly from the regiment's surviving radio 'logs' and the unit's after-action report, one gets a vivid impression of the combat: the extraordinary heroism of the frontline troops, trapped in their positions, unable to retreat – and the basic futility of their military task, as 'Corporal' Hitler played out his doomed role of the 'Greatest Field Commander of All Time' . . . .

In the late Horst Zobel's account of the tank battle for the bridge at Golzow, a small armoured unit with a hopeless mission pits its exceptional fighting skills against Zhukov's seemingly limitless Soviet armoured forces. Erich Wittor describes an encounter with history and a Stuka ace at Kunnersdorf, and returns later with a longer account of the confused action at Marxdorf. Harry Schweizer recalls his experiences as a schoolboy anti-aircraft gunner posted to the Berlin Zoo flak-tower; and how, briefly, he got a taste of tank-busting with the SS. Gerhard Tillery gives us a rifleman's account of the fighting in the Oderbruch, the retreat across Berlin and the eventual breakout of servicemen and civilians to the West. Karl-Hermann Tams describes the defence of Seelow, with a motley platoon of sailors and soldiers (who suffered over 90 per cent casualties) cowering under the greatest artillery bombardment in history. Rudi Averdieck, then a regimental radio sergeant, describes the harrowing retreat from Seelow to Berlin, and how he became involved with a newly-organised armoured brigade that had only one mission, to surrender to the Americans.

Quite properly, there are two Jokers in the pack. One is an account by Harry Zvi Glaser, a Latvian Jew who joined the Red Army and tells of his experiences at Halbe, where the remnants of the German 9th Army and its accompanying refugees suffered over 40,000 killed. (Harry, who became a US citizen, did not receive his medal until it was presented to him by President Yeltsin on a visit to the White House in 1995!) Finally, there is the insubordinate SS Sergeant Major Willy Rogmann, a born survivor (and the shortest man in his regiment) who, having 'done his bit' for Führer and Fatherland in some of the toughest theatres of the war, found himself leading an unlikely team of combatants through the ruins of Berlin, armed with a British Sten-gun (they didn't jam, like the German Schmeissers).

These exciting 'true tales' beg the ultimate question: what might we have done, With our Backs to London, or even Washington?

A H Le T
Frome, Somerset
January 2001

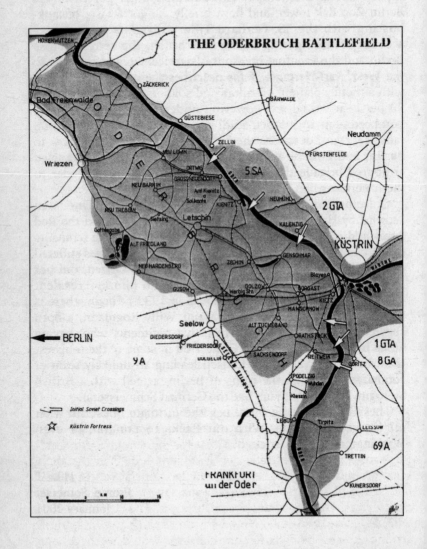

THE ODERBRUCH BATTLEFIELD

HOHENWUTZEN

ZÄCKERICK

Bad Freienwalde

GÜSTEBIESE

BÄRWALDE

ZELLIN

Neudamm

FÜRSTENFELDE

NEU LEWIN

5 SA

Wriezen

ORTWIG

GROSS-NEUENDORF

NEU BARNIM

Am Kienitz

NEUMÜHL

2 GTA

Solikante

NEU TREBBIN

KIENITZ

Letschin

Sietzing

KALENZIG

KÜSTRIN

Gottesgabe

ALT FRIEDLAND

GENSCHMAR

WARTHE

NEU HARDENBERG

ZECHIN

Blayen

GOLZOW

GUSOW

Warbig Stn

BORGAST

KIETZ

MANSCHNOW

← BERLIN

Seelow

ALT TUCHEBAND

DIEDERSDORF

RATHSTOCK

1 GTA

FRIEDERSDORF

REITWEIN

8 GA

DOLGELIN

SACHSENDORF

GÖRITZ

9 A

PODELZIG

Wuhden

Klessin

Initial Soviet Crossings

LEBUS

Tirpitz

LEISSOW

Küstrin Fortress

TRETTIN

69 A

FRANKFURT
an der Oder

KUNERSDORF

0   5   10   15
km

ONE

In the Steps of Frederick the Great

ERICH WITTOR

In 1945 Erich Wittor was a 20-year-old second lieutenant of three months' standing, leading a squadron in the Armoured Reconnaissance Battalion 'Kurmark', commanded by Major Freiherr von Albedyll, only son of the squire of Klessin (see The Siege of Klessin*). The Panzergrenadier Division 'Kurmark', to which his unit belonged, had yet to be fully formed on the basis of the Panzergrenadier Replacement Brigade of the famous Division 'Grossdeutschland'. This brigade had been sent forward from Frankfurt under Colonel Willy Langkeit a few days earlier to try and help plug the gap caused by the collapse of the German 9th Army on the Vistula, and was now itself trapped immediately east of Kunersdorf. Marshal Zhukov's troops, here elements of the 1st Guards Tank and 69th Armies, were rushing forward to close up to the Oder River, hoping to secure bridgeheads on the west bank before the ice melted.*

On 1 February 1945, I received orders to take Kunersdorf, a village directly east of Frankfurt an der Oder. This was the Kunersdorf where Frederick the Great fought a battle against the Russians and the Austrians on 12 August 1759. On the very same ground the cavalry regiments under General von Seydlitz[1] had attacked and the dead-tired Prussian infantry advanced against vastly superior numbers of Russians. The battle was lost with immense casualties. Now we were standing on historical ground, having to fight for our country. Would we have any better luck?

1

I drove out from Frankfurt an der Oder with eight to ten armoured personnel carriers (APCs). The enemy situation was unknown. All that was known was that the Replacement Brigade 'Grossdeutschland' was trapped in the Reppiner Forest northeast of Kunersdorf and was making desperate attempts to break out. We had to try and force a passage through to the west.

As we got close, I saw that fighting was taking place in Kunersdorf. We reached the edge of the village, where we stopped and I went forward to reconnoitre. I worked my way forward as far as the centre of the village, which was still held by our infantry, the eastern part being occupied by the Russians. T-34s and anti-tank guns were firing down the main street and Russian infantry were occupying the houses and gardens. An attack on our part could not have been successful and would only have led to severe casualties. I had my men dismount under covering fire from the APCs. The Russians were then unable to make any further headway.

While running across the street I ran straight into a burst of fire from the Russians and was scorched by a tracer bullet on my leg. We tried to drive the Russians out of the eastern part of Kunersdorf with shock troops but, after gaining thirty to fifty metres, we had to give up. The enemy forces were too strong and were far from idle: we had to keep on our toes throughout the night to avoid being surprised.

A new day began. Our comrades were still unable to break out of their encirclement. Our forces were too weak to break through the Russian ring. Then, towards midday, I was ordered to hand over my positions to some SS-grenadiers and to take the village of Trettin, about four kilometres north of Kunersdorf. The relief came, hand-over and briefing were soon completed and I got my men to mount up and drive off.

We drove continuously through the potentially dangerous terrain with all necessary care, having to reckon with enemy intervention at any moment, crawling unseen through the dips and hollows to Trettin. We reached to within a thousand metres of the village, from which we were concealed by a low hill. Trettin was already occupied by the enemy. We could see several enemy tanks. Although they were partly covered positions, we could still make them out. We did not know how strong the enemy was. What were we to do?

To attack across the open ground to the edge of the village in our lightly armoured vehicles would be suicidal, and to go round by a flank impossible. We had no artillery at our disposal and there were certainly still some civilians in the village. How could we take Trettin under these circumstances? It was a damnable situation, but a soldier has to have luck.

Suddenly we heard aircraft approaching. 'Stukas!' I shouted, 'Get out the identification panels!' We did not want to be attacked by our own aircraft.

They flew at medium height over us and banked round over Trettin. The village was flown over once more and then, with the next flight, we witnessed a unique display with deadly results for the enemy. From medium height the first machine flipped over on its wings and dived down with an ear-splitting noise. Was it the rush of air, or a switched on siren, or both?

The dive was aimed straight at the village, the pilot only pulling up again just short of the roof tops. One would have thought he would crash into the houses, he was so close. Shortly before pulling up again, he fired a single shot from his cannon, but the result was devastating.

A stab of flame shot up like an explosion and black smoke rose up into the sky between the houses. 'He's got a T-34!' we cried, for we were quite certain. Meanwhile the other two aircraft had done the same, diving and firing their cannon, and two more Soviet tanks were on fire.

Once they had climbed up again, they banked round once more and dived down on Trettin. The T-34s stood no chance against this attack from the air. They were not camouflaged from above and insufficiently armoured, and so could be destroyed one after the other by our Stukas. We were particularly impressed by the accuracy of the leading aircraft, which only fired one shot each time and each time scored a hit. Our delight was indescribable. Meanwhile the Stukas had destroyed eight or nine enemy tanks. Just think what they would have done to us if we had attacked twenty minutes earlier?

After their last attack the Stukas flew over us waggling their wings. That was the signal that they had finished their job and now it was up to us.

During the air attack we had been joined by a company of panzergrenadiers led by a dashing young second lieutenant. Now we attacked together, he taking the left of the road and ourselves the right, and we charged into the village. The Russian infantry had not fully regained their senses, having been completely demoralised by the loss of their tanks. We broke into the village firing on all sides, and had an easy job of it, the Russians losing many dead and prisoners. Some of them, however, managed to reach the safety of a prominent patch of woodland. I had only one wounded among my men, and that just a graze on his back. The grenadiers immediately took up defensive positions and we went into attack reserve.

After a dangerous night in reconnaissance behind enemy lines and an even luckier return to my own troops, I discovered several days later how the success in Trettin had been made possible. It was due to the famous Luftwaffe Colonel Rudel, bearer of the highest German decorations for bravery.[2]

That same day the 'Grossdeutschland' managed to break out, and we had done our bit towards it.

Erich Wittor's story continues in Marxdorf (p. 110).

1 This was an ancestor of the General Walter von Seydlitz-Kurzbach captured at Stalingrad, who became Chairman of the 'Bund Deutscher Offiziere' (League of German Officers) and Vice-President of the 'Nationalkomitee Freies Deutschland' (National Committee for a Free Germany), giving rise to the term 'Seydlitz-Truppen' given by the Nazis to those German prisoners of war who did propaganda work and even fought with the Red Army against the Wehrmacht, although he totally disassociated himself from those activities and was later exonerated by a West German court after the war.

2 Hans-Ulrich Rudel specialised in tank-busting with cannon-equipped Stukas, often working at turret-height and was credited with 519 Soviet tanks destroyed and 800 damaged, as well as the sinking of a cruiser and the severe damaging of a battleship. He was to lose a leg in action that same month and was treated at the Zoo Flak-tower hospital in Berlin.

TWO

The Last Defender of Schloss Thorn

ERNST HENKEL

I met Ernst Henkel while conducting a tour for veterans of the 94th US Infantry Division, when we visited Schloss Thorn as guests of Baron von Hobe-Gelting in September 1999. He had previously published this article, which I have translated with his permission, in the magazine Kameraden *and later wrote another short one about our encounter.*

The 94th Infantry Division had previously been employed in blockading the remaining German garrisons on the Atlantic coast of Britanny, so its first real combat experience came when it began deploying in front of the Orscholz Switch of the Siegfried Line on the 7th January 1945 (see diagram on next page). The Switch, built in the late 1930s, protected the base of the triangle formed by the Saar and Moselle Rivers and terminated on its western end at Schloss Thorn, opposite previously neutral Luxembourg. The German defences consisted of 'dragons' teeth', barbed wire and minefields backed by concrete pill boxes. This was one of the coldest winters of the century, the snow was deep, and the terrain high and exposed to the winds. The weather and the defenders, soon to be reinforced by the 11th Panzer Division (see The Surrender of the 'Phantom' Division) *exacted a heavy toll from the Americans, casualties being as high as 500 per cent in the rifle companies, where replacements tended to be killed before they had a chance to learn the ropes.*

By the time Ernst Henkel's division arrived, the Americans had secured the western end of the Orscholz Switch. The day it finally fell, the Americans were engaged in a major operation to clear the high ridge dominating the Switch from east of Sinz.

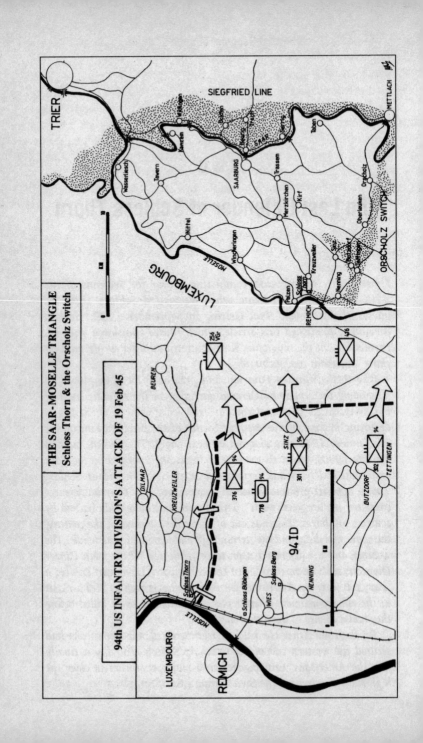

THE SAAR-MOSELLE TRIANGLE
Schloss Thorn & the Orscholz Switch

94th US INFANTRY DIVISION'S ATTACK OF 19 Feb 45

Towards the end of January, beginning of February 1945, the 256th Volksgrenadier Infantry Division, and with it Regiment 481 to which I belonged, was pulled out of the northern Vosges Mountains. We were all glad to be able to leave that sector. Four weeks of hard infantry combat in the snow and cold lay behind us.

Partly by rail and partly on foot over the Hunsrück Highroad, we reached Irsch, where I met a member of the 11th Panzer Division that we were relieving. The 11th Panzer were required elsewhere urgently. When I replied in some amazement to his query as to how many tanks we had with 'none at all', he laughed out aloud. 'Have fun,' he called behind him as he made off, 'you will never be able to hold on to the sector without tanks!'[1]

The sector in question was the so-called Orscholz-Switch, a section of the Siegfried Line between the Moselle and the Saar, that had been fought over for months. It got its name from the little place of Orscholz lying directly opposite the Saar Loop.

From Irsch we marched by night, as one could only march by night because of ground-attack aircraft, down the steep mountain road and across the Saar into Saarburg. Our platoon found accommodation in a building at the entrance to the town nearest the river, where an old man was still holding out, although Saarburg was supposed to have been evacuated. This was the last time we got a skinful.

On the evening of the next day we continued our march. The front was not very far off now with the lightning flashes of guns firing, exploding shells and the usual sounds of the front line. Here and there a fire glowed in the night. At dawn we came to an abandoned, half-destroyed farm. The enemy was firing at night on the roads and crossroads. After the previous day's drinking bout and the long march, we threw ourselves down anywhere and slept.

Next evening we moved on again. Smoking was strictly forbidden. Toward morning we came upon a well spread-out, destroyed village called Kreuzweiler, where we split up among the cellars. There were big wine cellars with massive, vaulted ceilings. There were also numerous wine casks of various sizes, but all were empty. Our predecessors had made a good job of it. As I later discovered, Kreuzweiler had changed hands several times, as the state of the village showed. My platoon spent the night in a big wine cellar where a guesthouse stands today.

We were a mortar platoon equipped with 80mm mortars. I was the platoon range-finder and so ended up a maid of all work, mainly, however, as a forward observer. I found myself a really good sleeping place in the cellar, sharing a worn-out sofa with two other soldiers. As I was dropping off to sleep, I heard two officers talking and my name was mentioned. I pricked up my ears and discovered that I was to go to Schloss Thorn as a forward observer with Staff Sergeant Witt. I nearly had a fit. Witt was about forty years old, a professional musician who had been conscripted into a Luftwaffe orchestra and gained the rank of staff sergeant with it. Then at the end of September 1944 the orchestra was disbanded and Witt was transferred to combat duty. I had never then or since come across anyone who lived in such a constant state of panic as Staff Sergeant Witt. His escapades in Holland and Haganau were known throughout the division, but that is another story.

From Kreuzweiler a narrow road twisted down toward the valley, made an almost ninety degree turn to the left, then about 150 m further on another similar turn to the right, then went straight on again to meet the road alongside the Moselle (today the B 419). In the angle formed by these bends lay Schloss Thorn, an imposing rectangular building, now, however, totally destroyed. It was not surprising, as this had been the front line for almost five weeks. The road leading from the valley had a small stream running parallel to it on the right that had cut down to about four metres at the deepest part, thickly overgrown but dried out at the moment. The light reverse slope, relatively good cover and road close by, ensured our ammunition resupply.

Several days later two enemy ground-attack aircraft made a low-level attack on Kreuzweiler and strafed our fire position as they flew off. They had apparently not seen our fire position as such, only some soldiers running around. However, we thought that we had been discovered and moved further to the right, where a track led to a small gully nicely concealed by a copse. There our mortars were to perform magnificently.

Neither Witt nor I had anything to do with the first fire position nor the change over to the new one, as we were by this

8

time already in Schloss Thorn. We followed the road to the first sharp turn to the left, where we turned to the right and came across two half-destroyed buildings. We went through a hole in the wall to the right again and along past a long, destroyed building to a big arched gateway (without the gates) through which we came to the castle's inner courtyard. As the whole area was strongly mined, we had to keep strictly within the denoted paths. As I said, it was a rectangular building with one side to the south and another to the west overlooking the Moselle. There were the remains of a thick tower, the top half of it shot away, and a long connecting building to a more slender tower, still intact, from where I was later to do my observing.

There were also two big cellars, the first used as a toilet, the second, reached by a flight of steps, served as accommodation for about fifteen soldiers. From the latter a passage led to another, smaller cellar, where Witt and I made our home. It had a small stove, for which our predecessors had knocked a hole through the ceiling. There was an artillery forward observer in the big cellar and a heavy machine gun team. The forward observer had two radio operators with him, through whom he had radio contact with his battery. From the big cellar a narrow flight of steps led to a platform with an arrow-slit-like view of the road leading down to the Moselle, and then a few more steps to the long corridor on the ground floor, from which one entered a big corner room with views to the south and to the west over the Moselle to Luxembourg.

We received almost exclusively only cold rations, occasionally also meat, which we had to cook ourselves, about which no one knew anything except Witt. He was an exceptional cook but, because of his permanent anxiety, had no appetite. I still remember him making a delicate goulash, which I stirred endlessly. Normally a cook would be pleased when others praise the food he has prepared, but not Witt. He even once called me a hog.

I spent a lot of time in the narrow tower, from where I had a good view of the destroyed bridge leading across to Remich. There was a small customs house on the German side with an American forward observer in it. When they changed men over, they would have to run about 50m across open ground, which they always did flat out. But my narrow tower required a special skill in climbing it. The spiral staircase leading up had long narrow windows on the enemy side under which one had to crawl on one's belly, or the Americans would see you and immediately open fire, something which would set Staff Sergeant Witt off into a panic.

For me it was like a holiday. The hard weeks in the Vosges Mountains with deep snow, icy temperatures and hard fighting in the woods, were forgotten. Here at Schloss Thorn we had shellproof accommodation, thanks to the vaulted cellars, and adequate rations. We did no sentry duties, as that was for the infantry, their heavy machine gun being in the big corner room covering the bridge and Nennig. I often chatted with the machine gunners. The No. 1 was a Sergeant Flinn (or Flint), the No. 2 a little chap with the Iron Cross First Class. Our mortar target area 'Anton' lay close behind the ridge beyond the road, in what was dead ground for me. My attempts at getting Witt to bring the target area directly on to the road were brusquely rejected.

There were also some incidents. Once an American reconnaissance aircraft, similar to our Fieseler Storch, circled over us and Kreuzweiler. We opened a ferocious fire on him and the lad hastily turned away and was not seen again. Now and then a couple of ground-attack aircraft would come back and strafe Kreuzweiler. Pulling up again they had to pass over Schloss Thorn, and we fired with everything we had. Staff Sergeant Witt threw a fit, saying that we should not provoke them, or the Americans would reply with their heavy artillery. However, nobody took any notice of him any more.

But there was an even better incident to come. One night two men from the Propaganda Company were brought to us, who naturally wanted to see some action. So the infantry had to creep through the rubble with grim expressions and weapons at the ready, jump up and lie down again, and occasionally fire a few bursts with their assault rifles. The shots had to be taken all over again, because one or other of them had grinned at the wrong moment. One of the Propaganda Company men also wanted to film a mortar bomb exploding in no-man's land, so we climbed up the narrow tower, I going on all fours as usual but not noticing that the Propaganda Company man was walking upright. I gave the order for a salvo on 'Anton' and the hits were easily visible in the foreground. The cameramen filmed eagerly away, even turning the cameras on me, but then I heard the incoming fire; 'Quickly down below! There's going to be a row!' I shouted, and we slipped down the spiral staircase, not a moment too soon, as some heavy shells landed on us. The propaganda men enjoyed their stay and that night were led back again through the minefields.

It must have been about 15 February that we had an experience with bad consequences. An extra heavy machine gun fired across from the Luxembourg side on Kreuzweiler and strafed the battalion command post. The battalion commander ordered us tersely to engage the machine gun immediately. Engaging a machine gun with mortars when it is firing from behind cover is almost impossible, apart from which the 80 mm mortar is intended for open spaces, with pin-point firing practically an impossibility. But orders are orders. If one drew a straight line from the crossroads in Kreuzweiler right past Schloss Thorn into Luxembourg, that would give the approximate location of the machine gun. I climbed the tower, taking the usual precautions. Staff Sergeant Witt remained below. My fire order was: '60 degrees less, down 200, key mortar one shot!' The fire position reported: 'Fired!' I heard the explosion but did not see it. I reported this to Witt, who exploded with anger and swore at our mortar crews. I repeated my fire order with one degree change and this time I saw the hit, which was on the slope of the Moselle, almost in dead ground. Now it was simple. Again: '15 degrees less, down 300, fire two salvoes!' The hits occurred either on the buildings or on their roofs. Marvellous! The machine gun stopped firing.

I reported to the fire position: 'Situation fine, cease firing!' Peace returned, but only for a moment, for the battalion commander had heard everything. We all depended on a single line, sometimes the whole regiment, as signal wire was in such short supply. The captain called Witt everything under the sun and, as the worst punishment, transferred him to the infantry. As he was being relieved of his post, the relief would take place that night. Witt asked me to escort him through the minefields that evening. He was a broken man. I was sorry for him. Although our relationship had not always been of the best, there was still a comradely bond between us. We shook hands on the road to Kreuzweiler for the last time and wished each other luck. He was convinced that he was going to his death, but in fact he was to survive, although, yet again, that is another story.

The relief was Sergeant Schultz. He was in his mid-forties, an East Prussian, a reserved type, but a good comrade. We were on 'du' terms, having survived the severe fighting in Holland, Hagenau and in the Vosges together. He had had a very sketchy education because of what had happened in East Prussia after the First World War, and his reading and writing were at best indifferent; a map was a complete mystery to him. As before, I left all these things to me. He was even more withdrawn than usual, as he knew what the Russians were doing to the unarmed civilians in East Prussia.

From 18 February onwards things began to happen. We could hear the artillery fire from the Saar to our left going on nearly all day, easing up a little at night and resuming fully on the 19th. Something was happening there, and although it was quiet where we were, we were on high alert. Shortly after dusk a sentry reported sounds of movement on the street leading from the Moselle. We peered out into the night from the big corner room. Things were certainly moving down there. Our heavy machine gun fired two belts into the gully, the noise stopped and it was quiet once more. I could not give any fire orders as the flashes from the firing mortars would have given their location away.

We went back into the big cellar. Shortly afterwards a runner appeared with orders for the heavy machine gun and the remainder of the infantry to go back to Kreuzweiler. Behind remained Schultz and myself, the artillery forward observer with his two signallers, and another two or three men, apparently signals fault finders. We stayed quiet. Outside it was exceptionally quiet.

I woke at dawn on 20 February to unusual sounds. I went through the small stairwell up to the big corner room, from where we had the best view of the gully and the road leading up from the Moselle. I leaned out of the window with a stick grenade. I caught my breath. The little road was buzzing with activity. American infantry, with the occasional Jeep, were making their way up. I hurried back to the cellar. A corporal from a section of infantry occupying a cellar outside our yard burst in from the inner courtyard, grabbed an assault rifle and left the cellar again by the outside steps. I told them in the cellar what was happening and slipped back up again. In the castle courtyard, seen at close range from the landing, an American tank drove in with a man on the back behind a heavy machine gun or quick-firing cannon. He was not being heroic, just damn' stupid. Only the fact that I had left my rifle in the cellar saved his life. So back to the cellar, grab my rifle and back up again, but the tank had gone.

Even today, after several post-war visits to the castle, I still cannot understand how it got in and then vanished again. It could not have come in through the arched gateway, as it was too narrow. But through the gateway I could see a Sherman tank with its gun pointing toward us. I turned round again, crossed the corridor and went down the narrow steps, stopping at the intermediate landing. Through the arrow-slit I had a good view of the road and the hilly ground beyond. American infantry were coming through a narrow gap in this hilly ground and jumping down on to the roadway. That was what we had heard the night before. Sheltered by the hills, the Americans had dug a communications trench parallel to the Moselle river bank road and made the last cutting during the night.

The first steep difference in height had to be covered with a two-metre jump down, the remaining four or six metres by sliding down as best they could. Strangely enough, the GIs were not even looking at the castle, where their enemy was. They saw their problem as being that first jump. Without hesitation, I set my sights at 100m and took aim at the first one. He looked down, jumped, and I squeezed the trigger. Hit as he jumped, he bent his knees and slid on his stomach down to the roadway, where he lay still. I reloaded and already the next candidate was preparing to jump. He was a small, fat chap. I squeezed the trigger and he slid down on top of his comrade. A third man had already appeared. The game was repeated; he jumped and I fired. Now some medical orderlies appeared. At the same time a Jeep drove up the road and an officer in the front passenger seat started giving instructions with many gestures. From the white stripe on his helmet I could see that he was a Lieutenant. After my shot he slumped forward and slid down. Because of the medical orderlies that attended to him straight away, I held my fire. Apart from this, I could hear the crunch of footsteps from outside. If the Americans were already there and one of them threw a hand grenade through the arrow-slit, that would be my lot. Despite these thoughts, I still tried to bring a machine gun into position, but the slit was too narrow. I could not set up the bipod properly, nor could I lean forward into it enough to take the recoil. My attempt failed miserably. The recoil ripped into my right shoulder and the machine gun fell clattering to the ground. Now I had had enough. I went down to the cellar, where the lads looked at me questioningly. I gave a brief account and concluded: 'We are sitting like rats in a trap!'

The artillery forward observer told me that he had ordered fire on our own position. I do not know whether we as forward observers for the mortars gave a similar order with Verey lights. It is unlikely, for the fire position must have been experiencing the same as ourselves. Schloss Thorn was being raked by our own weapons, and there was also heavy fire on the American infantry advancing on Kreuzweiler.

After a short discussion we decided to give ourselves up, otherwise we would be smoked out. One of us would have to go outside. Nobody wanted to be the one to go, but the lads picked on me as apparently I had once casually said something about speaking a little English. I opened the cellar door and climbed over the corpse of the corporal that had collected an assault rifle from us. He had been shot in the head by a sniper from the other side of the Moselle. The damaged screen that had sheltered us from view from the river had fallen down, and we had not found it necessary to put it up again last night. No one had felt responsible, and this poor devil died because of it.

My main problem was now the sniper across the way, for as I climbed the steps he would have me in his sights. Would the same thing happen to me as to the corporal on the cellar steps? I knew from my own experience how great the urge is to squeeze the trigger when one has an enemy in one's sights. I raised my hands as high as they would go, climbed the first step and shouted out aloud: 'American soldiers, we surrender!'

There was no reply. I climbed the next step with my hands

stretched up high and shouted again. Then the third step, and the lad must be able to see my hands now, I thought. Then step four. I was sweating. With the fifth step he would surely see my head. Did he have me in his cross hairs? Would he squeeze the trigger? He did not, so I slowly climbed the rest of the steps and stood in the castle's inner courtyard.

Calling out loudly I turned around and got a reply. From the adjacent cellar that we had used as a toilet came about ten Americans. They surrounded me and pointed their weapons at me. Their leader, whom I took to be a staff sergeant, cocked his big revolver and pointed it at my stomach. I was greatly relieved, for the sniper could not get me now. We looked at each other silently for a moment until I somewhat superfluously repeated: 'We surrender!'

The section leader pointed toward the cellar. 'How many?'

I shook my shoulders. 'I don't know, maybe six or eight. Some are dead like him', and I indicated with my head toward the dead man. The Americans stretched their necks and looked down. That satisfied the section leader. 'Let them come up, hands up and no weapons!'

So I called down below: 'Lads, unbuckle, weapons away and hands up, then come out!'

The first was the artillery forward observer, who grinned at me and threw me a knowing look. (They had meanwhile rendered the radio unserviceable.) With me included, we were six men in all. The war seemed to be over for us, and we had survived. They led us from the inner courtyard outside through the big arched gateway. The Sherman tank was there further up with three or four others. Several other men came out as prisoners from the outer cellars. It was clear to all of us that there was no way out of this trap.

Then we heard the first rounds of our 105 mm coming. Everyone threw themselves down in the dirt, Germans and Americans, trying to bury themselves in the earth. Here would have been a chance to escape. It would have meant running back through the fire of our own shells, hoping that they would not get me and that the Americans would not shoot after me. By the time I had thought it through, the opportunity was gone. One has to do these things without thinking, but today I am glad that I did not do it.

With our hands clasped behind our necks, they led us down the road coming up from the Moselle. The dead enemies that I had shot were lying there. One of the guards pointed to them with a threatening gesture. I was the last in the line. As we turned into the Moselle river bank road, I stopped and turned round once more, looking at the destroyed Schloss Thorn. It was a wretched sight and I vowed to myself never to forget it. This vow I have kept. My guard, a lanky, gum-chewing lad, struck me sharply in the chest with the barrel of his sub-machine gun and said: 'Let's go!', an expression I was to hear often.

They took us to Nennig for our first interrogation. There were already about ten men there, including the captain and battalion commander from Kreuzweiler, who had found their way into captivity surprisingly quickly. The artillery forward observer went in first, then myself about a quarter of an hour later. In passing, the forward observer whispered: 'Watch out for the blows!'

In the room were an officer who spoke good German and a bullish sergeant. They knew me by name, as the Americans had been listening in to our telephone line. That was easily possible technically, as we had no double lines, only one strand with an earth. His first question: 'Where is your fire position?'

I said: 'I will not betray it. You cannot force me to.'

The officer pulled back and the sergeant gave me a blow with his fist. All the same, it was not very hard and only meant as a warning shot. The officer then said: 'Now will you tell me? Here is the map. Show me where your fire position is on here.'

Then I realised what to do. Without hesitation I showed him the place where our first fire position had been. 'No,' said the officer, 'there is no fire position there. Our tanks are already there.'

I did not let my answer wait. 'Then we have moved it. I had no verbal contact any more. Fire was only called on with Verey lights and tracer.'

To my relief he accepted this outrageous lie and I was taken back to join the others. Although Sergeant Schultz was nominally the senior forward observer, they left him alone. Thus we survived the first critical hours. Towards evening they took us by truck to the rear. The battle for Schloss Thorn was over, and for us the war. And the most important thing was that we had survived!

EPILOGUE

To round off this account, a small postscript. I could not forget Schloss Thorn, the memories of 20 February 1945 were too strong. I first passed by again in 1953 when there was a fire brigade festival in Kreuzweiler. The castle still looked in a bad way, but at least the roofs had been restored. I returned to the Moselle in 1956 and 1959 and could see the progress made in the arduous process of restoration. Finally, in a visit to the castle in the autumn of 1995, I made myself known. The 'lord of the castle', Dr Baron von Hobe-Gelting made me very welcome and called me the 'last defender of the castle'. We talked in his office for a good hour then went on a tour of the premises that brought back old memories.

I discovered that several veterans of our former opponents, the 94th US Infantry Division, had also been here, the place having a similar meaning for them as it has for me. They had even funded and erected a Peace Monument at the strategic point between Sinz and Oberleuken, the inscription being signed by the then-President Bush. Veterans from both sides had come to the unveiling. Unfortunately I had not been among them, although I was apparently the only member of the 256th Volksgrenadier Division to have survived the fighting here and later.

The so-called Orscholz-Switch, the land between the Saar and the Moselle, had suffered a lot in the months-long fighting; all the villages had been largely destroyed, burnt, and the fields laid waste. But through the untiring industry of the inhabitants, the villages have been rebuilt and the countryside is flourishing. Schloss Thorn is a vineyard today. Even Kreuzweiler has been rebuilt. The evacuated inhabitants were only able to return to their destroyed village the following April. The men searched the neighbourhood for the dead that had been left lying around after the Americans had left. Twelve men were found and buried in the Kreuzweiler cemetery. When several years later the German

War Graves Commission wanted to move them, the villagers objected, so the fallen still lie in the earth that they defended. Today, above the cellar in Kreuzweiler where I spent the night, stands a magnificent guesthouse with comfortable rooms and excellent cuisine. Unfortunately, in the years after 1945 there was a string of deaths and injuries arising from our mines, but this is all now forgotten.

Many of my former comrades lie in the military cemetery at Kastell, where I spend many hours of reflection and also lay flowers. My former regimental commander, Lieutenant Colonel Gliemann, found his last resting place here. They fought and died in the faithful fulfilment of their duty in accordance with the oath demanded by the law. May the earth lie lightly upon you, comrades!

1 However, it was because the commander of the 11th Panzer Division felt so strongly that it was being misemployed here, the senior LXXXIInd Corps being unused to dealing with armoured formations, that he had appealed directly to the Inspector of Panzertruppen for the division to be relieved. In fact a battalion of Panzergrenadier Regiment 111 remained behind with some tanks to bolster the 256th Volksgrenadiers.

THREE

With Our Backs to Berlin

GERHARD TILLERY

I originally obtained a copy of Gerhard Tillery's manuscript from Joachim Schneider, an amateur historian from Frankfurt/Oder, and found it extremely useful in piecing together the events portrayed in my book Zhukov at the Oder. *Later I was able to establish contact with the author in Bremen and obtained his permission to reproduce this remarkable account of his experiences as a rifleman on the Oderbruch battlefront, in the retreat to Berlin, the fighting in the surrounded city and the breakout to the west.*

The potential officer course in Lübeck, which should have lasted until 15 March 1945, was broken off on 16 February. We were already in Cleverbrück on a ten-day field exercise when the orders came through. We had all hoped to become sergeants on 15 March and get some leave, but the Russians had already crossed the Oder, the Americans were also getting closer, and every man was needed at the front.

On 15 February I had gone with my comrade Hinnerk Otterstedt to a cinema in Bad Schwartau, and when we got back to the field positions at Cleverbrück at eleven o'clock our comrades were all ready to march back to barracks. We packed our things quickly and then marched back to the Cambrai-Kaserne, where we exchanged our old kit for new and gave away everything that was not absolutely necessary. I packed my personal stuff and had it sent to an acquaintance in Lübeck.

Then we marched in formation singing loudly to the railway station. Now that we were going into action, we were filled with enthusiasm. We were all young potential officers, most of us corporals, and 18 years old, and we could not wait to get out there. None of us would have believed that the war would be over and lost in the next three months and that soon, many of us would no longer be alive.

We were loaded into goods wagons and set off at last at dawn. We had been discussing whether we would be going east or west. Now at last we knew; we were going east. By midday we had reached Hagenow in Mecklenburg. Next day we reached Berlin and then Potsdam that same evening. Here we detrained and went to a barracks. Next morning we were inspected and issued with rations for the journey, weapons and ammunition. In the afternoon we could walk out. I went with Warrelmann and Gessner to the Garrison Church and then to the Palace. A few days later there was a heavy bombing raid in which much of the town was destroyed.

From Potsdam our journey took us to Werbig. The nearer we got to the front, the more heartily we were greeted by the inhabitants, who all hoped that we would be able to stop the Russians at the Oder and throw them back.

From Werbig we marched via Friedersdorf to Dolgelin, where the command post of the Division 'Berlin' to which we now belonged was located. We were assigned to the Officer-Cadet Regiments 'Dresden' and 'Potsdam'. Together with 15 comrades from Lübeck, I went to Regiment 1234 'Potsdam', where the others were from various training courses and officer cadet schools.

We marched to Sachsendorf, where our battalion commander, Captain Albrecht, greeted us. Sachsendorf lay in the Oderbruch, a completely flat landscape. We looked for something to eat in Sachsendorf, as our travel rations were long gone. At a bakery we each got half a loaf fresh from the oven, then sausage from a butcher's, and tobacco from a pub.

I sat down apart from my comrades in a roadside ditch, ate my bread, smoked my pipe and wrote a short letter home to my parents. It was my birthday. I was 19 years old.

The front line was still about four kilometres away. Several Russian fighters and ground-attack aircraft appeared in the cloudless sky, but soon fled when our own fighters appeared.

Our divisional commander gave a speech: 'It is the Führer's wish that the Lebus bridgehead be eliminated as soon as possible. Not without reason, our best regiments are here, and you can be proud to belong to these regiments.'

That evening we had to go to Rathstock, immediately behind the front line, to dig trenches. We left our packs with the company quartermaster-sergeant, taking only the absolutely necessary items, such as weapon, haversack and rations. We did not even take our washing and shaving kit, believing that we would be coming back.

That night a long convoy of carts removed potatoes and grain from Rathstock, which had been completely evacuated of its inhabitants. The Russians heard the noise and started laying down fire on the road, but long after the convoy had gone. We were marching silently forward in our ranks when several explosions bringing vile smoke suddenly struck quite close to us, and we vanished into the roadside ditches like lightning. As the explosions gradually got closer, our enthusiasm disappeared. Eventually Ivan quietened down and we could continue on our way. We had survived our baptism of fire well.

In Rathstock, which had been badly damaged by the shelling, we reported to the battalion command post. However, it was now two a.m., so we were no longer required to dig trenches. Instead we could take it in turns to sleep while some of us kept watch.

The battalion command post was located in the Rathstock manor farm, the only big farm in the area, and surrounded by small buildings. The Russians could naturally assume that soldiers would be accommodated in these buildings, which is why they shelled them from time to time. The previous day observers had established that the enemy were bringing forward reinforcements and an attack was expected, which is why we were being kept in reserve at the manor. We had to keep watch for two hours and then could sleep for four. I stood watch in the morning and had a good view of the area from a window on the first floor. However, I did not see any Russians, as we had snipers out firing at a range of 600 metres. I had just finished my watch when the Russians fired on the manor farm again. Hit after hit struck home, and gradually the building began breaking up. We had gone down into the cellar and were

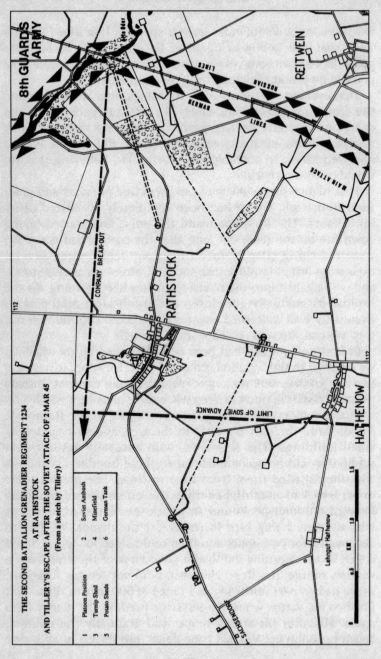

THE SECOND BATTALION GRENADIER REGIMENT 1234
AT RATHSTOCK
AND TILLERY'S ESCAPE AFTER THE SOVIET ATTACK OF 2 MAR 45
(From a sketch by Tillery)

1   Platoon Position   2   Soviet Ambush
3   Turnip Shed   4   Minefield
5   Potato Sheds   6   German Tank

8th GUARDS ARMY

REITWEIN

RUSSIAN LINES

GERMAN LINES

MAIN ATTACK

COMPANY BREAK-OUT

RATHSTOCK

112

112

LIMIT OF SOVIET ADVANCE

HATHENOW

SACHSENDORF

Lehngut Hathenow

KM

0   0.5   1.0   1.5

waiting for the firing to end, but it seemed that this would be the end of us instead. The cellar ceiling started to crack and chalk fell down on top of us. Another hour of this and we knew for certain that we would be buried under the rubble.

I had nothing left to smoke and so borrowed eight cigarettes from Hinnerk Otterstedt. I never got to return them. At last, when nothing was left standing of the building, the Russians stopped firing.

That evening we went into the front line and were divided up among several companies. Otterstedt, Hintze, Bebensee, Thode, Schoone, Meieringh and Borstelmann went to the neighbouring company, while I stayed with Gessner, Warrelmann, Erhardt, Bücklers, Pohlmeyer, Krahl, Gillner and Pfarrhofer in 4 Company, where our company commander was Second Lieutenant Reifferscheidt, and my platoon leader Staff Sergeant Lauffen.

The further forward we went, the heavier was the machine gun fire. Explosive bullets were going off all around us. We would get to know their horrific effect later. They were exploding with loud bangs in front, behind, near to and above us in the trees. We came to a communication trench that we had to crawl through on all fours and eventually reached the front line without casualties.

The company command post was in a dugout about two by three metres and one metre high. The company commander greeted us and divided us up among the platoons. Warrelmann and myself went to 2 Platoon. The position ran through a wood. There was no through trench system, just a foxhole every 12 to 15 metres. The Russians were about 30–40 metres in front of us. On the left of our position was a stream about eight metres wide, which was the Alte Oder, a tributary of the Oder River. A railway embankment formed our right-hand boundary. We were dug in on one side of the stream, Ivan on the other. That is where the company commander sent me first. My hair stood on end when I heard that the Russians were so close. We could only talk in whispers. Every sound from the Russians, every loud-spoken word could be heard clearly. Hand grenades were being thrown night and day, and casualties sustained here every day. Fortunately a machine gunner was needed on the left flank and I got the job. I was lucky, for several days later when the Russians attacked, no one survived on the right. I got my machine gun and moved across to the company's left flank, where I became the link man to the neighbouring company.

However, there was not much to be seen of our wood, as nearly all the trees had been reduced to stumps by the shelling. Branches and twigs lay around on the ground and were used by us as camouflage.

The other bank of the Alte Oder on which Ivan sat was higher than ours, so the Russians could always overlook us, and we dared not leave our foxholes during the day. I was paired with an old, front line-experienced corporal, Albert Schimmel, who had been in the Russian campaign since the very beginning. He showed me all the tricks that we newcomers had to learn. He had dug himself a hole about 1.60 metres long, 80 centimetres wide and a metre deep, but there was already ground water in the hole, so we constantly had wet feet. I had been issued with a camouflage suit in Sachsendorf that was very warm and rainproof. The weather was pretty bad; it rained a lot, and several times we had snow.

My feet froze and we never had a chance to tend to them. We could not leave our hole because of the snipers, who fired often. At night I had to make contact with the right-hand man of the neighbouring company every two hours.

When I went to make contact the first time, I became so lost in the dark that I could not find my way back. I came up to the Alte Oder and the Russians heard me and opened fire. I sought cover from their machine guns in a shellhole, but this was not so comfortable when hand grenades started coming over. Fortunately Ivan soon quietened down again, but the shellhole was full of water and I had to lie in it for about five minutes, getting soaked through. My teeth chattering, I carried on, cursing, until I made contact with the neighbouring company, which was only about 30 metres away. To my delight, I found Bernhard Meieringh there with Otterstedt and Pohlmeyer lying to his left. I said I would visit them again next day.

No one was allowed to sleep at night, and there were only four hours sleep in daytime, as we had to stand eight-hour watches. Thanks to plentiful cigarettes and good rations, we did not suffer too much from fatigue during the first few days. The body still had reserves, which, however, were soon used up.

There was always something going on at night, hand grenades flying here and there, rations and ammunition being issued. There was no movement at all in daylight, as the whole area behind the front line was under observation by the Russians.

I did not have to keep watch that morning and so could sleep, but I was frightfully cold in my wet uniform. Albert Schimmel had dug a small hole next to our foxhole, covered it with beams and lined it with straw, where I lay now. Albert had given me his greatcoat, but I still could not sleep. My clothes dried out slowly. Then punctually at 12 o'clock the Russians resumed their midday concert, plastering us with mortar fire as we crouched down in our dugout.

After about half an hour the firing eased off and Albert lay down to sleep, while I wrote a letter to my parents. Now and again a shot would whip past whenever one of us moved incautiously.

That evening I went back to our neighbouring company to see Meieringh. The first thing he told me was that both Hinnerk Otterstedt and Pohlmeyer were dead. Pohlmeyer had left his foxhole and been shot in the head by a sniper. Otterstedt had gone to help him and been shot too. So now after only two days we had already lost two dead, and when I spoke to Warrelmann and Bücklers later, they both said the same thing: 'Will I be next?'

Thoroughly depressed, I returned to our foxhole and told Albert Schimmel about it. He commented that they would not be the last.

I was then supposed to go back to the company command post and pick up the rations, but as I did not know my way around in the wood, Albert volunteered to go for me. I waited half an hour, an hour, but he did not come back. The Russians were firing again with all calibres, and we were not saving our ammunition either. I was firing at their muzzle flashes with my machine gun.

As Albert still did not return, I reported to the platoon leader, who sent off the platoon runner, Heinz Warelmann, to find him. Albert had been shot through the arm. As Albert's replacement, I got Sergeant Gillner, who had been posted into the company at the same time as myself.

There was no opportunity for us to get a wash or a shave. Gradually we became more relaxed, not ducking with every shot or explosion. You became hardened to it all, you got used to this kind of life and just faced up to whatever was coming. After a while, the effects of fatigue began to show. My face had fallen in and the fat that I had accumulated in the peaceful days of Lübeck was soon gone. But the rations were quite good. Every day we got half a loaf of bread and something to put on it, and every evening we got something from the field kitchen, although it was always cold.

The Russians shelled us regularly at noon, so that we could practically set the time by it. Werner Bücklers was wounded by one of these bombardments when he failed to reach the bunker fast enough, getting a splinter in the thigh.

By the time we had been out there three or four days, the third one of us Lübeckers, Bernhard Meieringh, had been killed and Bebensee wounded in the neighbouring company. We had not yet been a week at the front and had already lost three dead and two wounded.

Whenever the weather was favourable, the Russian fighters and ground-attack aircraft came and dropped bombs and fired their guns. However, they did not bother us much, as these attacks were mainly directed to our rear. The Russians resumed their concert punctually on 2 March, but much more heavily than before. When the bombardment had gone on for over half an hour and started intensifying, we knew that an attack would surely follow. There was a frightful noise out there. I sat in the bunker with Gillner. There was a howling and banging with splinters whistling around and striking the tree stumps, branches flying about, sand and muck flying everywhere, and a hot smell in the air. In between, one could hear the cries of the wounded. At last, after nearly two hours, the firing stopped abruptly. Then we knew: 'They are coming now!'

The next moment the Russian rifle and machine gun fire opened up, mixed with the 'Urrahs!' of the Ivans. The Russians leapt over the railway embankment on our right without encountering serious resistance. Only a few of us had survived the bombardment, which had been particularly heavy in that sector, and those that could not flee were soon overwhelmed by superior numbers. I could hear the din of the advancing Russians on the right, but could see none of them because of the wood. Nor could we leave our positions, for we had to expect the

Russians coming across the Alte Oder in front of us. They kept advancing and were soon behind us. They encountered little resistance from Rathstock and had soon taken the village. This made us uncomfortable, for the Russians were now in front, behind and on either side of us. They continued to advance and were only stopped just short of Sachsendorf.[1] Our neighbouring company had withdrawn and we were now cut off.[2] Heinz Warrelmann, our platoon runner, brought the order to withdraw, and we assembled at the company command post. Our platoon was now 26 men strong.

The greatest difficulty was getting out of our holes unseen. The Russians had naturally identified each hole and closed in around us. Of our four, Gillner and myself were the lucky survivors. Covering all sides, we came to the edge of the wood. What we then saw made our blood run cold. Thousands of Russians were streaming past unhindered, tanks, guns and carts, all going west. They were only 200 metres from us and had no idea that we were still in the wood, believing that we had retreated.

Staff Sergeant Lauffen gave the order not to open fire on any account, as it would only give us away. We dug in and waited for evening. The rest of the company was about 300 metres north of us and we could only communicate by runner.

Second Lieutenant Reifferscheidt ordered our platoon to break through with the company at nightfall. A reconnaissance party had found a position that appeared to be only weakly occupied and that was where the breakthrough would occur. When Second Lieutenant Reifferscheidt sent his company runner, Grenadier Reiffen, to us, he got lost in the wood and did not find us for quite some time. Meanwhile the company of about 60 men had split up.

Now our platoon was on its own and no one knew which way the company had gone. Nearly all the buildings in Rathstock were on fire and, although we were about 600 metres away, it was as light as day.

Before breaking out we destroyed everything that could hinder or betray us; without tent halves[3], haversacks, messtins and gasmasks. We only had our rifles as we left the wood when it was fully dark. In front was Staff Sergeant Lauffen, then the company runner, Grenadier Reiffen, Sgt Krahl, myself, Sgt

Gillner, Heinz Warrelmann and then the remainder of the platoon. We could expect to be spotted by the Russians at any moment and be fired upon. Not a word was said. At first we went through the wood, then crossed a road and came to a field that gradually sloped up to Rathstock.

Suddenly we were called upon in the middle of the field: 'Halt! Hands up!'. Twenty metres in front of us was a heavy Russian machine gun. They had seen us and immediately opened fire. Standing we would all have been killed, so we threw ourselves down, but we could not return the fire without hitting each other.

What now? Turn back? But that would offer the enemy a much better target. The Russians had dug in and were hard to see. However, before we could make up our minds, shots started landing among us and we had to lie still. It was frightening lying there, unable to shoot back. The Russians were using explosive bullets. I could see the shots exploding around us, and muck and sand was blowing into our faces. I thought: 'This is it!' I pressed my face to the ground, not wanting to look any more, and listened and waited for the end.

Then sub-machine guns could be heard firing. None of us cried out. I could not understand it. Were they all dead then? Then Staff Sergeant Lauffen started shouting: 'Comrades, stop firing, we are wounded!'

The Russians kept on firing. Staff Sergeant Lauffen shouted once more and then was silent. When the Russians reopened fire, I grabbed Krahl by the leg and said: 'Come on Krahl, fire, fire!' for he was the only one with a machine gun. He did not answer. I tugged him again. His face dropped from his arm into the sand. He was dead! Carefully I dragged myself toward Gillner. He lay with his head in the sand. I pushed his helmet back and saw his eyes: dead.

Something came flying through the air. Hand grenades! I lay still, unable to move. A hand grenade landed only two metres from me, and I could see the sparks. Then it exploded. I received a tremendous blow on my helmet, the blast taking my breath away, and sand pattered down around me, but I was not wounded. Apparently a splinter had struck my helmet, leaving a dent behind. The helmet had saved my life.

Several more hand grenades followed, then it was quiet. Then someone moved up in front. 'Now they are coming,' I thought, 'but they are not going to get me alive. Before I go, I will take someone with me!'. Preferring to sell my life as dearly as possible, I took the pin out of a hand grenade and was about to throw it, when I saw that it was Grenadier Reiffen. With his small body he had found cover behind Staff Sergeant Lauffen and so remained unwounded. 'Come on, back!', he said.

Then someone came crawling up from behind. It was Harry Warrelmann. 'Gerd, are you wounded?' he asked.

'No, are you?'

'Yes, four times – chest, stomach, bottom and thigh.'

'Come on, back!' I said, but he replied: 'No, it is pointless, I won't get through. But when you get to Delmenhorst again, please visit my parents and tell them what happened.'

I said: 'Nonsense, you are coming back!'

But he shook his head and said: 'Greet my parents.' Then he crawled off.

Reiffen and I crawled cautiously back. The Russians could not have seen us moving or otherwise they would have got us. All the comrades lying there were dead. Once we had crawled about 30 to 40 metres, we ran back to the wood, bent over at first but then upright, as we knew that there were no Russians there. We went back to the company command post and smoked a cigarette.

Now the hopelessness of our situation became clear. All around us were Russians and more Russians, the nearest Germans being four or five kilometres away. I thought that my end had come. I thought of my home and my loved ones, who would now be sitting safely in an air raid shelter. There was another air raid on Berlin going on, for although it was 70 kilometres away, we could hear the firing of the anti aircraft guns. Next day, the Russians would search the wood and find us. I did not want to surrender, as I had often heard that the Russians killed their prisoners. Suddenly we heard voices. Reiffen and I cautiously looked out and then realised they were German. It was another six men from our platoon that had come back, having failed to get away. Some were utterly despondent and wanted to go over to the Russians. The chances of getting through were very slight, but we decided to try anyway.

Meanwhile it was already one o'clock in the morning, so we

decided not to break through north of Rathstock, the way the company had gone, as the Russians would have been alerted there, but to try a route south of Rathstock.

We came out of the wood and reached the road and hid in a couple of shellholes to observe the traffic. The Russians were passing only ten metres from us and we could hear every word they said. Many were singing and trucks were driving back and forth. The sky was overcast, but the moon still broke through a gap in the clouds.

When there was a pause in the traffic on the road for a moment, we worked our way forward to the roadside ditch and prepared to run across. To our horror, we saw Russians digging in only a few metres away from us. They were so eagerly engaged that they did not notice us, but we would have to go back.

Then a horse-drawn cart came along the road. We lay in the ditch with our faces pressed to the ground, hardly daring to breathe. The cart went past only a few metres from my head, a marching column following behind. We dared not stay lying there, as they would surely have seen us, so we stood up and walked along with the cart as if we belonged to it, but then the moon came out from behind the clouds and the cry went up: 'Germans!'

We ran off as fast as we could across the field, the Russians firing wildly at us, but not hitting us, as we took cover in shellholes. We could see the Russians silhouetted against the burning village as they surrounded the field, but we all managed to slip out through a gap in their cordon.

By now the Russians had been alerted and we had to be more careful. It would soon be morning and the horizon was getting lighter. The cloud cover had broken up and the moon was shining uninterruptedly. We decided to look for a hiding place until the next evening and try to break through again when the Russians had settled down. We found a hiding place in a turnip shed, where we lay down on the turnips and covered ourselves in straw. After a short while, I realised that the cold was making my limbs stiff. I consulted with the man next to me in a whisper, and we decided to look for another hiding place.

We were just about to leave when some Russians approached and, after deliberating for a while, started digging a shelter only five metres from us. We had to stay. I was freezing and my legs had gone to sleep.

After we had been in this precarious situation for about an hour, I suddenly saw a Russian approaching our shed and go to where Reiffen was lying. Had he found him? The Russian only wanted straw for his dugout and removed it from where Reiffen was lying. In a flash, Reiffen thrust his sub-machine gun into the Russian's face. The Russian shouted and stumbled back, alarming his comrades. We ran as fast as we could out of the shed and across the fields. Again we had been spotted. Now the Russians were fully awake, running here and there and firing in the direction we had taken.

It was getting lighter in the east. We needed to settle down in a farm for the day. Then, about three kilometres away, we saw streaks of fire like comets into the sky and the explosions immediately afterwards. Rocket launchers! There were obviously Germans over there. We decided to go together and try to break through to them. We marched on toward the rocket launchers.

Suddenly we were called upon: 'Stoi!' There was a foxhole in front of us and we came under fire from a sub-machine gun. Fortunately, there were some shellholes to provide us with cover. The bullets whistled past our ears, but when we returned fire, the Russians ran away.

We made a detour and marched on toward the southwest. It was nearly daylight. We were about to cross the road from Rathstock to Sachsendorf when one of us suddenly called out: 'Stop! Mines!' Our eyes had been on our surroundings and not on the ground or our feet, and now we were in a nice mess. We were in the middle of a minefield. All around we could see the places where our sappers had buried their mines. We hardly dared breathe, thinking that we would be blown to pieces any moment. They often put anti-personnel mines between the bigger Teller mines intended for tanks and trucks, and connected them with wires so that the slightest movement would set them off. Crawling on all fours, we worked our way out centimetre by centimetre.

The minefield had delayed us for a long time and now it was full daylight. Right next to the road was a farm, alongside of which were four potato sheds arranged in a square. We established ourselves in these sheds with a man on watch on each side. The others could sleep.

Once the sun had come up, one of the sentries spotted a tank with its guns pointing toward us about 3–400 metres away. Was it German or Russian? Then we saw two men come out of the farm, one of them limping and leaning against the other. One of them had a gas mask case, so they must be German. They disappeared again into a farm next to the tank.

In order to reach that farm we would have to pass two others, the first about 100 metres away. We ran as quickly as we could to it, aware that it could have been taken by the Russians, but it was unoccupied, as was the next. The occupants had left some hours before and the cows were bellowing with pain in the stalls, as they had not been milked, but there was nothing we could do about it.

The house into which the others had gone was still lived in. A woman was crying interminably. One of the soldiers was wounded, so we bandaged him up and took him to the tank. The tank crew had seen no Russians. We were through!

It is impossible to describe our joy. No one could possibly understand what we had gone through, who had not been through it himself. We had wandered the whole night among thousands of Russians, often only a few metres apart, had fired at each other, been recognised, and yet had broken through.

The company had also managed to get through with only two lightly wounded out of about 60 men. In total, we had lost 16 dead out of our platoon of 24.

We now had only one desire; to eat something and then sleep, nothing but sleep. Later, we were taken by truck to our company supply section in Sachsendorf. The Russians were already firing on the village. Our company quartermaster-sergeant first attended to our stomachs and then we could sleep, but when we stretched out on the straw in a cellar I found that I was simply too tense and stressed to fall asleep. At last I got some sleep, but then immediately we had to go back into the line again.

We had hoped for a few days' rest, but the new front line had to be formed and this required every man. We were sent forward – without tent halves,[3] mess tins, gas masks or haversacks.

The Russians had been stopped behind Rathstock, and

between Sachsendorf and Rathstock was open meadowland through which the front line ran. Our platoon position was about 100m from the last house in Sachsendorf and we soon received reinforcements. Our new platoon commander was Staff Sergeant Buchal, a lawyer from Breslau.

During the first night (3/4 March) we dug our foxholes and during the following night crawling trenches were dug between the individual foxholes and later deepened until the trench system was complete.

The Russians had not dug trenches but were occupying the buildings in Rathstock about 400 metres away.[4] During the next few days we collected doors and straw from the ruined and deserted buildings. The doors we used to roof our dugouts, putting two at a time on made us safe against mortar fire, although not against a direct hit.

We were now getting our food regularly and on time. At dusk the wagon would come up the road as far as the front line. At first I would have to go back to the wagon to eat as I had no mess tins, but then I borrowed a mess tin lid. After the meal, ammunition was issued and the wounded and dead were taken back. The badly wounded were taken back straight away.

As soon as we had finished constructing our position, the company was replaced. In the meantime, we had gone on to build alternative positions, communication trenches and saps. We now got a not-so-well constructed position to the right of the road, where the same digging had to continue. A company of our battalion that had been in reserve replaced us in the old positions.

One day while fetching food, I met Jürgen Schoone from Lüneburg, who had been with me in Lübeck. He was now occupying my old dugout. Several days later I asked a member of his company for news of him and was told that he was dead. He had been sitting out a barrage in the bunker and had been killed instantly by a hit. If we had not been relieved a few days earlier, I would have been the one to be killed.

We expected the Russians to push their front line forward, so every night men were sent out to keep watch about 300 metres in front of our trenches. Each platoon would send a man. It was quite an uncomfortable feeling, spending four hours completely alone only 100 metres from the Russians. I always dug myself a shallow scoop to lie in. You began to freeze after a short while, despite the thick winter clothing. Everyone on this duty got a quarter litre bottle of schnapps, which was fine against the cold, but made you feel tired. The Russians also had men out but, fortunately, I never encountered one. I was always glad when my four hours were up.

Once we had completed this position we were again moved to another position about a kilometre further south. This position was quite horrible, for only 50 metres separated us from the Russian snipers, who made things very difficult for us.

Once I was given 24 hours' rest and went to the company command post, about 200 metres to the rear in a building. During the day I climbed up to ground level and could see far across the Russian lines. That evening we were sitting in the kitchen cooking something for ourselves when the barn suddenly burst into flames. The Russians had fired incendiaries at it. The fire soon spread to the other buildings and we had to flee. Sergeant Münz, a fine, older fellow, was wounded. He was always concerned about me. At night when I returned from the company command post I would walk across the fields rather than use the wet, dirty trenches. Although the Russians were always firing across the area, the chances of being hit at night were remote. But whenever Münz saw me he would complain: 'Tillery, don't be so careless!' However, he was the one that was hit in the brain by a stray bullet. He immediately lost consciousness, but was still breathing when he was taken to the Main Dressing Station that night. I do not know whether he recovered.

After a few days in this position we were moved yet again. We went even further south and each of the three platoons occupied its own farm, which had been developed into strongpoints. The farms formed a triangle and our platoon had the middle one. Only the foundations of these farms remained, the rest having been shot away by the Russians.[4] They had already dug a front line opposite us, and the farms offered the Russian artillery good targets. We had to suffer a lot of shelling and also take casualties.

I shared quarters with an old senior corporal who was a cook by trade. Every night he had to cook in the platoon command post and I would have to stand sentry duty alone. There was no question of getting any sleep, of course, for a lot went on at night. The rations arrived irregularly and always cold. The result was that I, like many comrades, got diarrhoea from the cold food and dirty water. The food was nothing special, there was plenty of bread, but little fat.

Here a Bavarian comrade was severely wounded and Albert Gessner from Bremerhaven was sent to hospital with hypothermia. The company had shrunk considerably during the past weeks and was barely 60 strong. On 15 March the regiment was relieved. We had noticed during the preceding days that the Russians were bringing forward reinforcements and were clearly planning an attack and in fact a few days later they attacked and took Sachsendorf.[5]

Once our relief, a newly established and equipped regiment, had been briefed by us, we marched to Sachsendorf, where carts were waiting to take us to Dolgelin. There we had a few hours free to sleep and, above all, to have a wash, which had been impossible in the positions we had come from.

SOLIKANTE

That afternoon we were taken by trucks to Neu Trebbin, where we stayed until the next morning. At lunchtime some comrades and I acquired two chickens, and the comrade that had shared a foxhole with me cooked them to make a tasty meal. It was just like peacetime for us.

Neu Trebbin lay about ten kilometres behind the front line and had not yet been cleared of its inhabitants, but there was considerable nervousness among them and we were often asked: 'Can you stop them?' Although they did not have much themselves, the inhabitants gave us some good things to eat.

In the evening we took a stroll. I even cleaned my boots and brushed my uniform for the event, but my eyes closed on me with the first glass of beer and I went back to our quarters, which were in a barn. I was very tired. I had not had a whole night's sleep for weeks, at most a few hours during the day. I slept in the hay as if in a feather bed, and no shelling or rifle fire disturbed me.

Next morning the trucks took us on to near Letschin, from where we marched to Solikante, about 15 kilometres north of

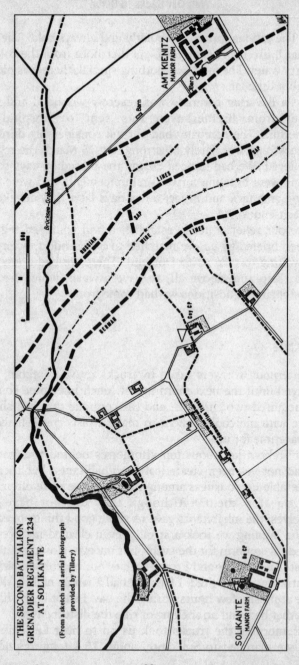

THE SECOND BATTALION
GRENADIER REGIMENT 1234
AT SOLIKANTE

(From a sketch and aerial photograph
provided by Tillery)

AMT KIENITZ
MANOR FARM

Barn

Barn

SAP

LINES

RUSSIAN

WIRE

SAP

LINES

GERMAN

Coy CP

Pub

Bn CP

SOLIKANTE
MANOR FARM

Brücksee-Graben

500
M

Küstrin. Our regiment was relieving another one that had suffered heavy casualties here. At first our company was left in peace. We moved into quarters in the Solikante manor farm. The manor itself was burnt out, but the stalls, farm labourers' cottages and barns were still standing. We made ourselves at home in the cellar of one of the barns, where we could look after ourselves properly for the first time. We received our rations on time and hot. We could also see to our weapons and equipment properly. Finally, we could get some more sleep.

How good it felt, sitting out in the open air in that lovely spring weather, or sheltering in our quarters when it rained. We also found various kinds of food, potatoes, peas, beans and corn, which we cooked and fried all day long.

It was then that I first noticed that my feet had been frozen. Often I could not sleep for the pain, and every step was agony. We had no duties during the daytime except weapon and equipment cleaning, but at night we had to dig trenches in the front line. The Russian air force was very active in this sector, but directed its attention to our rear and did not bother us much.

We were always very happy to get front line parcels with their contents of biscuits, sweets, chocolate, glucose, etc. Unfortunately, this was not very often.

After a week here, we had to take our turn in the front line, which ran between the villages of Solikante, which was in our hands, and Amt Kienitz, which was occupied by the Russians. There were about 400 metres of meadowland between the villages, with the lines running in between. The positions had already been prepared by the previous regiment.

The Russians were about 120 metres away. Our company command post was on the edge of Solikante in a farm that was partially burnt out. From there a trench ran forward to the front line and back to the battalion command post in Solikante. To the right of our company was a unit of Infantry Regiment 'Grossdeutschland'.[6]

The Russians had driven a sap forward opposite our communications trench to within 70 metres of our trenches, which had a barbed wire fence in front, and had laid mines in front of their positions. Our trenches were only weakly manned with two men every 80 to 100 metres, the distance to the enemy trenches being about the same. The Russians knew this and emerged at night to try and snatch people, so we always had to be very alert.

It was forbidden to sleep at night, and we hardly got any during the day. After dusk in the evening the food carriers would deliver our rations, bringing ammunition and mail with them, but the food was cold. We got three quarters of a litre of soup and half a loaf every day, but hardly any butter or fat to go with it.

I had received my last mail in Lübeck at the beginning of February, and now at last, at the end of March I had some more news, eight letters arriving at once. I had no writing paper left, and although we had asked the company quartermaster sergeant often, we still did not got any. In the end I took some empty pages from books to write on, or searched the abandoned houses for writing paper when I went back during the day.

I was appointed machine gunner. As my number two I had Ivo Pfarrhofer from Vienna, who had been with me since Delmenhorst. At first we were deployed to the right of the communication trench.

Here too the Russians gave us lunchtime concerts in the form of mortars and anti-tank guns. The Russians were firing directly at the trenches, and we had many casualties as a result. As the Russians already knew our positions, we built alternative positions to fire from, and I constructed several firing positions right and left of the communication trench. Often I would fire my machine gun from 30 metres to the right, then run quickly to 50 metres to the left and fire again.

There was a lot of firing at night. The Russians could see our muzzle flashes and fire at them, and we would do the same to them. So it went on endlessly. Whenever I fired, I would promptly duck my head, and sometimes the bullets would whistle only a hair's breadth over me.

By day, when the artillery and mortars were not firing, it would be comparatively quiet. Now and again a shot would ring out when someone moved incautiously and his head broke cover.

Gradually the supply of ammunition became shorter and, unfortunately, it was not much good. We got lacquered cartridges, which were always getting stuck in the breech. In case of attack, I always kept back a belt of 1200 rounds for my machine gun of which 300 were of brass.[7]

One of us was always on trench orderly duty, usually a section leader. I was always happy to get trench orderly duty, as the time passed quickly. By the time I had gone through the company's section, my watch was nearly up, but I stayed to chat with everyone, for there was always something to talk about. Often, it took me five hours to make the rounds.

My hole was not just a foxhole like at the previous location, but properly constructed and I had made myself comfortable in it. I had a proper machine gun mounting supported with planks, and we had nailed together a bench. Right next to the machine gun mounting I had a dugout in which we sat under heavy artillery fire so as to be close to our machine gun. The dugout in which we slept when we had a chance, was supported by thick beams. We had found some mattresses and feather duvets in a destroyed house and made a comfortable home that was the envy of our comrades sleeping on straw.

When the days became warmer, we dug a place to lie down in 30 cm deep, lined it with straw and sunned ourselves in it. We had planned it well, but Ivan, unfortunately, still had to be taken into account.

One day I had just finished trench orderly duty and wanted to sleep. It was just before noon and the Russians opened their concert, a short one but unusually heavy. When it was over the cry came: 'Alarm!'. I immediately ran to my machine gun and peered cautiously through the loophole, but there was no sign of any Russians. Some idiot must have been seeing ghosts, I thought. Two men, Dense and Brunkdorf, started screaming horribly. What had happened? One of them had mistaken a molehill for a Russian lying on the ground and shouted the alarm. Dense and Brunkdorf had run along the trench and were wounded by a shot that went through Dense's cheek and knocked out some of his teeth, then hit Brunkdorf in the chest and lodged there. Neither wound was serious.

The Russians had placed snipers in the roofs of Amt Kienitz that we could not see. They often sat in the attics from where they could easily see us. If you were not really careful in keeping your head down, you would be seen by them.

One day Sergeant Holst relieved me of trench orderly duty. Hardly any of us had cigarette lighters or matches left, so if you wanted a smoke you often had to go a hundred metres to get a light. I asked Sergeant Holst to bring me one on his way back. A long time past and I became impatient, as I wanted to have a smoke and then sleep. In the end I went to look for a light myself. About 30 metres from my dugout was a spot that was very damp, as a result of which it was only 60 centimetres deep, and it was there that I found Sergeant Holst. He had been shot in the head and was dead. A few days later Sergeant Behrensen, a nice chap, fell at practically the same place, also shot through the head. Both had been careless and had let their heads appear above cover, were seen and shot.

I was nearly killed myself one day as I was going back through the communication trench to the company command post. The communication trench was also very damp in parts and had duckboards in these places. There was a puddle about two metres long between these duckboards and all those wanting to cross it would make a run up and jump across, but it doing so they naturally had to stand up straight and could be seen by the Russians. The Russians had noticed this and fired at this spot. When I came up to it, I slipped on the wet grating and landed about 20 centimetres short of the next one. At the same moment an explosive bullet whistled past a hair's breadth from my head and exploded right in front of me. If I had not slipped, it would have hit me.

One night when all kinds of things were happening, Ivo Pfarrhofer was standing at the loophole. I had already fired a burst and was down in the dugout fetching another belt of ammunition, when suddenly I heard someone moaning and calling my name. I called Ivo but got no answer. I found him at the firing point. He had been wounded in the throat and paralysed. He was taken back to the company command post straight away.

Each section had a man watching the Russian lines through a trench periscope. Once when I was doing this the periscope disintegrated around my ears. It had been spotted by the Russians and a bullet had gone right through it.

One night when Sergeant Singer brought up the rations, he heard an unusual sound as if someone was cutting the wire. He went on as if he had not noticed anything and put the food container down, then went back and saw three Russians cutting through our wire by the light of a Verey cartridge. Unfortunately his sub-machine gun jammed and the Russians got away.

As a replacement for Ivo Pfarrhofer, I got Josef Wieser, a 35 year-old Bavarian. He was a decent chap, but unfortunately we did not get on well. He spoke in a dialect that I simply could not understand.

Although the situation was serious and our casualties too, we did not let it get us down. Every morning as soon as it was light, I would make my way to the company command post to report my ammunition state, singing loudly and strongly enough for Ivan to hear.

With our supply section was a crazy guy, whose name I have forgotten, who went around wearing a frock coat and top hat as a symbol of his individuality. He had the German Cross in Gold and was one of our most successful snipers, having shot over 130 Russians. He used to sit in a barn about 300 metres behind the lines and a man from the company would observe for him. Whenever he saw a Russian, the sniper would shoot him. One day I reported as the observer and was scanning the Russian lines through binoculars when I saw a dog running around about 600 metres away. I told him and he hit it with his first shot.

We had to suffer a lot from the Russian anti-tank guns firing at our positions. One day a direct hit killed Corporal Pestel in his dugout and wounded two others. The Russian heavy artillery fired mainly at our rear, thus sparing us. Even their air force, which was very active in this area, left us alone. There were always Russian fighters, bombers and ground-attack aircraft in the air attacking the rear. Once a German Focker-Wulf fighter appeared and manoeuvred behind a Russian aircraft flying back and shot it down. The Russian baled out.

On the other hand we often had to endure Russian 'bombers' at night. They would glide over our trenches about 100 metres up and drop hand grenades and bombs on us. We could see these antiquated biplanes quite clearly. I often fired my machine gun at the 'Sewing-Machines', as we called them, but they were indestructible.[8]

At night a reserve section was employed digging trenches behind the front line as a fall-back position should the Russians break through. One evening as the reserve section was coming from the company command post into the farmyard, they received a direct hit from a mortar bomb and all eight were injured, some seriously.

It was now the beginning of April and often proper spring weather. Once I was detailed off for potato-peeling to the company cookhouse located in a farm about two kilometres behind the lines. One day on the food-carrying detail I met Schammy Thode from Wesermünde, who had been with me in Lübeck, coming out of the company command post. We were now the only two left in action from our course there. Six were dead, five wounded, and one was in hospital with hypothermia.

We did not see or hear much of our artillery and air force, but rocket launchers fired often to the south of us, near Küstrin. Occasionally our artillery would fire a few shells at the Russians opposite, who would retaliate by giving us an incessant plastering.

By the end of March our reconnaissance aircraft had already confirmed that the Russians were reinforcing their troops and bringing forward more materiel. By the beginning of April we could hear this activity for ourselves. We could constantly hear tanks, trucks and singing. The Russians must have concentrated vast numbers of troops, and it was obvious that they were about to make a big strike toward Berlin.

We were getting ever more casualties, were not being relieved for weeks on end, and were exhausted. The Russian fire got stronger every day, while our own artillery was firing ever more sparingly, which meant that they were short of ammunition. Consequently the Russians were able to make their preparations for attack undisturbed.

The first attack came on 14 April. At 5 a.m. we heard the Russian mortars firing and seconds later the bombs fell on us. There was a howling and a banging, splinters whirled though the air, wounded screamed, and in between came the ratch-boom of anti-tank guns, the howling of anti-aircraft guns and hammering of machine guns. It was as if all hell had been let loose. After a few seconds we could not see five metres with the smoke and swathes of powder blowing in our faces. I sat in my dugout with my face pressed to the wall, waiting for the firing to stop. It only lasted ten minutes, but what had happened to our trenches in this time was beyond description. You could only wonder that you were still alive. What had been a properly constructed trench system was now a shallow scoop in the ground. The shells had completely shattered the trenches.

But then came the second instalment. The enemy rifle and machine gun fire started up and increased in volume. Pressed close to the ground, we waited for the enemy. That he would be coming now was certain. Suddenly the infantry fire eased up and a brown mass welled out of the Russian trenches. At the same time our own fire opened up, but even as many Russians fell, more came out of their trenches. Soon the first of them reached the trenches to our right with their cries of 'Urrah!' and broke into the communication trench. They then began rolling up our trenches. About 50 of them burst into the communication trench and more we coming all the time. We had to move ourselves. However, the way to the company command post was cut off, so we first went left and then back by another communication trench. But this trench was almost completely destroyed, offering us hardly any cover when the Russians opened fire on us, and my number two, Josef Wieser, was killed.

There was still a reserve section at the company command post, which now offered resistance to the Russians and checked their advance, enabling us to get away. But the reserve section was unable to hold the Russians and the company command post was lost. We occupied Solikante village, gradually amounting to about 40 men, supported by a machine gun section. Completely out of breath, I took up my position in a roadside ditch. Staff Sergeant Buchal lay in the ditch opposite. He called across: 'Tillery, have you got a cigarette?'

However, I only had tobacco and paper, so I slung my tobacco pouch across to him, but he too was out of breath and simply not ready to roll a cigarette, so I carefully rolled one for him and threw it across.

Meanwhile the Russians were busy sacking our company command post. We worked our way back toward it slowly and Second Lieutenant Reiffenscheidt gave the orders for a counterattack. I was wondering how we could throw back the ten times more numerous Russians. Would they mow every last one of us down? But orders are orders. We reached the communication trench exit about 200 metres from the command post and could see the Russians moving about. Then we charged. On the command, we ran forward loudly shouting 'Hurrah!' Once we got going, there was no stopping us. We charged full of enthusiasm, firing as we went, and it did not matter when my machine gun jammed. I tugged at the cocking handle, but to no avail. What could I do? Lie down and clear the jam? No, I could not do that either. So I charged on, not firing, but shouting all the louder. I was a bit to the left. Some of us went round the farm on the right, some straight into the farmyard and several, including myself, round to the left. The Russians sought safety in flight.

We thought that they had all left the farm. I turned and ran toward a liquid manure cart that stood in the corner of the garden. Suddenly there was a revolting smell from the manure cart as several bullets went through it right next to me. Twelve Russians were standing not more than ten metres from me in an extension to the communication trench, where previously a mortar had stood. One of them pointed at me and shouted something. At that same moment some comrades came out of the farm and threw hand grenades. Instinctively I pulled the trigger and the machine gun fired, all 50 rounds going off without jamming, as I aimed at the centre of the group. Some fled, but six lay there and two others only made it a short distance. I put in a fresh belt, but the gun refused to fire again.

Meanwhile my comrades had charged round the farm and we thrust forward again along the communication trench. The Russians promptly sought out their old positions and we re-occupied ours. The breach had been cleared. The Russians had suffered heavy casualties. We counted at least eighty dead. Apart from equipment, we captured one heavy, two light and several sub-machine guns. I took one of the latter. We too had suffered casualties; several dead, including Sepp Wieser, and several wounded. Second Lieutenant Gold, who had only just received his commission a few hours before, had been wounded in the charge. He had gone on ahead alone and screamed terribly when he was hit in the lower abdomen.

The Russians remained quiet for the rest of the day. We were relieved during the night. Shortly beforehand Sergeant Behrensen was killed by a shot to the head. The company was now only 48 strong, even though we had received several replacements.

The unit that replaced us was well equipped, combat experienced and rested. In contrast we had lost some of our weapons, were fought out, exhausted and filthy. In any case the relief was absolutely necessary and it was a stroke of luck to be relieved the day before the Russians' main offensive began.

The new troops arrived at the front line early on the morning of 15 April. We gave them a quick briefing and then marched back, happy to be out of that dangerous corner and not envying our reliefs their task, but we did not know that the Russians would be rolling over them 24 hours later. So we came to the rear positions that ran about three kilometres behind the front line.

Behind us lay the village of Altfriedland, in which there were still many civilians, most of them farmers. After several strenuous and wearying weeks, we were hoping to be able to have a proper break. First we saw to our weapons, then we could take care of ourselves. Once we had had a good wash we felt as fresh as new.

We were occupying a position that ran along in front of a manor farm and so did not have to crouch down in the trenches all the time, but lived in the buildings and took to the trenches only in an alert. At last we had time to write home. Many of the comrades' homes were in areas already occupied by the Russians or Americans, and news was reaching us only very sparingly at the front. I had read in the Armed Services Report that there was some heavy fighting in front of Bremen, but hoped that my letters would get through to my parents. Few of my parents' letters had reached me recently, and a lot of mail was not reaching its destination because of the many air attacks.

During the afternoon we worked on our position and at night we could sleep for the first time in weeks. However, one man from each platoon had to stand guard for half an hour at a time. The duties were given out and I got from 0330 to 0400 hours. I went to bed early in the straw that we had put down in the cellar and slept as if on a feather bed until it was time for my guard duty. This was the last time that I would have a whole night's sleep for weeks.

THE RUSSIAN OFFENSIVE BEGINS

I got up at 0330 hours, still half asleep, and took post, but did not have to be as alert as in the front line. It was very misty. I made the rounds of our quarters, and at ten to four woke up my relief and was happy that I could now sleep into the morning.

As I was going back down into the cellar, I heard the well-known sound; 'Flup, flup' coming from Ivan. He was firing his mortars. I took this to be the morning concert and carried on down. The first Russian salvos fell on the front line, but the hits started coming closer until they started landing in our vicinity. But there was more to it than that, more than the usual morning concert. Our building received several direct hits. Ivan was laying a violent bombardment down on us. Hit after hit followed the discharges and the din that came from their anti-aircraft and anti-tank guns and heavy artillery too could be heard.[9] Then the runner came from the company command post: 'Alert! Take post immediately!'

I reached the trenches, jumping from shellhole to shellhole under the heaviest fire. The earth was being ploughed up systematically, one crater overlapping the next. The trenches were already suffering and beginning to cave in. One of the comrades from my section was wounded with a splinter in his backside.

On the 14th, two days previously, I had thought it was the real bombardment, but what the Russians were giving us now was far, far worse. I did not think that anyone could survive. Every bit of earth was being churned over. I jumped in the holes where there had already been an explosion, as every soldier knows that no two shells land on the same spot. The minutes stretched into hours. At last after three hours the firing eased up and moved on behind us, but we knew that the second part was on its way. Now we could shoot back again, being no longer exposed to the shelling.

Men were running back from the front line, in a state of shock and without their weapons. Panting and trembling, they called out to us: 'Ivan is coming!'

Only a few had survived the shelling in the front line and been able to flee from the Russians, who were following close on their heels. One could not see them as it was so misty that you could hardly see ten metres, but you could hear them. The 'Urrahs!' were getting louder. I had handed in my machine gun for repair the day before because of the constant jamming, so Staff Sergeant Buchal sent me back to the company command post to get it. I found it, although the place was deserted, but when I came out again I could hear Russian voices in the immediate vicinity, and could not go back. The Russians had already reached our trenches. There was only one way out and that was to the rear. I ran westwards as fast as I could, but I had my heavy machine gun to carry. Apart from this, I had a box of ammunition, the Russian sub-machine gun, my pistol, hand grenades and all my equipment on me. Clearly I could not run very fast. The Russian voices were getting closer and soon they would be catching me up. I had to discard something. First went the Russian sub-machine gun, then the hand grenades went into the dirt, then the ammunition box, and finally I wanted to throw the machine gun away.

Suddenly I heard called from behind: 'Stoi! Ruchi verch!' The machine gun flew away in a high curve. I tugged at my ammunition pouches, but could not get them off. As I turned around I could see the outline of my pursuer, who already had his rifle up to his cheek. Then he lowered it again. 'Damn it, Tillery!' he said, 'Bring the machine gun with you!' It was no Russian, but a comrade from my platoon, Hans Kaldekowitz, who had a head wound. When the Russians arrived, they had not been able to get away in time and were overrun. Then they had mixed in with the advancing Russians and gradually got ahead. Later a large part of the company was to meet up again.

The next line was the rear defensive line, which ran between Sietzing and Klein-Neuendorf behind a four metre-wide ditch with 400 metres of open field in front of it, a very good defensive position.

Meanwhile the Russians had penetrated Klein-Neuendorf with their tanks. At the last minute some civilians escaped laden down with bundles of their possessions. The sun dispersed the mist at about 1000 hours and we could see the tanks. The anti-aircraft battery behind us then opened up and shot several of them. Here I met up again with several of my company, who had taken up position on the road to Klein-Neuendorf. It remained quiet in our area until about noon, although the sunshine had brought out the Russian ground-

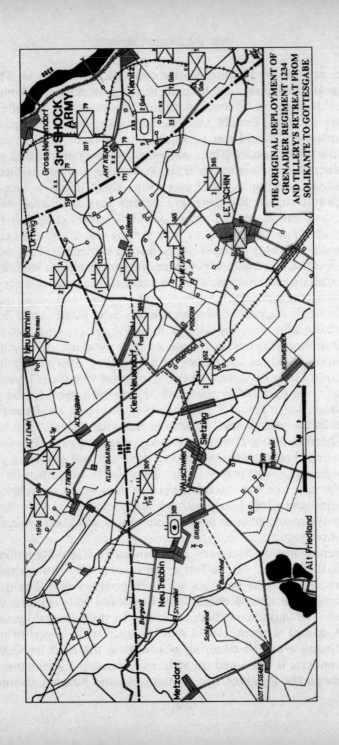

THE ORIGINAL DEPLOYMENT OF
GRENADIER REGIMENT 1234
AND TILLERY'S RETREAT FROM
SOLIKANTE TO GOTTESGABE

attack aircraft and fighters. The Russians had broken though in the neighbouring sector and we could see their tanks and trucks about two kilometres to the north. They were overcoming all resistance with the mass of their tanks and the following infantry were occupying the ground.

For a short while we had to occupy a sector further south. I went past a dugout that opened toward the Russians in which a soldier was sitting. I had gone past about 50 metres when it received a direct hit from an anti-tank gun. I went back to help the soldier, but he had vanished, having simply been blown to pieces.

As we were in danger of being surrounded, we had to move back again during the course of the afternoon. We could see how far the Russians had progressed from the columns of smoke rising in the sky wherever they were. In Wuschewier, to where we withdrew, we stopped for half a day. Then during the night of the 16th/17th we retreated again without getting a moment's sleep. Everywhere on the streets one could read the message: 'Berlin remains German!'

During the evening we prepared a new position but it was hardly finished when we had to withdraw again. We could only withdraw with difficulty, for the Russians had spotted our retreat and were trying to stop us with artillery fire.

The following morning, the 18th, we occupied positions on the north-eastern edge of Neu Trebbin, where our regiment gathered. Only 34 assembled, all the rest being either dead, wounded, captured or missing. Our company was still comparatively strong with about ten men remaining.

We deployed ourselves in front of the village. The Russians soon arrived and made an attack, coming to within a few metres of our positions and we even captured one. Suddenly the four self-propelled guns that had been supporting us vanished and now the Russians started coming at us with tanks. As we could hardly defend Neu Trebbin with less than forty men, we withdrew. We already had two men killed and several wounded in the village.

We withdrew about three kilometres over open fields until we came to a canal about ten metres across that ran between Neu Trebbin and Gottesgabe, and here we deployed once more. The self-propelled guns from Neu Trebbin reappeared in our support but, when the Russians attacked with tanks in big numbers, they had to be blown up as they were unable to cross the canal.

We pulled back to another ditch, where we were stomach deep in cold water, as otherwise the Russians would have seen us. My camouflage suit was soaked through and running with water, and I still had to carry my machine gun and box of ammunition, so I took off my padded trousers and threw them away; after all, it was spring. I could hardly get out of there. With every step my feet sank deep in the mud.

The Russians soon spotted us and brought the ditch under mortar fire. One bomb landed in the ditch and killed three men, including Corporal Kalteis. Then we had to cross an open field. The Russians were firing even when individuals crossed, using mortars – and accurately. At the end of the ditch lay a man wounded in the leg, who asked me to help him across. Although mortar bombs landed close, we managed to get across unscathed.

Then we came up against the military police and everyone who had a weapon had to go back into the line, but staff clerks and supply personnel were allowed to go, a factor that did little to raise our fighting morale.

I had become separated from my unit again. Although I knew that they were close by, the military police refused to let me find it. I was given a confused, thrown-together section to deploy along a line of trees in front of Gottesgabe. We had communication to the rear by means of a runner. When I sent a runner back with a message, he failed to reappear. I sent another runner back with the same result, so I went back myself to find out what was happening. I did not find a soul. They had all gone back without telling us.

A unit of 15 and 16 year-olds of the Hitler Youth had made an attack from Gottesgabe and been driven back with heavy casualties. I was deployed with my section along the eastern edge of the village. During the night the Russians thrust their way into the village with tanks and we had to withdraw.

We deployed again about 200 metres west of Gottesgabe. Suddenly about forty men came toward us. We opened fire, thinking they must be Russians, and by the time we discovered they were Germans, two of them were already dead.

At dawn on the 19th we occupied a position on the heights on the edge of the Oderbruch. It was a good position and we could see far over the valley. As it became light, we could see the Russians with masses of tanks and thousands of soldiers in and around Gottesgabe, and we were only a hundred strong. Slowly the tanks and the soldiers started moving. When they came to about 200 metres from us, we opened fire from the heights.

The Russians immediately started digging in while their tanks moved up. Then the tanks fired on us, later also mortars and anti-tank guns. When the fire became stronger, we withdrew, for the Russians had already bypassed us on either flank.

During the withdrawal I became separated again from the rest of my regiment, but then met up with five other men from my company. Properly formed units no longer existed, for they had either been split up or wiped out. Many had fallen. We six reported to the commander of a light anti-aircraft battery that had been deployed on the eastern edge of Ihlow. We deployed ourselves about 100 metres forward of the battery in a ditch that ran past a grocery. The village had been evacuated of its population only a few hours before. For once we could eat well; everything we longed for we found here. Abandoned cattle were roaming about everywhere.

When the first Russian tanks appeared the 20 cm anti-aircraft guns opened up and shot up several of them. As the Russians closed in on the village, we moved to the western edge, where there was a large manor farm, behind whose enclosing wall we took cover from the heavy shelling. We were also constantly fired at by low flying aircraft, and soon the Russians came in sight. Karl Danzer was severely wounded by a mortar bomb that exploded close to us, getting a splinter in his stomach. Once the Russians had crossed the road leading to Strausberg, cutting our line of retreat, the guns were blown up. Once more we were surrounded as we had been the day before, and would be again in the days to come.

That evening we withdrew under cover of darkness through a wood. Altogether we were about 60 men. After we had marched about four kilometres, we came to a road running east-west, along which trucks were driving westwards. We infantry marched with the battery commander, a lieutenant, at the head of the battery. The battery commander thought that this was a retreat route, but I noticed that nearly all the trucks had sloping radiators, and we did not have any like that. I reported my misgivings, but he told me off, saying that he was the commander and knew best. He had taken over the battery only the day before, after the previous commander had been killed. However, when trucks went past packed with singing soldiers, it was clear enough to me that they were Russian. I told my regimental comrades – there were now six of us – and we slipped back to the rear of the battery. To the left and right of us were ever thicker pine woods. Suddenly came some shouting and then the voice of the battery commander: 'Don't shoot!'

We could hear Russians shouting from in front and like lightning we vanished into the woods. The battery was captured virtually intact and now I realised that the commander was German but fighting on the Russian side and presumably a member of the National Committee for a Free Germany.[10]

Two men from the battery had come with us, so now we were eight. We forced our way through the dark woods toward the southwest. After we had been going for about three hours we came to the the village of Gross Wilkendorf, near Strausberg. We did not know if it was occupied by the Russians, so we crept cautiously up to it through an orchard, but could hear no voices. Then we heard the sound of an engine and someone calling out, so we knew that there were Germans here. As we entered the village, we saw a truck moving out with a heavy gun in tow. We appeared to be the only living beings in the village. We went into a house and had something to eat. We found enough food, for the inhabitants had moved out only a few hours before.

We moved on again. There was an ambulance at the other end of the village, but it suddenly drove off as we came up to it. There had been a field hospital in the school here that had been cleared. However, Karl Meinhardt was able to swing himself aboard as it set off. I ran along behind, but the vehicle was increasing speed. Karl stretched out his hand to me and I was able to grasp his fingers. He pulled me in and for a short while we were safe, although separated from the others. We were dropped off just short of Strausberg.

We then looked for a house a bit off the road where we could sleep for a few hours, but were soon disturbed by the sounds of tank gunfire, so again there was no sleep, and we had been almost a week without it. We debated whether to report to an infantry unit or to do as most troops were doing and simply make our way back. We decided on the latter and to try and get a day to relax and sleep in at long last. We had not washed or shaved for days, and looked more like vagabonds than soldiers. Our uniforms were encrusted with mud, and my hair had not been cut for weeks. The experiences of the last few days were etched in our faces. We had become pale and hollow-cheeked with dark circles under our eyes. When I happened to see my face in a mirror, I was shocked by my appearance. I certainly did not look like a 19 year-old.

We had only been going a few minutes when we were rounded up. A unit of 15- and 16-year-old Hitler Youths had deployed here, even though not all were armed. All soldiers going past were being rounded up by them and taken into their ranks. There were hardly any machine guns, but one thing you had to give them was their spirit, which was something seldom seen. They simply could not wait for the Russians to come. They knocked out several Russian tanks at ranges of four or five metres, and when the Russians realised that the resistance here was particularly strong, they brought up more tanks as reinforcements. Although the youngsters suffered severe losses, we only withdrew when the Russians came at us from three sides.

We then occupied a village that lay in a valley.[11] But here too we soon had to move, as we were too weak. We then occupied the high ground around the village, although some of the youngsters remained behind armed only with Panzerfausts[12] to knock out the Russian tanks. Whenever they succeeded they would return with happy faces to pick up fresh Panzerfausts. Nearly all were dressed in brown shirts, short pants and a much too large helmet. But as many tanks as they destroyed, the more took their place. There were at least ten Russians to every German soldier. As soon as the tanks had taken over the village, they turned their guns on us and inflicted more heavy casualties. Meanwhile the Russian infantry had caught up.

Suddenly we heard 'Urrah!' cries to our rear, so once more we found ourselves in a trap. We withdrew, hardly 30 of us, and somehow we met up with German soldiers again. The Russians had advanced a considerable distance to the north of us and we could hear heavy firing from there, but to the south it was quiet, so we headed in that direction.

After we had been going for some hours through a wood that had big swamps in it, we came to a road leading to Rüdersdorf. There, hundreds of vehicles were streaming back, all to the west. It was the night of 20/21 April and the vehicles had driven into each other so that they could neither go forward nor back. At last we got some sleep in a school, where we lay on the hard floor until morning. Then we carried on along the Frankfurt/Oder road to Berlin.

Karl Meinhardt and I had had enough of this marching, so we simply swung ourselves onto a field howitzer going past and had ourselves carried along, thus becoming separated from our unit. There were constant hold-ups. The road was over-filled with vehicles and refugees with handcarts, prams and horse-drawn wagons. The Russians were pressing so hard that we were unable to stop and deploy. At Hoppegarten the flood came to an absolute halt. Here, immediately before Berlin, the Russians had to be stopped.

There were some military police standing at a crossroads who rounded up all those that were still capable of fighting into companies. Our names were taken down in a pub and then we were sent to our positions right of the main road. On the way Karl and I were invited into a house where the people gave us food and we also took time to have a wash and shave. Strengthened and refreshed, we went on to our positions.

There was a Volkswagen standing by the famous stables[13] and on its mudguard was the armoured bear sign of our division. I asked the Colonel there about our unit and was told that this was our divisional supply column and that the fighting troops had been scattered everywhere. We were the first of our division that they had seen for days. He advised us: 'Make sure that you get home safe and sound. There is no sense in this any more.'

That evening we withdrew on orders to Mahlnow, a suburb of Berlin, and deployed in a cemetery. The trenches were already dug, and we were reinforced by Volkssturm[14] and a police battalion.

The Russians continued to push their way forward slowly. When they came up against resistance on our right, where the police were, they plastered us with mortars. Our company commander was a gunner second lieutenant with no previous infantry experience.

Karl Meinhardt became the headquarters section commander and I the company runner. For a week now Karl and I had had no regular meals, so the company commander sent me off to scrounge something. I rode a bicycle back and came to a school where the ladies were cooking, and got two milk cans full of food. Once I had satisfied my hunger, I rode back to the company with the milk cans hanging from my handlebars. As I came up to the company bullets suddenly started whistling past my ears, so I turned sharply into a sidestreet. I then had to carry the cans forward through the houses.

During the afternoon of the 23rd the Russians thrust forward again. The police battalion occupying the neighbouring sector departed without informing us, leaving that flank open. The Russians used this opportunity to close in on us. We pulled out as soon as we recognised the danger. The company on our left had also pulled out. Fortunately, there was still a way out open.

The company commander sent me off to re-establish contact with the company that had left just before us. I had gone about 200 metres when I suddenly heard voices coming from a side street. I stopped and listened, as night had fallen and I could not see anything. Russians were coming along the street. I stayed where I was and called to the company commander to come over, but he misunderstood and walked straight into the Russians at the crossroads. Some that still offered resistance were shot down by the Russians and others taken prisoner.

More Russians arrived. If I had opened fire, it would have been suicide. When they got to within 20 metres of me, I ran off. I could hear Russians shouting and singing everywhere. After I had run about three kilometres I met up with our supply section. I was completely exhausted.

PANZERGRENADIER

In front of me were trucks, tanks, guns, all fleeing to the west. I went on for a few more kilometres. There was a traffic jam when we came to a crossing over the railway.[15] I had had enough of marching and asked the commander of a tank if I could have a ride. I had hardly slept in the last few days and had travelled over a hundred kilometres. My eyes kept closing with fatigue and I was footsore. The commander of the tank, Second Lieutenant Lorenz, allowed me to climb aboard, and now the journey went faster.

Several hours later, after being held up by numerous traffic jams, Second Lieutenant Lorenz ordered the tank to stop. The crew had been in action for weeks with little sleep. We lay down somewhere in a hallway and slept well into the next day, 25 April.

It had been dark the previous night and we had seen very little of the city. When I came out into the open air I was astonished to see that we were in the middle of Berlin in a shopping street with several large buildings all round us. We were bombarded with questions from all sides by the inhabitants. Their electricity supply had failed, all sorts of rumours were circulating in the city and no one knew anything for certain. The place was like an ants' nest.

The Russians had thrust past Berlin, and many people were trying to get out of the city, but I gave it no thought. I felt myself quite safe. I could see what weapons there were around and that there were sufficient supplies for months. That Berlin would fall within the next ten days, I would never have believed.

Second Lieutenant Lorenz asked me if I would stay with them as an escort infantryman, a panzergrenadier. The tank was a 38(t), a Czech model known as the Hetzer, which had made quite a good name for itself; it was small and manoeuverable, very fast, had a 75 mm gun and a machine gun. The crew consisted of four men: commander, gunner, driver and radio operator. There were also four panzergrenadiers attached with the task of defending the tank in close-quarter combat. Two of their panzergrenadiers had been killed in action. With my arrival we were a trio.

The tank was part of the Panzer Division 'Schlesien'. Only a few tanks of this division were still in action. We first looked for our regimental headquarters, driving up and down through Berlin.

We went past a big warehouse and saw large packing cases being removed. Second Lieutenant Lorenz sent me in to scrounge something. I got a large box with bottles of wine, schnapps, liquors and sekt, something for everyone. I also found a copy of the *Völkische Beobachter*[16], which had the headlines 'The Bolshevik horde's attack will founder on Berlin's walls', 'The Führer is with us', and so on. The newspaper was only half the size of a normal newspaper sheet. Having found regimental headquarters, we were tasked with securing a street, but nothing happened. Then in the afternoon we had to secure another street, but again heard nothing from the Russians. I went off on the scrounge, as we had had nothing to eat all day. There were soldiers wandering around all over the place, but no kind of order. There were hardly any proper units left, just stragglers everywhere and no leadership. A soldier asked me for a cigarette. I had plenty, having been given 300. In exchange I asked him for something to eat and he gave me seven cans of pork, one for everyone with the tank. I went back and we opened the cans with our bayonets. Meanwhile the Russians had brought up their artillery and started firing, at first sparingly, into the city. I ate my meat sitting on the steps of a burnt-out building, the other two panzergrenadiers were leaning against the tank and the crew sitting inside. Suddenly there was a roaring in the air and I saw forty to fifty Stalin-Organ rockets coming toward us. These rockets had a diameter of 10.5cm, as I later discovered, and left a fire trail behind them. I vanished into the building like lightning at the same moment as the rockets crashed down around us. Stones, dirt and dust clattered down around me. When the dust cleared, I saw where the rockets had been aimed: the tank was buried under about two metres of rubble with just the top showing. The ruined buildings had collapsed and fallen into the street, burying the two panzergrenadiers alive. The entry hatch had been left open, but no one inside had been badly hurt. They had bruises and scratches, and everything inside was covered in thick dust. Fortunately the engine was still intact and the driver was able to drive out of the rubble. I too was thickly covered in dust and had some minor scratches. My pork was now inedible, of course.

Next day, the 26th, we had a day off, as the tank urgently needed overhauling and cleaning. We could stretch out on a lovely plot of land in western Berlin and relax while the mechanic saw to the tank. It was lovely spring weather with greenery everywhere and the fruit trees in blossom. We made ourselves comfortable on our nice plot of land and could sleep undisturbed and wash ourselves properly in peace. However, next day we would have to go back into action.

Meanwhile the Russians had completed their ring around Berlin and we no longer had any communication with the west. From now on the Russians fired on the city with all calibres of artillery, while aircraft dropped their bomb loads on us. One risked one's life going out on the street. Everywhere buildings and vehicles were burning and dead soldiers lying around. The water supply had collapsed and the population had to queue for hours at the few pumps as the shells fell, killing women and children.

Next day, the 28th, we went to the Tiergarten, where the regimental headquarters were located. Our tank parked close to the Victory Column (Siegessäule), where all hell was let loose. The Russians had worked out that our heavy artillery must have moved into the area, for they had fired a few times, and now were bombarding the area with artillery, mortars and bombs. As the firing intensified, I ran across to the Victory Column, under which there was a cellar, where I felt relatively safe. The Russians were already at the Brandenburg Gate, which I could see from there. There were four 37mm anti-aircraft guns near the Victory Column, but no longer firing, and Russian bombers were flying over at 200 to 300 metres in close formation without being fired at.

The firing continued to intensify and we could not afford to stay any longer. We drove off westwards along the East-West Axis. I preferred to run alongside the tank rather than sit aboard, as there was no cover on top. But as the tank could be seen by the aircraft, Second Lieutenant Lorenz drove ahead and waited for me. Suddenly a squadron of nine twin-engined bombers flew right over us and dropped their bombs in our immediate vicinity, so I took cover in a shellhole.

That night we were able to sleep again, with everyone taking turns at one hour of sentry duty. We moved into private accommodation in Mommsenstrasse, which was mainly undamaged. The inhabitants pestered us with questions, and when we said that we were looking for accommodation for the night, they mustered round us. However, we did not get much sleep, as during the night we received orders to go back into action. We were sent to Wilmersdorf, where we had to secure Barstrasse, where it led off Mecklenburgische Strasse. Our tanks stood at a crossroads and covered toward Mecklenburgische Strasse. Behind us were some shops, a small lake with a bridge going over it, and beyond it a cemetery and a crematorium. The Russians were already occupying the other end of the street.

Suddenly a T-34 appeared. Our gunner had spotted it and it burst into flames with the first shot. Meanwhile the Russian

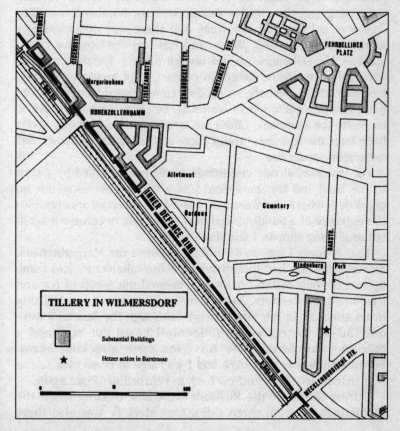

infantry could be seen in the buildings, so we had to withdraw over the bridge to the cemetery.

On 30 April we changed position again to the Margarinehaus on the Hohenzollerndam, where there was also a Mark IV tank from our regiment. In the Margarinehaus were thousands of civilians who had lost everything in the last few days, mainly women and children. There were no supplies and the children were crying for bread. Unholy chaos reigned. There were also many soldiers here, and the Russians were only 100 metres away.

On the afternoon of the 30th we moved back to Fehrbelliner Platz, where there were some large administrative buildings. Most of the city was now in Russian hands and we were being pushed in closer together. The Russian artillery fire was steadily increasing and the city lay under constant bombardment. For days we had not had any sleep and there was no longer any warm food to be had. We would have to see how we could survive. Nevertheless, we did not go hungry, for the civilians, with whom we were always in contact, kept giving us snacks. However, these were the worst days in my experience, for in the front line one knew where Ivan was, but here we had always to be ready for surprises. Often we would be in a building and a little later the Russians would come and bring the windows and cellar exits under fire.

For instance, at one crossroads a soldier was killed by a shot in the head and lay there dead just a few metres away, but no one knew where the Russians were. I disappeared quickly into the entrance of a building, and how I was able to come out again without being shot at, I still don't know.

That evening I was in a building opposite the Margarinehaus. The Russian fire had diminished and the inhabitants had come up out of their cellars. A woman brewed me a cup of tea and gave me a few biscuits. As if in normal peacetime, I was sitting in an armchair in her sitting room, although the Russians were only 30–40 metres away. Suddenly I heard our tank and a machine gun firing. The Russians were attacking again. Fortunately it was very dark and I was able to cross over to the Margarinehaus. We withdrew back to Fehrbelliner Platz again.

During the night the Russians were able to close in on the Margarinehaus from three sides. Our Mark IV was also there and could not withdraw, because it was not known which streets were occupied by the Russians. On the morning of 1 May, Second Lieutenant Lorenz sent me to look for a way out for them. 'Don't miss anything, though!' he said. At first I tried to reach the Margarinehaus via Eisenzahnstrasse. I ran across and was shot at by a Russian anti-tank gun, but was saved by diving into a cellar entrance as the splinters smashed into the wall above my head. Then I tried again via Cicerostrasse and Nestorstrasse, but I was spotted in both of them and shot at. The only route remaining was via Osnabrücker Strasse.[17] I ran from cellar entrance to cellar entrance and when I had to cross an open space, I opened fire on the Russians. There was not a single German soldier to be seen anywhere around. The last stretch was over open ground, but I was not shot at as I had expected, and I covered it at the run. I reported to the commandant of the Margarinehaus, a lieutenant colonel who had already given up hope of further contact with the outside world. There were now some 800 men in the building and when I explained to him that there was still a chance of getting away, he immediately ordered the building to be cleared.

The Mark IV tank had left during the evening and driven back. I had now to return to my tank, which was about 300 metres away. Explosions, bangs and whistles were going on everywhere and I was only about 100 metres from my tank when suddenly a shell howled close by. I instinctively dived for cover, but too late. I was intending to take cover behind a window sill, but the blast caught me and blew me on top of it instead. At the same moment I felt a burning pain in my upper left arm and in my rear. I felt around with my right hand and found blood. I had splinters in my right arm and rear. I hobbled into the building, feeling quite numb. After shouting several times, someone answered from the cellar and two young girls of about 18 came up and took me down into the cellar, where they applied first aid dressings. After about half an hour, I hobbled back to the tank. Second Lieutenant Lorenz let me sit aboard and took me to the battalion command post, where the medical centre was located, and there I was bandaged properly.

This was hardly finished before Second Lieutenant Lorenz came for me and took me to report to the battalion commander. The battalion commander commended me for what I had done and awarded me the Iron Cross Second Class. As the doctor who had bandaged me was afraid I might get tetanus from my wounds, I was given an anti-tetanus injection. Shortly afterwards I developed a terrible itch that got worse and worse, and then I lost consciousness.

I was taken in the tank to an emergency field hospital in a cinema. When I came to again, I was lying on the floor of the cinema with a frightful itch and a terrible thirst. The nurses had removed my weapons, as no one was allowed to keep them in hospital. Several hours later, after I had been through some hallucinations and stumbling around, Second Lieutenant Lorenz came to see me. He wanted to say good-bye to me and said: 'I would have liked to have kept you with us.' Then he shook his head and said: 'Tonight we are going to break out to the west to the Americans.'

'And what will happen to us remaining here?'

'Berlin will be surrendering in the morning.'

No, the Russians were not going to get me. 'Sir, I am coming with you, even if I have to tie myself to the tank. I am not stopping here!'

He grinned and said: 'Alright, then!'

Those comrades that were coming with us supported me as I hobbled to the tank. The rear of the tank sloped a bit and I could hold on. The engine was beneath me and it was quite hot. Suddenly the woollen blanket I was wrapped in because of my fever caught fire.

During that night of 1/2 May, all available vehicles were deployed for an attack to the west to force a way out of the encirclement. In fact the troops fought with contempt for death, for they knew that the only possibility of getting away from the clutches of the Russians was by driving them back about ten kilometres. But only a narrow corridor was fought free, less than 100 metres wide, with the Russians on either side of it. The latter quickly brought together all their guns and mortars to bear and waited for us to come. Naturally, they were expecting us to try and break out.

The stream of vehicles rolled incessantly along this corridor to the west. Our tank was one of the last, as we had to secure the rear. Thousands of vehicles forced their way along this one free route. Ever more vehicles forced their way along, were shot up and caused traffic jams. We came through Spandau, which was already occupied by the Russians. A vast number of the inhabitants decided to come along with us to the Americans, telling us what chaos the Russians had caused. More and more vehicles fell out, and panicky confusion reigned on the streets. Thousands of dead lay around amid the burning vehicles and constant shelling. The wounded cried out for help, but no one heeded them.

In Spandau the stream of vehicles had to cross a bridge over the river.[18] The Russians were sitting only a few metres away and brought down everything possible to inflict more casualties. The bridge was already half destroyed by artillery fire and only one vehicle at a time could cross, but thousands wanted to. Every man opened fire on the Russians. Hundreds of dead and wounded lay in several layers on top of each other. At first there were twenty men clinging to our tank; all but four were shot off.

The route went on via Staaken. While there had been ten thousand wanting to break out through Spandau, there were now hardly a thousand at Staaken, and only a few hundred left when we came to Döberitz. We crossed the Döberitz Training Area with a Russian biplane keeping an eye on us and warning of our coming.

Our force was getting smaller and smaller. We saw no more infantry, only three Mark IVs and three Hetzers and several armoured personnel carriers were still together. Suddenly our tank stopped and refused to go any more. I was able to get aboard a Mark IV as our tank was blown up. The crew stayed behind. We then drove through a Russian artillery position before the Russians realised it and were away.

When we came to about 20 kilometres from Brandenburg, we went through a village that was swarming with Russians. This village lay deep in the Russian rear, the front being far distant. In any case the Russians had never expected us to appear here, but before they could recover from the shock and get hold of their weapons, we were away again. Then we had to drive round a corner and, as we drove round slowly, a fat Russian came out of a house on the corner and pulled up his sub-machine gun and started shooting at us. I already had my pistol out and fired back. As we turned the corner there was a sudden bang and I flew in a high curve off the tank. It had received a direct hit from an anti-tank gun and burst into flames. I thought to myself: 'If you don't want to be caught here, you are going to have to play it cool.'

But where should I go? There was thick smoke all around me, and a few metres away was a ditch with a bridge leading over it, so I hid myself in the reeds of the ditch until it was dark. Then I went further along through the reeds. The ditch opened out into a reed-lined lake. With two other soldiers that I found in the reeds, I stayed here four days. We hid ourselves in a willow bush. The ground was so wet that puddles formed whenever you put your foot down. None of us had anything to eat. I developed a high fever and was unable to think clearly about continuing our flight. It was very cold at night and my clothing was wet, so with the fever, no food, and Russians all around, there seemed no point in hanging on.

After four nights I was so weak that I could not last out any longer. Nearby was a farmhouse a little apart from the rest, at which I asked for something to eat. I was given some bread, a few potatoes boiled in their jackets, and a pan full of milk. The farmer's wife also gave me a civilian suit, quite an old thing, but I put it on. I sank my uniform in the lake together with my pistol, medal, papers and letters. Then I slept in the hay for a few hours.

Next morning, 7 May, I set off with one of my comrades. Although every step was painful and I was still very weak, we left the farmhouse in good heart and marched off to the west. As far as we were concerned, the war was over and we hoped to get back home soon.

Unfortunately it did not work out this way and one and a half years in Russian captivity were to follow.

Tillery was captured on 6 May and released again after a week because of his wounds. He stayed with a farmer near Rathenow for about four weeks only to be arrested once more and sent to a camp near Brest-Litovsk, where a third of the 800 prisoners died, and he himself lost over 40 lbs in weight. He was repatriated in the autumn of 1946 as unfit for work, and obtained a job as an interpreter in an American hospital kitchen, where he soon regained his strength. He then made his career in the German Post Office. He married in 1954 and now has a son and a grandson serving in the Bundeswehr.

1 In fact the German counter bombardment separated the Soviet infantry from their accompanying tanks by the time they reached Route 112 and their advance came to a halt just beyond Rathstock.
2 I have a report on this by Herbert Tegeler, a platoon commander in the neighbouring 2 Company, commanded by Lieutenant Dr. Hoffmann, which broke through north of Rathstock to arrive back in Sachsendorf intact that same night.
3 These also served as rain-capes.
4 These foundations were usually of 'Feldsteine', ice age boulders recovered from the fields, and were immensely strong.
5 However, Sachsendorf was retaken by the Germans and was in their hands as a major strongpoint until the 16th April.
6 This was the honour guard battalion from Berlin.
7 Shortage of brass led to the introduction of steel cartridges, which had to be protected from rust with lacquer, but the latter melted once the breech of a weapon became hot and caused the cartridges to stick. Machine gunners would have to change their barrels after every burst and riflemen to force open the bolts with their entrenching tools, a tedious business that drastically slowed down the rate of fire.
8 The Po-2 was armoured against infantry fire.
9 Marshal Zhukov had ordered every available gun to be fired, whether they were targeted or not, in order to add to the psychological pressure.
10 Otherwise known as 'Seydlitz-Troops'.
11 Probably Gielsdorf.
12 A hand held anti-tank weapon.
13 Hoppegarten is a famous German racecourse with its own stables and training facilities.
14 The Volkssturm was raised by a decree of 25 September 1944 forming a Home Guard under Nazi Party auspices from all men aged 16 to 60 capable of bearing arms. The Hitler Youth were also armed and exploited in the defence of their country.
15 Presumably where Frankfurter Allee crosses the S-Bahn ring.
16 The official Nazi Party newspaper.
17 Now Bielefelder Strasse.
18 This was the Charlotten Bridge over the Havel, which had been severely damaged when an ammunition truck blew up while crossing. Horst Zobel (see The Bridge at Golzow) led the break-out here in an armoured personnel carrier, the break-out having been organised by Luftwaffe Major General Sydow.

FOUR

The Siege of Klessin

Tony Le Tissier

I have pieced together this account from an after action report and extracts of a radio log provided by Lieutenant General Hans-Joachim von Hopffgarten, who was Ia (chief-of-staff) of the Panzergrenadier Division 'Kurmark' at the time. Further information was provided by Herr Helmut Jurisch, then a radio operator in the Tank Regiment 'Brandenburg'. Prewar photographs and the diary of Herr Otto Karl Paul von Albedyll, the then 57-year-old squire of Klessin, were kindly provided by Dr. Reinhard Schmook of the Oderlandmuseum, Bad Freienwalde, plus additional photographs and material supplied by Dr Jürgen Freymuth OBE.

To find Klessin on the map, one has to follow the road running north out of Frankfurt on the Oder to Lebus and then look for the first turn-off on the right, where this tiny hamlet sits on the eastern edge of the Reitwein Spur, a good hundred feet above the Oder valley. The Klessin of today bears little resemblance to the Klessin of early 1945, the few remaining houses having been resited, but the geographical features are the same, with two tracks rising steeply from the Oder valley on either side of the promontory on which the Schloss, or manor house, once stood. Capping the promontory between these tracks, the house had magnificent commanding views over the valley that gave it its military significance, but today its site and former gardens are completely overgrown with trees.

The metalled road from Podelzig ran directly toward the main entrance to the house, being flanked by labourers' cottages and outhouses either side of the approach to the courtyard entrance. This long rectangular courtyard was in turn flanked by barns, cowsheds and stables with access to the external parallel streets. A further group of cottages and outhouses lay at right-angles to the north of this formal grouping.

The owner of the Schloss, Otto von Abedyll, kept a diary from which it is clear that the Klessin Gut, or manor farm, was a prosperous concern with a variety of livestock, including dairy cattle, pigs and sheep, and considerable stocks of grain and other produce stored in its various barns. When the Red Army closed up to the line of the Oder in early February 1945, von Abedyll was able to evacuate the civilian population and most of his livestock, but the produce was lost when the area came under shellfire and the barns caught fire.

Then on the late afternoon of 15 February the Soviet 69th Army launched a surprise attack across the last of the ice into Lebus. Unheralded by the usual preparatory bombardment, two infantry divisions, supported by tanks, broke through the German lines to threaten the rear of the Reitwein Spur position, but were contained in time by elements of the Panzergrenadier-Division 'Kurmark' under Colonel Willy Langkeit, which had meanwhile taken over the defence of this sector. To reinforce the 'Kurmark' had come several two-battalion officer-cadet grenadier regiments raised from potential officers at the Reich's various Kriegschule (KS), after which they were named. Thus the core of these units was of unusually high calibre, for the officers were instructors from these schools and the potential officers all experienced NCOs, but numbers and replacements had to be made up from all sorts, including Volkssturm.

With the ice melting, the Soviets had to resort to bridge-building against which the Germans turned their air and artillery resources with varying success. During the second half of February the 'Kurmark' received formidable artillery reinforcements and could eventually summon up to 250 guns in its support, the cooperation in providing defensive fire for the infantry working extremely well. With unusually plentiful supplies of ammunition readily available, these resources could lay up to 8,000 shells on an area of 11,000 square metres to support or quell an infantry attack. Bombardment conditions on the Reitwein Spur from the artillery of both sides were described by some First World War veterans as comparable to those experienced at Fort Douamont near Verdun in 1916. In the severe winter weather of 1945 the Wuhden and Klessin positions were of particular value as observation points.

On 2 March a night attack by elements of 8th Guards Army sweeping down the Reitwein Spur forced the German lines back to the eastern edge of Podelzig, leaving a battalion of the 1st Grenadier Regiment 'KS Potsdam' isolated in Wuhden, where it had to set up an all-round defence. A counterattack next day stalled under heavy Soviet fire and failed to get through. A Führer Order was then issued declaring Wuhden a 'fortress', which meant defending it to the last man, but it was totally unprepared for this role, its only supply resources being a potato store and a single well. Air supply was decided upon and a transport aircraft allocated for making night drops, but the Soviets promptly brought up their anti-aircraft artillery and soon rendered this means of supply impracticable. The Corps Commander, SS-General Matthias Kleinheisterkamp, then ordered an armoured thrust to relieve the garrison, but this met such a hail of anti-tank gunfire that the tanks hardly got across their start line. A subsequent dash at night by three of the 'Brandenburg's' Panthers was more successful. Although one tank was knocked out and another damaged, the latter got through with the third tank, which happened to be a communications vehicle manned by radio operators and thus provided good communications for the beleaguered garrison. However, the first message out reported the majority of the battalion either dead or wounded, leaving a combatant strength of only 150–160 men. They had no medical officer with them to tend to their wounded and they were under frequent attack by Soviet infantry and being heavily shelled day and night.

Corps turned down all requests by Colonel Langkeit for permission for a break-out as being contrary to Hitler's orders. Eventually Colonel Langkeit decided on his own responsibility to order a break-out on the 12th March, by which time the potato store and the well had been destroyed, only 80 of the original

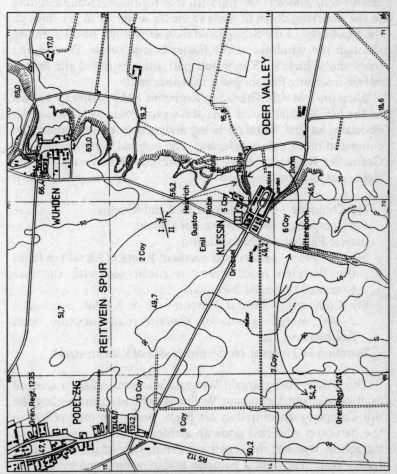

The Deployment of the 2nd Battalion Fahnenjunker-Grenadier-Regiment 1242 on the 7th March 194?

The Target areas indicated are based upon interpretation of the radio log.

400 men were still on their feet and the wounded had to be abandoned. Nevertheless, the 'Kurmark' continued to report Wuhden held for a further four days until formal permission to break out finally came through. The survivors were then rewarded with their commissions as second lieutenants and fourteen day's leave.

A similar fate was now to befall Klessin, which had also been declared a 'fortress' at the beginning of March while defended by elements of the Panzergrenadier Regiment 'Kurmark'. Franz Schaberich, who was serving with that regiment, recalls assisting in the knocking down of walls to enable a Hetzer to get through ·the front door of the Schloss and manoeuvre into position to fire through the windows at the Soviet bridge below. Several hits from the vehicle's 75 mm gun partially destroyed the bridge before returning fire obliged it to withdraw.

Then on 7 March, Grenadier Regiment 1242 (formerly known as the 'KS Wetzlar') took over the sector Point 54.2-Klessin-Alt Podelzig, its 2nd Battalion being assigned to Klessin under the command of a Captain Wiegand. The original deployment, with Grenadier Regiment 1241 (also formerly 'KS Weslar') on its right, was as follows:

7th Company – between Point 54.2 and Klessin
6th Company – southern front of Klessin
Bicycle Platoon – Schloss Klessin
5th Company – eastern and northern fronts of Klessin as far as the Wuhden road, where it connected with the 2nd Company of the 1st Battalion
8th Company + Mortar Platoon + 2 or 3 HMG Sections – 3–400 metres south of Klessin road junction with Reichsstrasse 112
Battalion HQ – cellar on the north side of Klessin street

Three days later Captain Wiegand was sent off on a General Staff course and Lieutenant Wolfgang Schöne, commanding the 8th Company, appointed in his place, being the only officer in the battalion who had done an artillery spotting course, even though he was not the senior subaltern. One of his subsequent letters read: 'Far right a pontoon bridge, submerged by day and refloated at night when they bring their tanks across cheekily with their headlights full on. We have to count them and report the number to Regiment. That is our main task.'

On his first afternoon in command, the Soviets advanced up the sunken road from the south with the aid of tanks to reach the Klessin-Podelzig road, but a counterattack by the regiment that evening re-opened the route and destroyed a T-34 tank. Again the following afternoon, 11 March, the Soviets in battalion strength attacked the German positions north of the hamlet and were only forced back by committing the last of the regimental reserves. That night the Soviets broke the German lines at the juncture between Grenadier Regiments 1242 and 1235 west of Wuhden and thrust south, cutting off and surrounding Klessin. Those German troops that had been fighting north of Klessin were forced back into it, adding elements of the 2nd and 3rd Companies of the 1st Battalion to the garrison strength. Only a weak and by day untenable line of positions now connected the Klessin garrison with Point 54.2 and the rest of the regiment.

During the night of 12/13 March it was possible to re-supply the garrison once more using tanks and armoured personnel carriers, which were also able to remove the wounded, but came under heavy artillery fire on their return journey.

Temporarily reinforced by the remains of the Replacement Battalion 'Feldherrnhalle'[1], Grenadier Regiment 1242 made a bid to re-open the link to Klessin on the evening of the 13th March, but failed with heavy losses attributed mainly to heavy anti-tank gunfire coming from the direction of Wuhden. Only a few Soviet tanks were engaged in this action.

The only well providing water for Klessin was destroyed by shellfire that day and there were to be four waterless days for the garrison before some enterprising individuals managed to re-open the well and discover a second one. The garrison remained under constant artillery and mortar fire with mounting casualties. The wounded were tended by the battalion medical officer, Junior Surgeon Dr. Gehre, who worked untiringly under the most difficult circumstances, not least a lack of medical supplies. The accumulating wounded spread from the neighbouring cellar into the battalion command post itself.

The supply difficulties were partly eased by some calves,

several lambs, a quantity of potatoes and a sack of peas left behind by Herr von Albedyll after the evacuation of the property.

Communications were provided by the regimental signals platoon with a radio section under Corporal Hopp, later to be promoted sergeant, whose radiomen fortunately had a faster speed of transmission than those usually encountered with the infantry. Then there was the Armoured Artillery Regiment 'Kurmark''s forward observer, Sergeant Hennecke, who was later to be recommended for promotion and the award of the Iron Cross First Class for his brilliant work in directing artillery fire under the most arduous conditions, and the forward observer of the SS-Artillery Battalion 101, Sergeant Hagen, whose radio failed to function throughout. However, there was an acute shortage of batteries for the sets, and expired batteries were supposed to be returned to Regiment for recharging whenever possible. Extracts of Sergeant Major Baier's radio log at the regimental command post survive and provide a comprehensive background to events.

At 0941 hours on the 13th March, Klessin garrison reported the massing of Soviet anti-tank guns, mortars and infantry northeast of the hamlet and called for a fire concentration. At 1320 hours 5 Company holding the northeastern perimeter came under attack but managed to beat the enemy back. The garrison reported a fighting strength of 196 with six severely wounded awaiting collection.

At 1416 hours the Soviets repeated their attack from the northeast and then minutes later the position came under attack from the southeast as tanks and infantry emerged from the hollow below the Schloss. Because of the steepness of the approach, this latter group could only be countered with mortar fire, but the request for this was closely followed by a call for a complete fire bell around the battalion position. By 1520 hours the garrison was calling urgently and repeatedly for water, which was promised for delivery by tanks that night.

The Soviet attacks continued, causing the garrison to call for heavy machine gunfire over the position, as well as artillery, rocket and mortar fire on specific target areas. Three and a half hours later the garrison was able to report a complete defensive success by 5 and 6 Companies, but tetanus inoculations and bandages were urgently needed.

At 0210 hours next morning, 14 March, Regiment announced the armoured relief attack would commence at 0245 hours assisted by infantry. As soon as the tanks broke through, the 2nd Battalion was to push out on the flanks to re-establish contact with its neighbours on either side. The 2nd Company of the 'Brandenburg' provided fire cover for the 3rd Company, but then a Panther hit a mine and the tank in which Matthias Hamedinger was the radio operator was ordered to recover it. He reported: 'The Russians were firing at our tank with Panzerfausts without hitting it. Then one hit the petrol tank alongside the engine and our tank burst into flames and the ammunition started exploding. I baled out through the radio operator's hatch without difficulty, but the Russian infantry closed in and started firing at us with their sub-machine guns. The tracks cut by the tank into the meadow provided us with good cover, but our tank commander, Sergeant Räth, was hit and wounded.'

As Helmut Jurisch commented: 'That first night the enemy put up such a hail of fire that, although it did not penetrate, the closer we got to Klessin, the greater was the danger that they would penetrate the side armour. Eventually the attack was broken off at dawn.'

The attempt at relief had failed and at 1000 hours the Soviets resumed their attacks from the north and south. Again this was eventually checked by artillery fire. That evening Regiment called on the garrison to hold out for one more day. The garrison was now down to 37 officer cadets, 8 senior NCOs, 116 other ranks and 27 wounded, already on their fourth day without water.

At some stage during the siege, the Political Department of the 8th Guards Army produced a special leaflet to try and get the garrison to surrender, which started as follows:

NOBODY WILL GET THROUGH!
SOLDIERS of the Klessin garrison!
You are now sitting in your pocket waiting for help.
Forget it! Help is not coming any more!
The attempts to break through to you have cost the German command several dozen tanks and armoured personnel carriers.

Tanks and armoured personnel carriers will not get through!

No one will get through!

You may hold on for another day or two, perhaps even a week – that changes nothing.

Sometime during the course of the fighting it was discovered from prisoner of war interrogations that the Soviet attacking division so outnumbered the German defence that, although all their mortar resources were kept in action, they were only fielding one regiment at a time out of three on a three-day exchange system of one in the line, one in reserve and one resting!

During the night of 14/15 March Klessin reported hearing the enemy digging in either side of the Podelzig road and called for heavy artillery fire on that area. The garrison suffered no casualties during the night.

That afternoon Regiment announced the mounting of a second relief operation and in the evening some tense signalling began in which a forward observer with the relief force, 'M', reported progress as recorded in the radio log. (I and II denote the 1st and 2nd Battalions respectively.)

To II	1940	Watch out! Our own relief operation. Pull back. Illuminate battlefield.
M	2002	Strong anti-tank fire. Tanks rolling forward. Strong anti-tank fire right of road to KLESSIN.
M	2012	Own tanks rolling forward.
M	2018	Tanks continuing to advance. No sign of own troops at the moment.
M	2033	Tanks 300-400m before position. Remainder on high position.
To II	2035	What is the situation?
M	2036	Fire from big mortars could be laid down in front of tanks.
M	2038	Infantry right of road advancing well.
From I		What is the situation?
To I		Head of advance has reached KLESSIN. Wing companies advancing.

M	2041	Own troops left of road advancing.
M	2047	Heavy artillery fire on own troops right of road.
M	2051	Lieutenant Wilken wounded. Coming back.
M	2055	Sounds of fighting quieter.
To I	2100	An officer to immediately go forward and clarify situation.
M	2100	Groups of our own troops are coming back right of road 200m from the position.
M	2105	Tanks still advancing. No sign of own troops.
From I	2107	Some tanks now behind village. No infantry companies to be seen. Where is artillery fire?
M	2110	Tanks now in hollow 400m from own positions. 3 tanks going further forward on right.
M	2120	Have some elements gone back?
To I		Second Lieutenant Lehner to take over 3 Company and attack.
M	2118	Since last report at 2054 hours no returning troops seen.
From I	2125	KLESSIN reports via 8 Company: We are free.
M	2126	One tank returning.
M	2130	KLESSIN reports: We are free.
M	2137	Up to 8 men seen returning.
To I	2215	Breakthrough must be forced with tanks under all circumstances. Tanks have orders to this effect.
To I	2220	Has an officer gone forward from 1st Battalion to clarify situation?
From I	2223	Attack on the hollow stalled. Tanks partly ahead of own infantry companies without contact to the platoons. Partly covered by considerable mortar fire.
From II	2236	Contact to right re-established, to the left still unclear. Still enemy on the road.
From I	2238	Remove 7 wounded from 8 Company Command Post. 4 stretcher cases.
To II	2250	Urgently need to know whether contact to southern front has been completed.
From II		If 1 Company/1242 left PODELZIG-KLESSIN road is not going to advance, fire on DROSSEL[2] from all artillery resources requested.

To II		Report immediately when armoured personnel carriers arrive.
From I		7 Company has contact with KLESSIN. If a frontal advance not possible, 3 Company is to drive forward to the Russian trenches that 7 Company has blocked off and roll them up to north. Brief the tanks and let them support us from you.
From I		7 Company has contact with KLESSIN. If a frontal advance not possible, 3 Company is to drive forward to the Russian trenches that 7 Company has blocked off and roll them up to north. Brief the tanks and let them support us from you. Report immediately whether attack frontal or from south.
From II		6 Company has contact with left platoon 7 Company, not with right of 7 Company. Armoured personnel carriers not yet arrived.
To I	0025	Prepare Engineer Platoon immediately. Platoon to roll up trenches from south to north. Lieutenant Rossmann to command platoon.
From II	0045	What is the situation?
To II	0105	Frontal thrust along the road now stalled. Engineer Platoon tasked with clearing enemy trenches from south to north. 2nd Battalion is to send an assault troop along 7 Company's front from 6 Company to re-establish firm contact with 7 Company. Armoured personnel carriers are on their way.
From I	0125	Engineer Platoon briefed and already under way.
To I	0135	As soon as the Engineer Platoon is there, roll up the position from south to north. Also commit 3 and 1 Companies. The enemy must be chased out of these trenches.
M	0135	Wounded transport to here.
From I	0135	Wounded transport to 8 Company. Numerous wounded there.
From II	0150	2 Company on right at the moment including No. 1 Platoon of 7 Company at Grid Reference

		69660/14000. Request closure of still open gap by rest of Feldherrnhalle or 7 Company. Note coordinates.
From II	0045	What is the situation?
To II	0158	Query: have the armoured personnel carriers arrived yet?
To II		Request Hopp to establish: a) How many pack radios in KLESSIN? b) How many of these intact? Reply immediately. Baier.
From II		From Feldherrnhalle: One armoured personnel carrier and 2 heavy armoured personnel carriers driven on mines in renewed attack, also strong infantry fire.
To II	0745	Lieutenant Schöne: Undertaking failed due to enemy anti-tank mines. Recognition of your steadfastness and that of your men. I will personally not rest until we are reunited.
From II	0732	Request yet today another drop of ammunition, Verey lights, hand grenades, water, food, lead and nickel batteries, anodes, tetanus, bandages.
From II	0920	Situation Report: Battalion is holding KLESSIN in old positions. One platoon 7 Company in battalion reserve broke back through to us after a short fight after being cut off. Right wing of battalion about 150m north of shot-up Russian tank. Gap to 7 Company about 500m. Also possible to close the gap with specific bombardment of the intervening hollow without putting tanks on stand-by.
From Div		For Combat Team Klessin: Report approximate casualties immediately. Have you a doctor in KLESSIN?
To II	1153	Report immediately for Division: fighting strength, casualties and whether you have a doctor in KLESSIN.
From II	1230	In KLESSIN there are in all five pack radios and one unreliable Sender/Receiver. Four of the sets

are on their last batteries. Regimental set has still duration of 24 hours in receiving mode. 2 Company cannot communicate with 1st Battalion, but I have secured their batteries.

We will only transmit when we need you. Please note.

From II 1327   Fighting strength 5/182. Casualties: 15 (6 dead, 9 wounded). Doctor best possible.

To II   1740   Expected supply drop 1745-1815 hrs. Shoot white and green. Mark drop zone SCHLOSS yard.

From II 1902   To Commander: Re your message of 1730 hours. Messages that through encoding cannot be acted on in time are pointless and endanger confidence in the leadership. Drop zone not SCHLOSS but village street.

To II   1940   Supply bombs coming tomorrow morning. Timing will be passed on to you.

Thus another attempt at relieving Klessin had failed. Helmut Jurisch with the Panthers reported that, although two of their tanks managed to break through the Soviet lines, they were both soon brought to a standstill in a hail of fire. Attempts to recover them and their baled-out crews were equally unsuccessful because of the volume of fire. Even though there were some dead and wounded among the crews, the majority were captured alive.

However, two Panthers commanded by Second Lieutenant Eimer and Sergeant Stephen had got through to the garrison, although they were not included in the strength return until the 19th. Most importantly, they brought with them a useful addition to the radio link for directing artillery fire.

Early next day, 17 March, Klessin reported visible signs of deterioration in the state of the men as a result of the failure to resupply. The supply drop by Luftwaffe aircraft at 1600 hours coming in from the direction of Podelzig in the face of considerable anti-aircraft fire from the ample Soviet resources resulted in all the supply containers falling east of the Schloss into the Soviet positions. That evening Klessin reported: 'Visible drop in physical capacity of men after six days without resupply. Already two men have collapsed from physical exhaustion in 6 Company. Today three wounded. Totals 19 severely and 30 lightly wounded. Fighting strength 184.'

On 18 March the radio log continued:

To II		I promote with effect from 1 Mar 45 all officer cadet sergeants to officer cadet staff sergeants, Sergeant Lippmann to staff sergeant, Corporals Hopp and Herbert to sergeant. Those unqualified are not to be informed.
To II		The Commander-in-Chief of the Army Group and the General Officer Commanding have announced their special recognition of Officer Cadet Grenadier Regiment 1242 for exemplary fortitude at WUHDEN and KLESSIN. From Div
	1630	Combat Team Klessin! How much longer can your radios function?
From II	1833	Another 2 days on 'Receive'.
To Div		Another 2 days on 'Receive'. However, when traffic continues like today and yesterday, only one more day on constant 'Receive'.
To II	1910	Division wants to know whether there were 2 pigs in KLESSIN when it was surrounded and whether the potato store there has been entered. Reply immediately.
From II	2045	2 pigs destroyed by enemy action before encirclement. Potatoes available have diminished. Amount consumed as rations will be accounted for upon relief.
From II	2130	Situation unchanged. Day-long harassing fire from mortars and anti-tank guns. Last night a storm troop was repulsed by 5 Company and papers captured. Enemy constantly reinforcing encirclement positions.
		Fighting strength 178.
		Casualties: 3 dead, 3 wounded,
		8 severely wounded have died so far.
		Resupply urgent: ammunition, Verey cartridges,

hand grenades, food, flares, bandages, medicines, tetanus.
Emergency water supply re-established.

Later Wolfgang Schöne was to comment: 'The tactical radio, partly through my fault, was loaded with unnecessary traffic (i.e. recommendations for medals and promotions, detailed strength returns for routine traffic, the especially grotesque questions from Division about Herr von Albedyll's two pigs and my ironically intended reply).'

On 19 March the Luftwaffe succeeded in dropping thirteen containers on the village street at a cost of two aircraft shot down, but the containers could only be recovered at night due to the heavy enemy machine gun and anti-tank gun fire. These containers brought welcome relief to the garrison and proved a considerable boost to morale, as the radio log shows:

From II	0512	Attack on 5 Company. Barrage requested.
To II	0540	Supply bombs again today.
From II	0652	Strong movement and noise during the night, apparently in preparation for attack on 5 Company. Quiet in front of 6 Company. Watch out for green flares.
		Where is the resupply?
From II	0823	Enemy has dug his way in during the night to hand grenade throwing distance on the boundary between 5 and 2 Companies and close east of the WUHDEN-KLESSIN road. Expecting attack today from several directions.
From II	0845	To 13 Company: Request from 0900 hours onwards harassing fire on TONI during the morning.
From II	0925	To 13 Company: Harassing fire on TONI falling too short. Up 50m.
From II	0942	To 13 Company: Request irregular harassing fire on TONI until noon with up 50m.
To II	0950	Can barrages on MÜHLE-MARS be thickened up? If so by how much?

To II	1016	Please report daily fighting strength and casualties from 18 Mar onwards.
From II		Reply to 0955 hours. 13 Company: MARS and MÜHLE cannot be drawn in closer. Command MÜHLE unchanged. Command MARS up 50m. Combine fire.
To II	1042	How is the fire on MÜHLE-MARS?
To II	1150	Expected supply drop 1400-1430 hours. Fire Verey lights as per last time. Hopefully it will work.
From II	1342	Checked fighting strength of 18 Mar 45: 5 officers, 55 officer cadets, 17 senior NCOs, 121 other ranks, plus 2 tank crews. Casualties: 2 officer cadets, 1 other rank wounded. 1 officer cadet, 2 other ranks dead.
To II	1448	There has been a delay. Exact time is coming through.
To II	1520	Delicacies arriving 1630 hours. 24 aircraft. Light signals. Mark drop zone.
From II	1605	Enemy attacking. 1 salvo on MARS.
From II	1620	Query: Has barrage on MARS been fired?
From II	1625	Request barrages on MARS and TONI up 25m.
From II	1655	Own bombs here. Detailed report follows.
From II		We thank you for the help. Detailed report follows.
From II	1719	Beaten off in front of 5 Company.
To II	1722	Well done, Schöne.
From II		Forward Observer 13 Company to 13 Company: Guns on bearing 190 more WUHDEN one shot.
To II		Report immediately how many supply bombs on target.
From II		10 bombs on target.
To II		Query: Was shooting down of two of our aircraft observed?
From II		Yes, in the direction PODELZIG.
From II	1745	Without prejudice to further commendations, request award of Iron Cross 1st and 2nd Class to Second Lieutenant Heinrich of 5 Company. From the first days of the encirclement he has

		beaten back numerous attacks, some severe, with his company, held his position steadfastly and on 10 Mar personally led a counterattack to restore the old front line.
To II		Lieutenant Schöne: On the instructions of the Divisional Commander Second Lieutenant Heinrich is awarded the Iron Cross First Class. Heartiest congratulations.
From II	2047	Fighting strength: 5 officers, 54 officer cadets, 18 senior NCOs, 115 other ranks, plus 2 tank crews. Casualties: Wounded 5 officer cadets, 5 other ranks. Dead 3 other ranks. 7 light wounded back on duty.
To II	2245	Lieutenant Schöne: How did the food taste?
From II		Lovely, we thank you!

The resources of the Panzergrenadier Division 'Kurmark' being recognised as inadequate to break the deadlock at Klessin, Grenadier Regiment 300, commanded by Lieutenant Colonel Helmut Weber, was detached from the 303rd Infantry Division 'Döberitz' and given two or three days to prepare. Its task was both to relieve the Klessin garrison and re-establish firm defensive lines back to Grenadier Regiment 1242, at the same time apparently taking over control of this sector from the depleted 1242nd. Then, at the last minute, the promised armoured support was withdrawn.

The regiment advanced behind a heavy artillery barrage at 0515 hours on 20 March, only to find themselves heavily shelled in turn. However, moving fast, the commander of the 2nd Battalion, Captain Böge, managed to break through along the track to the hamlet with some of his men and some sappers of the Armoured Engineer Battalion 'Kurmark' within fifteen minutes. Losses among the attacking force were considerable and only 45 men eventually got through to Klessin, where Lieutenant Schöne handed over command of the garrison to Captain Böge, but was instructed by Regiment to continue reporting as before. The Soviets followed up their counter-bombardment with attacks from both north and south and soon regained their blocking positions as they systematically destroyed the 300th's troops in their path.

At about 0900 hours a Volkssturm man of 7 Company who had been captured in the previous day's fighting appeared with a Soviet demand for the garrison to surrender by 1400 hours. This demand. signed 'The High Command of the Red Army', was set out in proper German and promised, should they surrender, immediate attention to the wounded and immediate release to their homes once the war was over. It was ignored and the Volkssturm man rearmed and put back into the line, only to be killed later on. The radio log continues:

From II	1545	Request immediate recce along road to here whether trenches are free of enemy. Green flares if trenches free of enemy, otherwise red.
From II	1615	From 6 and Assault Companies. Trenches reoccupied by enemy. One to one and a half companies. An energetic attack with supporting fire could still regain these trenches today. Reserves close by. After break-in, strong protection to right and left.
To II	1656	Immediate radio silence except for urgent matters.
To II		Request strengths of Böge elements there.
From II	1800	To Commanding Officer 300: Strength of 2nd Battalion 300: HQ 2/3/10, 5 Company 1/2/7, 6 Company 0/1/7, Engineers 0/0/4, Storm Company 0/0/4, 2 Company 1/4/4.
From II	1948	Request running harassing fire on SPERBER during the night.
To II	2025	Where is your strength and casualty report?
To II	2055	We are trying again. Time 2300 hours.
From II		To Regiment: Fighting strength 5 officers, 56 officer cadets, 17 senior NCOs, 110 other ranks, plus 2 tank crews. Casualties: 3 other ranks wounded, 1 officer cadet dead.

Total wounded 64.
Air supply tomorrow necessary with batteries,
food, flares, Verey cartridges, machine gun
ammunition and hand grenades.

The 300th launched a second attack at 2330 hours with its
greatly diminished resources, but this again was stalled by Soviet
artillery fire with heavy loss. Attempts at relief involving some
heavy fighting resumed on the 21st, as these extracts from the
radio log show:

From II	0832	To Armoured Artillery Regiment 'Kurmark': from Forward Observer, 2nd Battery. Possibility exists that codes have been blown. Use new codes.
From II		What is the situation?
To II		New countermeasures being prepared.
From II	0935	To Commanding Officer 300:

1) Enemy is digging in from direction of
WUHDEN in a second trench running from the
shot-up Panther to here from the direction of
the main road. Thus there is a danger that this
trench will eventually lead to the track and form
a second continuous trench between you and
us.
2) Fire direction is being tried via tank, as own
set is u/s.
2) Request permission to fire upon identified
heavy weapons.
The ODER is clearly visible.

From II	0946	For establishment of new fire direction it will be necessary for the command tank to drive to the firing position of the 2nd Battalion, Armoured Artillery Regiment 'Kurmark'.
From II	1026	To 13 Company: Prepare for orders to fire.
To II	1037	Give short basis for commendation of Sergeant Hennecke.
To II	1055	Fire direction will be conducted via tank. From 1130 hours reciprocal callsign is ROTHKELCHEN.

From II 1132	To Regiment: Sergeant Hennecke has as Forward Observer in heavy fighting under the heaviest artillery fire so outstandingly conducted himself, that a considerable part of successful defence is attributable to him.
From II 1218	To Regiment: Request urgent running harassing fire on SPERBER, EMIL, DROSSEL by all available artillery resources.
To II	Still no orders from Corps.

There followed recommendations for the award of the Iron Cross First Class for six officer cadets, and Second Class for a further 38 officer cadets, 26 other ranks and eight Volkssturm men, the promotion of Second Lieutenant Heinrich to lieutenant and Gunner Brandenburg to bombardier for his outstanding conduct as a radio operator under the heaviest enemy fire.

All the while Colonel Willy Langkeit, the 'Kurmark' divisional commander, was doing his utmost to get permission from the XIth SS Panzer Corps commander, the fanatical Nazi SS-General Matthias Kleinheisterkamp, to give permission for the garrison to break out, but so far without success.

The log continues:

From II	Where is resupply?
	To Commanding Officer 300: Request further harassing fire during the whole night on DROSSEL, SPERBER, GUSTAV.
	Query: Where is 6 Company? Conditions for wounded bad.
From II 1910	Strength of Grenadier Regiment 300 and Engineer Regiment 309: 4/11/30, plus 1/9 wounded.
From II	To Commanding Officer 300:
	Some enemy barrages from heavy mortars, otherwise quiet.
From II	Artillery working well. Request once more urgent artillery action during night on GUSTAV, DROSSEL and EMIL. Greetings please from 6, 7 and 8 Companies. The fire has not gone out yet.

From II 2118   To Regiment:
                 Fighting strength: 5 officers, 55 officer cadets,
                 17 senior NCOs, 107 other ranks, plus 2 tank
                 crews.
                 Wounded: 1 officer cadet, 3 other ranks.
                 Wounded of 2nd Battalion/1242 in KLESSIN
                 54.
                 Request supply of following: flares, batteries,
                 machine gun ammunition, Verey cartridges,
                 replacement machine gun, food.

There was a second successful supply drop by the Luftwaffe that night with thirteen containers recovered.

The whole of 22 March Klessin lay under heavy bombardment from artillery, mortars, anti-tank guns and heavy machine gun fire. The situation had become almost untenable, as the radio log records:

From II 0500   Barrages on GUSTAV and TONI.
From II 0510   Barrages up 100m and 100m more to left.
From II   To 13 Company: Once TONI fired, one barrage
                 on MARS, where enemy forming up.
From II   Order to 13 Company cancelled.
To II   0555   Has enemy broken in?
From II 0618   What is the situation on the left?
From II 0621   Russians broke in 2 Company at 0500 hours. 7
                 Russians in trench left behind a machine gun
                 when thrown out again. 1 dead and 2 wounded
                 in this. 2nd Battalion/Armoured Artillery
                 Regiment 'Kurmark' fired well-laid
                 bombardments during the night. Situation
                 restored.
                 Waiting urgently for food, Verey cartridges, hand
                 grenades and machine gun ammunition.
From II 0920   Request one salvo harassing fire on
                 RITTERSPORN, from where sound of tanks.
From II 1003   Enemy bombardment with heavy mortars.
                 Situation for wounded bad.
From II   To 13 Company: Request harassing fire on

	MARS and ILONA from 11 to 1300 hours. Timing from Regiment.
From II	Expecting enemy attack. Under running artillery bombardment. Conditions for wounded unbearable.
From II 1000	KLESSIN fortress boundaries: From crossroads at western exit SE 300m, NE 250m, N 300m, W 150m, S 150m. Please pass on to Luftwaffe.
From II 1111	To Regiment: Prepare barrage all round.
From II	Is barrage ready?
To II	Barrage is ready.
From II 1148	MARS, GUSTAV, ILONA, one salvo.
From II 1200	Bombardment of own positions by Russians.
From II 1203	Query: Has salvo been fired on MARS, ILONA, GUSTAV?
From II 1209	One salvo on DROSSEL.
From II 1217	Prepare barrage all round once more.
From II	Enemy attack. Fire barrages on GUSTAV, TONI, RABE, MARS and keep firing.
From II	Barrage on GUSTAV urgent.
From II	Barrage on GUSTAV urgent. Keep on firing, and DROSSEL.
From II	Enemy attack. Barrages on DROSSEL, GUSTAV and SPERBER.
From II	Fire again on GUSTAV urgent. Enemy attacking!
From 7 Coy	Enemy attack on KLESSIN clearly visible. Barrage on hollow!
To 7 Coy	Where exactly is enemy attack? Give exact areas.
From II	Fire rockets 600m further to north.
From II	Fire on GUSTAV again.
From II 1247	Enemy is attacking from directions of 49.7, 56.2 and 16.8, from north and northwest.
From II	Request concentrated fire on GUSTAV. One running barrage on RITTERSPORN 2.
To 7 Coy	The enemy attacking KLESSIN is most urgently to be forced to ground with machine guns.
From 7 Coy	Enemy attack from WUHDEN toward west swung round on KLESSIN and from the dip in front of our own Sector on KLESSIN.
To II	Do you have lamps for a night supply air drop?

From II	1344	To 13 Company: 2 salvoes on MARS.
From II	1347	Situation re-established, cleared up. Casualties from enemy artillery fire expected.
To II	1350	Query: Have all attacks been beaten back?
From II	1355	Prepare for further all round fire.
To II	1419	How was the last rocket barrage?
From II	1435	To 2nd Battalion/Armoured Artillery Regiment 'Kurmark': One salvo on GUSTAV immediately.
From II		Query: Is the barrage ready? Command TONI 100m up, otherwise in own trenches.
To II	1448	Barrage ready.
From II	1448	. . . and thrown out again in a counterattack. The enemy was being driven on by commissars. Current statements from prisoners. We are expecting further enemy attacks. Casualties not yet reviewed. Conditions for wounded very, very bad. Cover hardly possible. Reserves fully committed. Urgently request fighter aircraft support.
To II		What is situation?
From II	1540	Relief today urgently necessary. The enemy is occupying the eastern part of the SCHLOSS and is constantly reinforcing. Forces for a counterattack not available. Please relieve urgently.
From II		Barrage all round.
From II		Continual barrage all round urgent.
To 7 Coy		Force the enemy now attacking southern KLESSIN to the ground with all your weapons.
From II		Barrage all round urgent.
From II		Where is the barrage?
To II		Where is the main enemy point of attack?
From II		East and south of SCHLOSS.
From II	1630	Heavy losses. We are fighting to the last man.
To II	1643	Hold on. Decision applied for.
From II		One battery on GUSTAV. Own artillery firing too short.

From II		To 2nd Battalion/Armoured Artillery Regiment 'Kurmark': one salvo on SPERBER.
From II		One salvo on GUSTAV.
From II	1711	Situation difficult. We must fear the worst this evening.
From II		To 2nd Battalion/Armoured Artillery Regiment 'Kurmark': one salvo on GUSTAV.
From II		To 2nd Battalion/Armoured Artillery Regiment 'Kurmark': Harassing fire on SPERBER, GUSTAV and RITTERSPORN 2.
From II		Where is the harassing fire on areas GUSTAV, SPERBER and RITTERSPORN 2?
To II		Harassing fire being fired constantly. Report where and how strong enemy penetration.
From II		Enemy has penetrated SCHLOSS and southern part of village with one company.
From II		Where is the harassing fire?
To II	1754	Artillery report that they are firing constantly. What is the situation?
From II	1800	Prepare all round barrage.
To II	1805	Barrage ready.
From II		Request constant harassing fire all round.
To II	1821	Own artillery doing everything possible.
From II	1825	Wounded can no longer be provided shelter in the position. Considerable collapse of trenches. We are using the last of our strength. Enemy preparing to attack.
To II		Tell Lieutenant Schöne of concern that all the divisional Radio codes, including the most important, be destroyed in radio station HOPP. Report immediately if code blown. Corporal Hopp is already aware.
From II	2000	Fire barrage!
From II	2001	Request last orders.
To II	2036	Is there an enemy attack?
From II		No!
From II		Mortar fire landing on own positions.
From II	2055	Heavy artillery harassing fire on position.
To II	2104	Decision whether KLESSIN garrison is to

		continue fighting has been passed by Division to Army Group.
From II	2101	To Regiment: Old command post blown up.
To II	2126	Through a direct hit or demolition?
From II		Several direct hits. Burnt, then exploded.
From II		One salvo on all blocking areas.
To II	2206	KLESSIN can be assured that the Regiment is doing everything possible.

The garrison's fighting strength fell dramatically through losses in dead and wounded, and both tanks were knocked out by direct hits during the course of the day. That evening Second Lieutenant Greib of the Bicycle Platoon knocked out a Stalin tank with a Panzerfaust at point-blank range. However, the situation demanded constant artillery support, which did not stop the Soviets getting a foothold in the eastern corner of the Schloss that evening that proved of considerable tactical value to them.

Although the situation in Klessin was now desperate, both the Corps and Army commanders regarded Hitler's orders as sacrosanct, so Colonel Langkeit apparently decided to bypass them and appeal direct to Colonel General Gotthardt Heinrici at Army Group. Meanwhile decorations and promotions were used as morale-boosters. Years later Schöne was to comment that they had never lost confidence in their regimental and divisional commanders in this situation.

On the morning of the 23rd March the Soviets broke through into the main part of the Schloss after a long and heavy artillery preparation and after several failed attempts. The defence were by now too weak to mount a counterattack and were obliged to form a cordon west of the building. The Soviets then brought in two tanks, an anti-tank gun and several heavy machine guns with which they began to dominate the hamlet from the Schloss, causing trenches to collapse and inflicting heavy casualties to the extent that nearly everyone of the defence were wounded.

Two breaches in the northern defences had to be cleared during the morning, and by noon the last fifteen to twenty unwounded soldiers formed a hedgehog around the battalion command post, into which a number of the wounded had to be carried. Then, during the late afternoon, the Soviets forced their way into the centre and the northern part of the hamlet, splitting the garrison into several groups. The radio log shows how the situation developed during the day:

To II	0036	All officer cadet staff sergeants in KLESSIN are promoted second lieutenant with immediate effect.
		Heartiest congratulations.
From II		To Commanding Officer 300:
		Enemy is pressing in ever closer on inner defences from all sides.
		One tank destroyed in close fighting. The wounded are lying in the trenches. Everything can be expected to be overrun in the next attack. No reserves left. Is it possible to break out or be relieved by 0300 hours?
From II		Tanks are ready with infantry.
To II		Send further recommendations for Iron Cross.
From II		Where are the barrages on ILONA and RITTERSPORN 2?
To II		Barrages coming.
From II		Decision presses until 2300 hrs. This combat team cannot take another attack without reinforcement and will be overrun.
To II		Highest recognition of your brave conduct. Hold on!
		Langkeit, Colonel.
From II		Request harassing fire on DROSSEL.
To II		Men of KLESSIN! One looks on you full of pride and admiration. You are the decisive wave-breakers against the Bolshevist storm on the Reichs capital. Heil our Führer! SS-Obergruppenführer and General of the Waffen-SS Kleinheisterkamp.
From II		To 2nd Battalion/Armoured Artillery Regiment 'Kurmark': one salvo on RITTERSPORN 2. Enemy forming up point.
To II		Lieutenant Schöne: The Führer has awarded you

		the Knights' Cross. Heartiest congratulations from the Regiment.
From II	0410	Strength 90 men.
From II	0445	Request permission to break out. Russians ready to attack.
To II	0515	To Captain Böge: High Command insists position is to be held under all circumstances.
From II		Enemy attacking. Barrages on ILONA and RITTERSPORN 2.
From II		Enemy attacking. Barrages on ILONA down 50m and RITTERSPORN 2, for 13 Company.
From II		All artillery resources on RITTERSPORN 2. To 13 Company: on SCHLOSS and 8 Company.
From II		ILONA up 200m. Barrages on ILONA and RITTERSPORN.
From II		Enemy attacking from east via SCHLOSS (one company). Request running barrages on ILONA and RITTERSPORN.
To II		Query: whether one can fire on the SCHLOSS?
From II		The SCHLOSS can be fired on. Not too short!
From II		What is the situation?
To II	0750	Hold on! How is it, Lieutenant Schöne?
From II		Where is barrage on ILONA? Schöne OK.
To II		ILONA fired on several times.
From II		Prepare barrages on ILONA and RITTERSPORN 2.
To II	0826	Ready.
To II	0910	Is it known that Schöne has been awarded the Knights' Cross?
To II	0952	Award all those recommended for Iron Cross First and Second Class, also Iron Cross First Class for Christ, Second Class for Hohenstein, Ackermann and Scherzinger.
From II	0957	Why no fire on ILONA?
From II		Artillery firing too short. Up 100m.
From II	1000	Enemy in company strength in SCHLOSS. No reserves left to throw them out with. Situation of wounded hopeless. One cellar of wounded in enemy hands in SCHLOSS. Fire support from

own arms especially lacking. Artillery radio unserviceable through battery, also Panthers. Transmitting with last battery. Desperately need ammunition, food, batteries, flares.

From II	1100	To Regiment: Recommend Iron Cross First Class for Second Lieutenant Zeller (twice wounded) and Second Lieutenant Plonka.
To II	1103	What are hedgehog coordinates now?
From II	1130	Prepare barrages for ILONA and RITTERSPORN 2.
To II	1130	Artillery fire on ILONA. Give corrections immediately.
From II	1137	Fire barrages.
From II	1142	Fire barrages immediately.
From II		3 salvoes on RITTERSPORN 2, 100m left.
To II		Where enemy attack? Give bearing.
From II		Enemy attack from east.
From II	1200	Two shots were too short.
To II	1302	Please report whether codes for all radio stations in KLESSIN (apart from the valid sheets for the 23rd and 24th) have been destroyed or have fallen into enemy hands.
From II	1345	When is relief coming? Own artillery especially tired.
To II	1349	Highest Command have yet to give orders.
From II		Urgent barrages on RITTERSPORN 2 and ILONA.
From II	1440	To Regiment: Enemy counterattack in northern part. No reserves available. Cutting off hardly possible. Repeat request of this morning as last possibility. Dead and wounded mounting by the hour.
From II	1510	Direct hit on command post. Fighting to the last man.
From II	1535	Urgent barrages on MARS and RABE.
From II	1549	Barrage on MARS.
From II	1559	Mortars firing too short, up 100m.
To II	1738	The decorations and promotions are evidence to

		you of Highest Command's recognition of your exemplary fight. The Division is proud of you. Langkeit, Divisional Commander.
To II		How many enemy have penetrated northern and western parts?
From II		I cannot encipher as I have no codes.
To II		Are the codes destroyed?
From II	1759	Yes.
From II	1810	Request barrage on Schloss.
To II		Are there no more codes available?
From II	1822	Correct, none.

At last at 2120 hours the message from Division was passed to Klessin by Regiment: 'Mission accomplished; fight your way through!'

Captain Böge ordered those men immediately to hand to assemble at the potato store at the western edge of the hamlet with the intention of breaking through during the night as a compact group. As many as possible of the severely wounded were taken along to the assembly point. Meanwhile Lieutenant Schöne took a group to the east to create a diversion and, due to the heavy enemy mortar and machine gun fire, contact with him and his group was soon lost.

Using the cover of the thick smoke and dust of an artillery barrage, Captain Böge's group reached the hollow southwest of Klessin just ahead of a group of twenty to thirty Soviets and were able to use captured Panzerfausts found in the hollow to blast their way through and reach the unoccupied first and second lines of Soviet trenches. By this time the Soviet troops were fully alerted and using flares and Verey lights to illuminate the breakthrough point, which was brought under heavy machine gun fire from both north and south. But Böge's men, using the last hand grenades and Panzerfausts stormed the third, heavily-manned Soviet trench and broke through, just 26 of them reaching the German lines.

Meanwhile Lieutenant Schöne's group reached the potato shed and then followed the track west across the fields for about thirty minutes before they too had to storm the last of the Soviet trenches. Using the last of their strength, some 30-35 men, including some severely wounded, got through to the German lines. Several others were to slip through the Soviet lines during the course of the night and reach the neighbouring Grenadier Regiment 1241.

The Political Department of the Russian 8th Guards Army utilised the victory over Klessin to issue a special pamphlet aimed at the 1242nd with the text:

THE LESSON OF KLESSIN

SOLDIERS of the Officer Cadet Grenadier Regiment 1242! More than 300 German soldiers were surrounded in Klessin. On the 23rd March 1945 the entire garrison was destroyed. No man broke through to their own lines. 75 men raised the white flag and stayed alive. All the others died senselessly.

Who is to blame?

HITLER IS TO BLAME!
He began this senseless war. He demanded in his orders: *"Hold out at any price!"*

YOUR COMMANDERS ARE TO BLAME!
They did not withdraw the troops from Klessin when they should have done and then condemned them to death with lying promises. With their futile attempts at relief they sent hundreds of other soldiers to their deaths, as well as squandering many tanks and self-propelled guns.

When the war ended, just part of the front portal of the Schloss remained, together with the rusting hulks of the destroyed German and Soviet tanks. Tens of thousands of mines littered the landscape. The mines and hulks were removed and the remaining ruins collapsed. Later the hamlet was revived with the construction of a row of houses along the Wuhden road and two cottages on the old site.

In 1995 a stone was unveiled in Wuhden commemorating those who had fought and died on the Reitwein Spur, with the inscription:

He who lives in the memories of his comrades is not dead
Only those forgotten are dead
We remember our fallen comrades and all that died in the war
1945
Reitwein Spur with the villages
Podelzig, Wuhden and Klessin
1995

1 The Division 'Feldhernhalle' was the only SA (Sturmabteilung) formation in the Wehrmacht. Its replacement battalion had been sent to the Oder front as an emergency measure, much against the wish of the SA leadership, which kept pressing for its return. The battalion ended up with only 60 men in the line.
2 Only a few of these target areas have been identified on the ground, as per the drawing.

FIVE

The Bridge at Golzow

HORST ZOBEL (6 MAY 1918 – 3 OCT 1999)

Horst Zobel, as a captain, commanded the 1st Battalion of Panzer-Regiment 'Müncheberg' in the fighting in the Oderbruch. Here he relates his experiences near Golzow as the Soviet 5th Shock and 8th Guards Armies united their bridgeheads, isolating the fortress of Küstrin. Zobel's newly-formed battalion was under threat of disbandment at the time.

Suddenly the division was allocated a sector of the front and, as the preparations for our proposed disbandment were not yet complete, we were committed intact. At the commanders' conference at Division, I was able to establish that at least two of my squadrons would be included, although our mixed 2nd Squadron would have to detach its SPG (self-propelled gun) Troop to secure the Küstrin 'corridor'. It had unfortunately become the practice for the tanks to be split up on the ground in order to reinforce strong points. This tactic had been born out of the necessity of the time, the tanks being needed to bolster the fighting spirit of the infantry, and was known as 'corsetting'. Only after I had pointed out that the completely flat terrain with its kilometres-long visibility enabled me to guarantee that I would be in a position to repel any attack promptly, were my proposals for deployment accepted. Fortunately, I had enough time to inspect my squadron commanders' individual areas and to give them explicit instructions before we drove out to our positions on what must have been the night of 20/21 March 1945. That same night the individual tanks were dug in and camouflaged. I was able to assure myself next day that the tanks were superbly camouflaged from view both from the front and above, and that many had a field of fire of from two to three kilometres.

The 2nd Squadron, less one troop, was located in Gorgast, the 3rd Squadron in Golzow, while the 1st Squadron blocked the highway at the Tucheband level. I and my staff were located with the 3rd Squadron at Golzow. My command post, there being not much of a choice, was located in a cellar that was spacious, but unfortunately very high-ceilinged. The tank crews were also sheltering in cellars when not required to be in their tanks, as the Russians were using harassing fire and heavy bombardments at irregular intervals on the villages, which had been almost completely cleared of civilians.

We believed the danger of being detached from the division was over, but the very next day the new regimental commander, Major Marquand, visited us with his staff to see our positions and be briefed, as he would be taking over command the day after. There was nothing we could do but accept orders and await our fate.

So we came to 22 March, the day of our intended relief. We were all in our improvised lager – it must have been about 0600 hours – when the morning quiet was torn apart by a chain of powerful explosions that caused us to leap up in shock and take cover in the corners of the room, as the house rocked down to its foundations. The next moment the windows blew in and a whole flood of plaster and stones swept into the cellar, followed by a thick cloud of dust that darkened everything around us. Our lovely, high-ceilinged cellar threatened to be our undoing. The explosions and splintering continued, hit following hit. With an effort, we were able to hang some rugs over the windows. Now we crouched in the dark while the shells crashed down around our house. Whenever the house sustained a direct hit, everything shook around us. It was simply impossible to leave the cellar and climb into our tanks. The telephone lines were already shot through. We sat close together and waited for what was to come. How long this lasted, I cannot say, all sense of time having left us.

Quite suddenly a feeling of unease came over me. This unease I knew of old. Its meaning was quite clear; we had to get out of here and into our tanks. It was high time. The shells were still hailing down on our house, which unfortunately lay in the middle of the

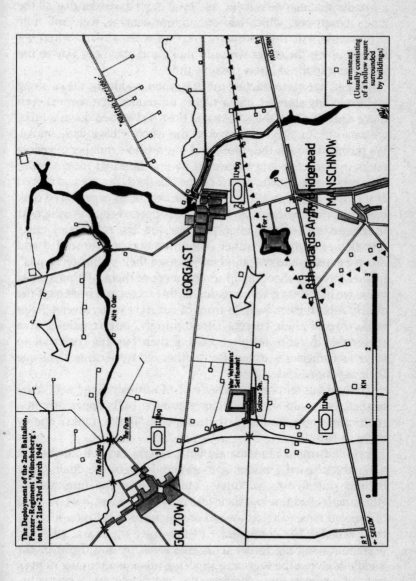

The Deployment of the 2nd Battalion, Panzer-Regiment 'Müncheberg', on the 21st–23rd March 1945

Farmstead (Usually consisting of a hollow square surrounded by buildings)

KÜSTRIN

Küstrin corridor

MANSCHNOW

11/Abtlg 2

Fort

8th Guards Army Bridgehead

GORGAST

Alte Oder

The Farm

11/Abtlg 3

The Bridge

Isbr Veterans' Settlement

Golzow Stn.

11/Abtlg 1

GOLZOW

KM

R1

SEELOW R1

village. One by one we leapt out of the cellar into our tanks. It was a wonder that no one was hit, and even more a wonder that all the tanks except one, which had only minor damage, were still fully serviceable. All the company's crews were aboard when we formed up on the street with our tanks and made our way to the village exit in the shortest possible time.

We had not quite reached the exit when, suddenly, the crashing and exploding stopped, and a silence descended that seemed even more sinister. Once the smoke and dust had settled down a little, we saw the Russians had covered the whole village with smoke. We pushed through the smoke and saw a whole number of enemy tanks opposite coming toward us several hundred metres away. This was a proper mass attack by the Russians, but we had moved at the right moment. With the routine drill of an experienced tank man, Second Lieutenant Strauss, who happened to be driving next to me, assessed the situation and shot the first two enemy tanks into flames with his Panther. The others became unsettled and drove excitedly into one another. We used their confusion to push further forward, shooting up several more of them. Within a short while we had cleared the situation in this sector and beaten off the attack. A bit further away, in front of our right wing, several Stalin tanks raised their turrets threateningly, but remained at a reasonable distance from us, leaving their burning comrades to serve as sufficient warning. But neither did we wish to challenge their superior 125mm guns.

Then to our left, on the other side of a stream lined with alder bushes, we could see our infantry coming back, apparently in a rush, and soon we heard their shouts: 'Tanks, tanks, enemy tanks in front!'

I turned round immediately with several tanks from the left wing and crossed a bridge and advanced left of the ditch. Close behind our fleeing infantry, who, despite the outstanding Panzerfaust, had not lost their fear of tanks, we saw a whole herd of Russian tanks coming toward us. We were in collision within a few seconds. The commander of my Tiger squadron, who had been following me in his tank, overtook me and drove in the middle between the Russians, shooting up tank after tank right in front of my nose. Once the first tank had caught fire or blown up, the Russians became confused here too and drove excitedly all over the place, and then in fast flight to the rear, seeking to gain distance, leaving a whole number of them behind.

At this point I recognised, or thought that I recognised, that we could now use the Russians' confusion to launch a counterattack and strike a wonderful blow. It was important for me to re-establish contact with my 2nd Squadron in Gorgast, which the Russians had already thrust past, although I already had a good understanding with the commander of this squadron. I had just given Division my proposal, when I received orders to hold on to our present position and not advance any further. So we took up a suitable defensive position right and left of the stream, having to use all the tanks, including the command vehicles. The adjutant, with his tank, secured one corner, facing east, of a lone farmhouse that had an orchard, while I secured the other corner facing north. The commander of the 3rd Squadron was also with us.

Once we were more or less in order, the Russians brought us under heavy artillery and mortar fire. From the very beginning, their favourite target was apparently our farm, with its orchard, which they kept under constant fire from heavy calibre weapons. However, it was absolutely essential that we remained in this position, as from this farm the bridge was barely 100 metres away, and whoever held the farm had the bridge in hand.

Toward evening we were again attacked in our position by tanks. The adjutant told me that some seven to ten enemy tanks were advancing toward him. As I was myself fully engaged, I had him passed the reply that he should shoot his attackers, because ten tanks attacking over open ground posed no big problem for a well-sited Panther. Then I heard the adjutant open fire and the problem seemed resolved. Only after dark did I discover, to my dismay, that his turret had been jammed and so things could have gone very badly for us.

It was late evening before I could sum up the day's events. The Russians had attacked along the whole front with equal force, the main thrust in the morning having been south of Gorgast, where the 2nd Squadron with its self-propelled guns and one troop of Mark IV tanks was located. Lieutenant Ziehmann, the commander of the 2nd Squadron, had his tank outside the defensive position pointing directly south, where he was able to shoot us a considerable number of enemy tanks.

With his very short, in comparison to those of the Panthers', 75mm gun, he was even able to shoot into flames several Stalin tanks from the flank.

Unfortunately, there was still no report from the 1st Troop of the 2nd Company, which had been sent forward to secure the 'corridor' to Küstrin. Not even the squadron had heard from them but, according to statements from returning infantry, the troop had in fact been commandeered by the commandant of Küstrin.

Despite all the strength and the heaviest artillery support used in the Russian attack, which I later discovered had the aim of breaking through our front and at least occupying the heights around Seelow, it had been wrecked by our tanks up front. The enemy's only achievement had been in severing the land connection to Küstrin. Excluding the fate of the 1st Troop, 2nd Squadron, we had sustained only minimal material damage and had two men wounded that day, and had shot into flames 59 enemy tanks, not counting others rendered immobile.

On the other hand, our infantry had been decimated. Major Steuber had been severely wounded in the first hours of the battle. That evening a battalion commander and his adjutant reported to me that he had lost his whole battalion. I later saw him in our position manning a machine gun like an ordinary soldier. Of my officers, only Lieutenant Ziehmann had been wounded.

I sent my report back to Division by Second Lieutenant Henatsch, who returned with the Division's congratulations to my battalion. Unfortunately, I could not talk to Division myself, as I could only leave my command post with the express permission of my immediate superior, which the situation here did not warrant.

It was gone midnight before everything had quietened down and we could take some rest beside our tanks.

Then that same night the 25th Panzergrenadier Division, which we had relieved to go into reserve, conducted a counterattack along the Seelow-Küstrin highway, but became stuck in the Russian minefields. The commander of their tank battalion later told me in jest that they had not encountered any enemy tanks, we having apparently destroyed them all, but had seen numerous wrecks littering the ground. Unfortunately, we were not to have the same feeling about the day that was to follow.

We resumed our positions of the previous day around the lone farm at dawn. During the night the returning infantry, some of whom had stopped by our supply column, had been reorganised and sent forward again. Of these 200 soldiers were allocated to me for the defence of our small bridgehead.

It was to prove a very, very hard day indeed. The previous day, although not lacking in drama and tense moments, had above all brought visible success. This day, however, was different, far more tense, and demanding extensive effort from all of us. Throughout the whole war I never had such a long and exhausting experience as on this day, 23 March 1945. What success the previous day had brought through luck and perhaps also routine drills and experience, had come relatively easily, but this day I had to earn it the hard way.

We were about 100–150 metres from the stream and bridge, with completely flat and open country in front of us. We had four tanks in the orchard of about 75 square metres. There was a massive single-storey building on the north side of the orchard with several outhouses. We were supposed to, and had to, hold this farm, for once the Russians crossed the bridge, the divisional front could easily be rolled up from that flank. The fruit trees were very young and had no leaves at this time of year, so we had no cover from view at all.

This little plot of land became the Russians' goal for their artillery, mortars, anti-tank and tank fire. At first we pressed our tanks close to the buildings, but these were soon shot to pieces. The hits were so accurate and so dense that we were constantly having to change position. In the end we moved from one corner to another, hour after hour. Between the loud explosions of the heavy and extra-heavy calibre artillery came the lighter sounds of mortars and the sharper crack of tank and anti-tank shells. And all the time, as the shells were landing so densely that we kept thinking the next one must be a hit, we kept changing location again and again, back and forth, here and there. So it went on the whole day long, and a day can be dreadfully long.

The infantry too were suffering under this heavy fire. Instead of digging in about 50 metres from the orchard, they bunched around the tanks like grapes, and consequently were hit more often, but they could not see this. Even before midday the 200 men of that morning had been reduced to a second lieutenant and six men. On the other hand, our few tanks were still in full fighting order, although we had had to switch off our radios to preserve our batteries. Only if a direct tank attack against our position was identified would our radios be switched back on.

That afternoon our situation did not improve one iota. Again and again I asked myself whether this spot of ground was really worth it. Several times I was close to giving the order to clear the orchard, but then convinced myself once more that there was no other possibility of preventing the Russians from occupying this ground with their tanks by surprise, and that would mean the loss of the bridge. So I was actually pleased that I had this inner conflict about the orders given by Division to hold on to this present position to the last man. Orders of this kind were not unusual at this time.

With these orders – perhaps it was meant as a small sop – I was also permitted to hand out the awards given for the day before. (Experience had shown that awards should be handed out as soon as possible after the event concerned because, firstly, it gave pleasure and had a greater educational effect; and secondly, because decorations had unfortunately often arrived too late. A posthumously awarded decoration can no longer be regarded as a reward, only as a nice gesture.) So I called the tank commanders concerned to come to the rear of my tank and climbed out myself. Even this slight movement must have been spotted by the Russians, for I had yet to pin the Iron Crosses on the commanders when two shells exploded right and left in front of my tank, so close that the blast threw us to the ground. It could have been a disaster, but fortunately no one was hurt.

At dusk the Russians attacked with tanks again, but it was not difficult to repel their attack. Then it was dark at last, and we were just thinking that we had made it, when such a ferocious barrage from weapons of all calibres clattered down on top of us that it was simply impossible to take. As the shells burst with showers of sparks and flashes of light all around us, everyone sought to reach open ground with their tanks as quickly as possible. The crews had held out bravely the whole day long, but what came now was more than they could bear. Had it only been an artillery or mortar bombardment, we might perhaps have held on, but the rockets and the flat-trajectory tank and anti-tank shells forced us to flee from the orchard. We had clearly identified that the Russians, under cover of this terrible bombardment and the darkness that had meantime overcome us, were aiming to take over our positions with their tanks. But even if we had lost the orchard, I wanted at least to prevent the bridge falling into Russian hands. I therefore formed up my tanks immediately around the bridge. The shells continued to shower down on the orchard, then it quietened down again. Before it became completely dark, I formed a semi-circular defensive belt behind the orchard and looked forward to a quiet night, although this position would be untenable next day.

We would have to throw Ivan out of the orchard again. About midnight I obtained two sections of infantry under a staff sergeant from the infantry commander to carry out a reconnaissance in force. Beforehand I had brought my tanks close up to the orchard to provide covering fire for the infantry should they come into contact with the enemy, When everything was ready, the infantry set off. We stared intently into the darkness, the gun layers having their eyes pressed to the optics, ready to cover the infantry with fire at any moment. This intense concentration lasted a quarter of an hour, and then another quarter of an hour, without anything being seen. Then suddenly shadows appeared right in front of us that immediately identified themselves as our scouts, and to our great surprise, the staff sergeant reported the orchard free of the enemy. It would seem that the enemy found the situation too critical for them in the dark and had withdrawn back to their start-point. Nothing could have pleased me more. We immediately reoccupied the orchard, and then had peace for the remainder of the night. Even the following morning passed without incident. The Russians had apparently decided that further attacks on that position were pointless.

At about midday on 24 March I received orders for our relief. We were to return to the tank field workshops, while our position would be taken over by another unit.

Once the relieving commander had been briefed on the details of the hand-over, I drove back to Division, where the Intelligence Officer (Ia) told me of two Russian radio transmissions that had been intercepted. In the first the commander of the sector opposite the orchard had been rebuked for not pressing home his attack. In the second the sector commander reported that he had counted eight dug-in Königstigers in the orchard, against which he could make no progress. This was too much of an honour for us for, firstly, we only had five tanks in that position, and secondly, we had absolutely no Königstigers with us, and we were certainly not dug-in! But we often got similarly nice confirmations of success from Ivan over the radio.

Zobel lost his 2nd Squadron to the Küstrin Garrison. On 16 April he had his two remaining squadrons deployed behind the Hauptgraben water obstacle east of Seelow, where his battalion claimed over 50 Soviet tanks destroyed that day for a loss of four; the four that he had sent forward to support the infantry being knocked out in error by the German anti-tank gun screen. Having been outflanked on his right he withdrew his battalion that night to replenish in the woods behind the Stein-Stellung. Again on the third day of battle the battalion claimed to have destroyed another 50 Soviet tanks caught in the flank advancing north of Trebnitz. The battalion then covered the retreat to Berlin, where it became involved in the defence. Zobel was promoted major on 20 April and then led the breakout to the west over the Charlotten Bridge into Spandau (see With Our Backs to Berlin) *on the night of 1/2 May. When the last vehicles ran out of fuel, they abandoned them and continued on foot. Unable to swim, Zobel nevertheless got across two rivers, ending up naked on the west bank of the Elbe, where he persuaded a mayor to provide him with civilian clothing and a pass stating that he was 'visiting his pregnant wife in the next village'. Armed with this, he traversed American-occupied territory until he found his wife working for the British in Braunschweig, where he joined her as an interpreter, never having been taken prisoner.*

In due course he received an invitation to join a German team to help train the Egyptian Army, which he did until another letter arrived inviting him to help found the Bundeswehr. On his way home he learnt of the defeat of the Egyptian Army in the Six Days War with Israel, in which virtually all the armoured troops he had helped train had been wiped out.

Zobel subsequently became a full colonel and Inspector of Panzer Troops in the Bundeswehr and, after his retirement from active service, went on to edit a technical journal on armoured subjects.

SIX

The Defence of Seelow

KARL-HERMANN TAMS

I met Karl-Hermann Tams at the reunions of the 20th Panzergrenadier Division's 'Mook wie' old comrades' association held on the anniversary of the battle for the Seelow Heights, which were held at the Seelow Museum each year after the reunification of Germany made such events possible. He was always the life and soul of the party, a great raconteur, and his death on 16 April 1995 was a great loss to all his friends there.

My thoughts go back to March 1945 when the situation on all fronts was relatively stable and the feeling among us young soldiers could still be described as confident. We had not been brought up to political contemplation. The situation appeared different at home in the now surrounded remains of the Reich, where there was already a widespread feeling of defeat, although the transport system was intact and food supplies still reaching the population.

I was already 21 years old and had passed a company commanders' course at the Boehm-Kaserne in Hamburg-Rahlstedt, when on Good Friday, 30 March 1945, I received my orders to join the troops on the Eastern Front. I said farewell to my family and remaining circle of friends with truly mixed feelings; as, the longer the war lasted, the more difficult it was for a soldier to return to the front. I had already been wounded twice in action in Russia. The feeling of parting was, in view of the strange situation, hard to describe, inwardly burdened with the uncertainty of the future, yet outwardly confident nevertheless.

For us the collapse of the Reich and of the Wehrmacht was unimaginable and one's own ignorance about what was happening was deliberately suppressed and played down. So I set off with three other comrades full of inner tension on the adventurous route to Berlin, a city which, even in the sixth year of the war, had not lost its appeal and radiance as a metropolis.

Naturally we had a night out 'on the town' in Berlin at a small bar on the Kurfürstendamm. Next morning, Easter Saturday, 31 March 1945, we continued our journey to Fürstenwalde, until then still a delightful little town. It made a great impression on us, being accustomed to living in one destroyed city after another. (Just three weeks later I came through here again freshly wounded and found only a dead town of smoking rubble.) At the Movement Office in Fürstenwalde we were directed to exactly where our unit was at the moment, namely in Seelow and in positions in the Oderbruch eastwards of there opposite Küstrin. Our destination was Seelow.

There was a train laden with supplies for our unit (20th Panzergrenadier Division) at the railway station. Departure was expected at dusk, as Seelow already lay in the combat zone. The designation HKL (Hauptkampflinie = Main fighting line) had been given up at the end of the war and replaced by a new term 'Kampfraum' (combat zone) covering an area about 3 kilometres deep. Thus Seelow was in the front line and the population had been evacuated.

Our train moved off and groped its way, fully blacked out and without any lights at all, almost step by step through the night; part of the route being visible to the enemy. Familiar flares stood in the sky above the front; single tank gunshots bellowed through the night, and heavier gun barrels boomed and thundered their greetings from here and there and all around, while machine guns rattled sporadically in the distance. Although the train rolled on, the front had already bypassed us, and our senses adjusted once more to a different reality from that to which we were otherwise normally accustomed.

Finally the train drew up at a siding, a branch line to an agricultural barn on a small slope on the southwestern edge of Seelow, where we were cheerfully welcomed by our comrades. Suddenly we were hearing our Hamburg dialect again and the odd familiar smiling face with the right jokes on their lips. After my frightful experience in the bombing of Dresden and having avoided the general rounding up of those heroes that had been grabbed and commandeered for a wild, emergency unit raised on the spot, I was happy to be back in one piece, with my unit at last. We used to call it 'our gang'. People today would hardly credit it, but we young soldiers felt at home being back in our unit.

The reception and disembarkation went quite quietly, briskly, without noise or excitement. We were quickly briefed and told to report to our Commanding Officer, Colonel Reinhold Stammerjohann, at the regimental command post on Easter Sunday morning. Father Stammerjohann was no stranger to me and I was delighted at the prospect of seeing him again. Assigned to him as a second lieutenant, of course I immediately requested a combat command. With a grin, he clapped me warmly on the shoulder and said: "Son, you have only just got here from the slaughter-house, stay here with me for a while!"

Naturally I thought this was an excellent Easter present. The staff officers greeted us young second lieutenants with vodka, as was the custom.

The next few days were full and passed quickly, although the front remained quiet. I was assigned to the regimental combat reserve, i.e. as a general dogsbody. The days were filled with inspection visits, ground familiarisation and looking at the possibilities open to us, and to infantry close combat training of the sailors in our Field Replacement Battalion. One would hardly believe it, but these men had been assigned to us because of the lack of ships for them to man, there being no other alternative for them. They were all experienced in naval warfare, many of them having had their ships sunk under them, and I should stress that these sailors generally made an outstanding impression on us. They were a very likeable lot, as were our own soldiers, who were all up to Ivan's cunning tricks and knew how to turn them to their own advantage. In a short time, however, all of them were killed in action. I still maintain that our regiment in Seelow was undermined by the faulty assessment of these men's ability to convert into infantry. That applies above all to the employment of two Volkssturm companies in our sector. Their losses were devastating. Certainly we could never have foreseen the stubborn doggedness of those troops facing us. We were to lose our last optimistic assumptions pretty quickly.

If I can quote from a report in 'Stern' magazine of April 1975 – thirty years after – the scale of the differing force strengths in this battle can be properly evaluated.

> . . . it became clear with a visit to the socialist shrine[1] on the Seelow Heights, where the decisive battle for Berlin began on the 16th April 1945. 33,000 Red soldiers fell in the attack on the strongly fortified German positions. 10,000 alone are buried in the main Soviet cemetery. How many German soldiers fell cannot allegedly be established.

We survivors can give our own troop strength estimates. In the roughly twelve kilometres-wide sector concerned, there were certainly not more than 5,000 German soldiers lined up for the defence, of which apparently only five to ten individuals survived. So we can calculate troop strengths of twenty to one confronting each other on the Seelow Heights in April 1945.

But to return to our experiences and impressions.

On the Friday, 6 April, I was attached to the combat commander of Seelow, Helmut Wandmaker – then Major Wandmaker – i.e. allocated to the Seelow Combat Group. Out task was simple: to defend Seelow, if necessary to let it be surrounded and to tie down enemy forces as long as possible. This was a suicide mission, but Helmut and I survived it.

First I set up quarters with Second Lieutenant Günther Reimers and another comrade in the building of a grocery store right on the market place. Naturally, standing on this market place in the middle of the town, there was also a church with a tower. That this church tower would or could eventually become the aiming point for the Russian artillery we simply ignored in view of what this building offered, with all the amenities in the world. Not only enough food for us three for a whole year, but comfortable furnishings, beginning with the feather beds and the intact bath on the first floor behind on the east side. The building had been left by its inhabitants as if they had just gone off for a short holiday. Certain rooms were locked and sealed and so unavailable to us.

So we first heated the bath water and had a proper bath, one after the other. Günther Reimers willingly took over the kitchen and served us up one luxurious dish after another. For a few days we did not appear at the field kitchen. The wine and spirits supplies were inexhaustible. We became overconfident and shot pigeons off the roof with our pistols for the eventual pleasure of eating them.

One day the Russian artillery opened fire. We noticed during the course of the day that at regular intervals single shots were being aimed at the church tower in the town centre. We first realised that our building lay right in the line of fire late that afternoon, after duty, when we were all sitting in our quarters.

I had already started running my bath water and was standing naked in the bathroom doorway, Günter was busy in the kitchen over our supper, and our third comrade was sorting out his kit for the next day in his bedroom, when we became aware of the familiar noise of a gun firing. Involuntarily we froze, as we tried to determine the direction of flight. Missing the great roar and howling of its passage over us, it suddenly became crystal clear that the hit must occur in our vicinity in the next three or four seconds. The combat experienced soldier recognises this immediately – CRUNCH! We all ran to the centre of the first floor of the building as it landed under the shop. We were completely covered in brick dust, glass splinters and falling plaster. It lasted at least two minutes or longer until the dust settled and we could recognise one another again and see our tensed faces. Although none of us were wounded, we were shocked and released our tension with laughter at our appearance and funny situation. The shell had exploded at the back of the building on the windowsill of the office under the bathroom. The partition wall with the shop, with all its shelves and their contents, lay on the market place in front of the building. All our 'luxuries' had been brought to an end with one blow. We had to retire to the cellars, as were the instructions. Once more we had got away scot-free.

A further example of how a soldier took things easy when there was an apparently stable front, we felt fully tactically secure; for, as defenders on the Seelow Heights, we thought we could overcome any attacker through our geographical advantage, especially as they first had to break out of a bridgehead. So it was decided to hold a social evening. I cannot remember who was the host, but it certainly was an excellent party. All the officers and NCOs of the regiment who could get away for the evening were invited, including those of the Field Replacement Battalion of our 20th Panzergrenadier Division. Where exactly in Seelow we then sat down together at table, I cannot remember. Nevertheless, I recall a large banqueting room with tall Roman windows, a table laid for thirty to fifty persons with white tablecloths, place settings for many courses and the same number of glasses for various drinks, and radiant, festive electric lighting.

We felt quite at home in this officers' club. We talked about the war, and what would happen to Germany after it had lost it. Why couldn't somebody kill Hitler? Was it right for the oath of loyalty to be made to an individual, and did our building in Hamburg escape the last air attack? Then we discussed politics: how long would the Western Powers continue as unequal partners with the Soviet Union. Would we have to have another go to the east along with the Western Powers? How long can we hold the Russians on the Oder, etc.? Finally, we heard it from our Commanding Officer's own lips: 'We shall stay here if necessary until the American tanks drive up our arse! Understood?'

The conversation was cut short suddenly as we found ourselves the target of a Russian artillery salvo. The shellfire brought us back to reality. The electric lights went out. Yet nearly everyone remained seated at the table. We lit the candles that had been laid out for emergencies and the celebration continued unhurriedly, although the prettily coloured Roman windows were now without glass. Fortunately we had already finished our meal and the table had been cleared. Fresh glasses were quickly brought out and the congenial atmosphere was enhanced by the candlelight. It just shows how thick-skinned soldiers can be!

Next morning, 14 April 1945, we were awoken by loud sounds of combat. Heavy fire was falling on our forward positions. Could this be the beginning of a new major offensive? The 'Hurrah!' cries of the Ivans were smothered everywhere one after the other by the concentrated defensive fire of our troops.

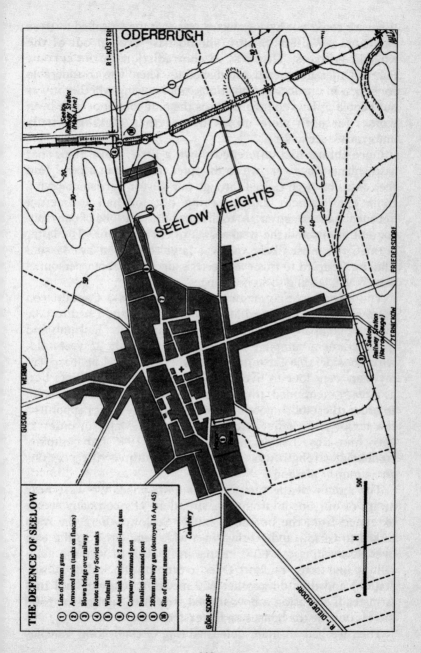

THE DEFENCE OF SEELOW

① Line of 88mm guns
② Armoured train (tanks on flatcars)
③ Blown bridge over railway
④ Route taken by Soviet tanks
⑤ Windmill
⑥ Anti-tank barrier & 2 anti-tank guns
⑦ Company command post
⑧ Battalion command post
⑨ 280mm railway gun (destroyed 16 Apr 45)
⑩ Site of current museum

ODERBRUCH

SEELOW HEIGHTS

What we could not have expected was that the so-called fortress garrison, a Waffen-SS unit, should have broken out of the Küstrin Fortress. This was in contradiction to the current Führer-Order and greatly astonished us. There was considerable confusion in our forward positions, not knowing whether it was our people or Ivan coming towards them. It could not have been worse, for both were mixed up together, making a truly unfortunate scene for us.

Once things had quietened down a little, came the sober assessment. How were we to interpret the Russian attack? Had the confusion been caused through our Küstrin garrison blowing their encirclement and breaking out, or had it been a 'reconnaissance in strength' to discover the locations of our main concentrations and the weaknesses in our positions? The latter seemed the most likely and was later confirmed by Marshal Zhukov. Coupled to this event certain decisions about personnel were made, leading to some changes.

The new battle commander of Seelow was a Captain von Wartenberg, who relieved Major Wandmaker, and I had to take over the company detachment of Sergeant Major Eiskamp and thus became a company commander. I was only 21 years old, with considerable Eastern Front experience, and at least half my men were four to five years older, experienced sailors but, as already mentioned, totally inexperienced in fighting on land. In order to establish good relations with these men I appointed the senior petty officer Company Sergeant Major in order to keep him close beside me. On 14 April 1945 our company combatant strength was 136 divided into three rifle platoons and a mortar platoon.

The morale of the company was quite good. We were fully aware of our uncompromising situation. The company sector extended from the northern exit of Seelow, where the road forked to Gusow and Werbig, in a wide semi-circle to the east over Reichsstrasse 1 (200 metres in front of us was the main railway line from Frankfurt/Oder to Stettin with Seelow railway station) and then on another 500 metres past a windmill to a farmstead, enclosing a bow-shaped stretch of land about 1500 metres outside the houses on the eastern edge.

Then we had an inner defensive ring of connecting trenches

between the houses over a distance of about 700 metres, and here in the middle I established my command post. We were on an elevation and about 200 metres east of us the land dropped steeply eastwards towards the Oder. The railway line and station lay beneath us in a cutting running across our front. Küstriner Strasse, as Reichsstrasse 1 here was called, led in a straight line away from the bridge over the railway and past a waterworks across the Oder marshes to Küstrin.

My task was to prepare both these objects, the bridge and the waterworks, for demolition, and to blow them should there be a threat of a breakthrough by Russian tanks. Set back a bit in the entrance to the town, we built an anti-tank barrier and placed two anti-tank guns behind it.

I divided the mortar platoon into two sections and deployed them to cover the eastern and northeastern exit roads. On the slopes along and in front of the railway cutting in our sector were six or eight 88 mm anti-aircraft guns dug in in the anti-tank role. The anti-aircraft gunners gave us an impression of great confidence.

The Luftwaffe were very active on 15 April. No doubt as an adjunct to reconnaissance for the SS unit that had broken out, they flew continuous attacks with so-called 'pick-a-back' units, i.e. a fighter aircraft mounted over the airframe of a worn-out Junkers 88 packed with explosives, and releasing it over the target in the enemy lines.[2] Each time there was a tremendous explosion and a gigantic fireball. Each hit was a source of great satisfaction to us.

That these were only drops in the ocean, we could not have believed at that time. Our time was filled with preparatory measures for defence, expecting a major Russian attack at any moment.

At 0300 hours on the morning of 16 April 1945, forty thousand guns opened fire simultaneously. It seemed as if the dawn was suddenly upon us, then vanished again. The whole Oder valley bed shook. In the bridgehead it was as light as day. The hurricane of fire reached out to the Seelow Heights. It seemed as if the earth was reaching up into the sky like a dense wall. Everything around us started dancing, rattling about. Whatever was not securely fastened down fell from the shelves

115

and cupboards. Pictures fell off the walls and crashed to the floor. Glass splinters jumped out of window frames. We were soon covered in sand, dirt and glass splinters. None of us had experienced anything like it before, and would not have believed it possible. There was no escape. The greatest concentration of artillery fire in history was directed immediately in front of us. We had the impression that every square yard of earth would be ploughed up. After two or three hours the fire was suddenly lifted. Cautiously we risked a peep over the Heights down into the Oderbruch, and what we saw made the blood run cold. As far as we could see in the grey light of dawn came a single wave of heavy tanks. The air was filled with the noise of tank engines and the rattling of tank tracks. As the first row came closer we saw behind them another, and then hordes of running infantry.

The first shells had already been hurtling past over our heads for several minutes. With their barrels fully depressed the anti-aircraft guns dug in on the ridge along the chain of hills directed their murderous fire on the Soviets. Tank after tank went up in flames, the infantry sitting on them being swept off. The survivors charged on with piercing cries. The Luftwaffe gun crews were firing into the packs of Red soldiers and the attack began to collapse in front of our eyes. Several T-34s had broken through and were now being knocked out by our troops as they tried to roll up the slope of Reichsstrasse 1 into Seelow. As it became full light, the attack was beaten back with heavy losses for the Soviets.

Now we were in a hurry to prepare for the next Russian attack. Our foremost positions were evacuated and the survivors of our regiment withdrew as quickly as possible to the top of the hill. This had to be done without the enemy seeing in order to surprise him in the next assault. This was successful. Under my direction the waterworks and the road bridge over the railway were blown up, both demolitions going smoothly.

During the course of the morning the Russians increased their artillery support of the land battle with heavy bombers and ground-attack aircraft. They were feeling out our positions on the Heights. All day long we formed a catchment line for stragglers from our forward lines.

About midday a sudden, heavy artillery barrage fell on our positions on the Heights, lasting about thirty minutes and hitting us hard. It was indescribable. Immediately after the bombardment came a Russian attack, this time directly on my company's positions. A bigger breakthrough could only be prevented by considerable sacrifice on our side. The situation was catastrophic for me. Every fifth man in my company was either killed, missing or wounded, including Staff Sergeant Kühlkamp with 18 men.

About 1800 hours contact with my No.1 Platoon on the south side of Küstriner Strasse was lost. With dusk the Ivans secured the cottages on either side of the street up to our anti-tank barrier.

Then there was another incident on the left-hand side of our sector opposite the railway station. Here I came across a Waffen-SS staff sergeant with some other stragglers that had originally belonged to the Küstrin garrison and were now already in their fourth day of combat since the break-out. They were coming out of the defile that led toward us from the railway station from the northeast and reported that the station was swarming with Russians. This was only 120 metres directly in front of us.

The Waffen-SS men looked completely exhausted, both physically and mentally, and I had to force them at gunpoint to make a stand and accept my orders. I put them on my left flank, and was delighted to be able to make up my losses with these combat-experienced soldiers. Unfortunately, in the haste and excitement of the moment, I did not take down their names and so could not be surprised next morning when I found that they were no longer there. It was if the earth had swallowed them up, leaving a gap in positions that was to prove fateful next day.

Then back to Küstriner Strasse at about 2100 hours. How had the connection to my No. 1 Platoon been lost? I set off with my company sergeant major. We crawled up to the main road then darted across to the side wall of the building opposite. Here we recovered our breath and listened for the reaction to our move. To our horror, we could hear Russian voices in the building where we were standing. Suddenly a Russian hand grenade landed right at my feet. I instinctively kicked it away, and we ran off into the back garden. Following the explosion of the hand grenade, there was a burst of sub-machine gun fire behind us. The nature of the terrain and darkness had protected us. Even using a flare, Ivan could not see us.

A few metres further on we were challenged by our own sentries. There was great astonishment on the faces of our comrades, who were expecting the Russians and not us from this direction. No. 1 Platoon was in good fighting order. The men had blown up the windmill in front of their positions to give a better field of fire. I joined with Second Lieutenant Rebischke in the forcible clearance of the cottages on Küstriner Strasse, which lasted until daybreak. This went quicker than expected, the Russians pulling back without serious resistance.

Shortly after midnight, Captain Rosenke of the 1st Battalion, Panzergrenadier Regiment 76, appeared with the news that we were now directly under his command. From then on we would be called Combat Group 'Rosenke' on the orders of the regiment.

In the early hours of 17 April I had things relatively under control once more. Contact on either flank was established, the last fighting strength of my company was about eighty soldiers, and I could pass this figure on to my superiors. What would the day bring us now? Consideration had to be given to the state of our troops, most of whom had now been in action for three or four days. The losses in men and weapons could no longer be made good. It was impossible to relieve our men.

Dawn brought yet another blast of artillery fire, which was supplemented and supported by wave after wave of bombing attacks by heavy aircraft. It was horrific. I was at my command post in the cellar of the same house. At one point there was a tremendous explosion, and the whole building rose and settled down again a little tilted to one side. We found a man-sized hole in the exterior wall opposite, and outside a crater deep enough to have taken the whole house before being levelled off. One petty officer went crazy, started foaming at the mouth, and had to be forcibly restrained.

The artillery fire ceased abruptly. Now the moment had come to get out of the house and occupy our positions. Our main point of aim was toward Küstriner Strasse. The sounds of combat led me to make my way to the northern part of the company sector, which had been quiet until then. Something was wrong here. I was accompanied by our petty officer, Sergeant Lohmann, Lance Corporal Bayers and Corporal Liefke. To our surprise, the positions, partly demolished by artillery fire, were empty. As already mentioned, the Waffen-SS men had vanished. Our No. 3 Platoon no longer existed; Staff Sergeant Kühlkamp had fallen the day before. Our northern flank was open and contact with our neighbouring unit, a Volkssturm company, could not be established. If I was going to save anything, I would have to act fast. Lohmann, Bayers and Liefke were tasked by me to maintain visual contact with Küstriner Strasse, to hold the position and to fall back on the centre of Seelow if necessary, where we could meet up again. I would go with our petty officer and ask our Commanding Officer for the reserve platoon and bring them to the rendezvous.

Now everything seemed to move at the double. Our goal was the battalion command post at the manor farm. Our route took us via the street leading in from Gusow, which, to our surprise, was under direct fire. Then we recognised some T-34s close by and coming toward us. I had not expected to be attacked from the north so soon. I still remember a long white wall about two metres high leading past the knacker's yard, which gave us cover from fire from the north.

The Russians must have seen us, for the wall received a broadside from the barrels of several tank guns and disintegrated briefly in smoke as soon as I had passed. Our sympathetic petty officer immediately behind me was buried by the wall and disappeared in the smoke. I felt powerless, as if hypnotised, and rushed across Reichsstrasse 1 into the gateway of the manor farm.

The yard was about a hundred metres square and surrounded by barns, stalls and storehouses with loading ramps. Our battalion command post was in the cellar of a storehouse and reached via the loading ramp through a large sliding door. I reached the top of the steps out of breath and called down: 'Everyone outside, the Russians are here!' The faces that I saw were apathetic, virtually defeated. The command post as such had already been evacuated, and the soldiers remaining there were seeking shelter and cover from the bombardment. One of the soldiers told me that our Commanding Officer, Colonel Stammerjohn, was dead. This event had caused something of a sensation, paralysing the leadership for a while. His body had already been sent back.

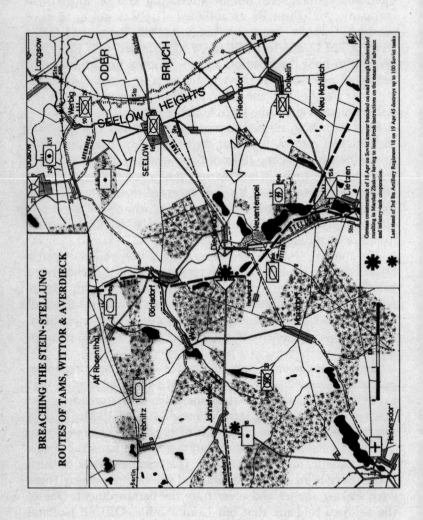

BREACHING THE STEIN-STELLUNG
ROUTES OF TAMS, WITTOR & AVERDIECK

German counterattack of 18 Apr on Soviet armour bunched on road through Diedersdorf resulting in Marshal Zhukov having to issue fresh instructions on the means of advance and infantry-tank cooperation.

Last stand of 3rd Bn Artillery Regiment 18 on 19 Apr 45 destroys up to 100 Soviet tanks

Soviet troops outside the Brandenburg Gate.

German youngsters being marched off into captivity.

Schloss Thorn from across the Moselle River.

Erich Wittor in the uniform of a subaltern of the Grossdeutschland Division.

American troops survey the dead after the fighting for Nennig near Schloss Thorn.

Ernst Henkel in 1943.

Volkssturm at Frankfurt/Oder.

Top left: Schloss Klessin before the battle.
Middle left: The two German 'Tigers' destroyed at Klessin.
Left: All that remained of Schloss Klessin after the battle.
Above: German dead in their smashed trenches below Seelow.

Inset right: Karl-Hermann Tams as a sergeant major with the Iron Cross Second Class.
Right: The first visit of the 'Mook wie' Old Comrades Association to Seelow on 15 April 1991. Tams in raincoat on left, the author far right.

Major von Hopffgarten revisits the 'Kurmark' battlefield as a retired Lieutenant General of the Bundeswehr.

Soviet T-34 tanks on the battlefield.

Opposite: The Klessin position as seen from the German lines at Point 54.2. Thick trees cover the site of the Schloss in the centre, with the new houses on the Wuhden road to the left.
Right: Horst Zobel on a battlefield tour with the Royal Welch Fusiliers in 1993.

Stalin II tanks under fire on the Moltke Bridge, turrets closed, as seen from the Diplomatic Quarter on 29 April 1945. The demolition hole is indicated by the missing parapet. Two SU-100s and a T-34/85 have their guns trained on the far bank, and a dog sledge for evacuating wounded can be seen centre left.

The overgrown site of Schloss Klessin today.

The Wuhden memorial to those who fell on the Reitwein Spur.

Gerhard Tillery on home leave in 1944.

Hinnerk Otterstedt's grave in Sachsendorf.

Harry Zvi Glaser in 1945.

40,000 soldiers and civilians died in the attempted break-out at Halbe.

Harry Zvi Glaser in conversation with President Clinton at the White House after being presented with the 'Order of Glory' by President Yeltsin during a state visit.

The Zoo Flak-tower from across the Landwehr Canal during dismantling. Crowned with four twin 128mm gun mountings and twelve multi-barrelled 20mm or 37mm 'pom-poms', this bunker formed the core of the defence while sheltering up to 30,000 civilians.

Harry Schweizer in Hitler Youth uniform.

Soviet anti-tank guns in action in Berlin.

SS-Sergeant Major Willi Rogmann wearing his Close Combat Clasp in Gold.

A wrecked Soviet T-34 facing the Reichstag on Moltkestrasse.

Adolf Hitler and Youth Leader Artur Axmann congratulating Hitler Youths on their awards for bravery on 20 March 1945.

Soviet tanks push through the rubble.

Rudi Averdieck as a
sergeant with the Iron
Cross Second Class in
1944.

Rudi Averdieck in France, 28 May
1940.

Wrecked Soviet armour on Charlottenburger Strasse.

Soviet troops with a panje wagon and a Stalin II converging on the rear of the Reichstag to sign their names on the walls.

The author with Willi Rogmann in Berlin in 1994.

The staged hoisting of 'Red Banner No. 5' of the 150th Rifle Division by Sergeants M.A. Yegorov and M.V. Kantaria on the rear parapet of the Reichstag on the afternoon of 2 May 1945. (Imperial War Museum)

The soldiers came back to life when Sergeant Stein aimed a shot at a Soviet officer as they were leaving the storehouse through the sliding door. Two T-34s were standing in the yard with their engines running and their gun barrels aimed in our direction. The man on the tank with a red band on his hat fell, apparently hit. The shock caused by the Russian presence spread among the men emerging from the building along the ramp. The ensuing unequal exchange of fire caused panic among us, so that my original intention to lead the men back to the centre of town to redeploy them was forcibly abandoned. Meanwhile a third tank entered the yard, and there being no anti-tank weapon ready to hand, the men disappeared. Only Sergeant Stein remained beside me. We went back behind the building to the railway siding where I had arrived seventeen days previously.

There I found three men of my company headquarters, who, knowing what I had intended, and having experienced the collapse of the remains of the company on Küstriner Strasse, had worked their way back through the town to the manor farm. It was a real joy to see them again. They brought news of the wounding of Lieutenant Ludwig.

We moved about 200 metres further south to the Seelow-Diedersdorf railway line. Here our Captain Rosenke (or was it Captain von Wartenberg?) was lying on a mound observing the movement on the battlefield. In fact Seelow had been surrounded and cut off from the north, giving us the feeling that the stricken ship was sinking. From here we could see khaki-coloured figures enveloping and attacking the town. The sounds of combat rose sharply once more in the southern part of the town, and then all was quiet again.

I was given the task of occupying the heights in front of Diedersdorf. Lieutenant Schäfer, badly wounded in the lungs, was led past us by two soldiers on their way to the Main Dressing Station. I was able to speak to him and wish him a speedy recovery. So we pulled back in a sad column under cover of the railway embankment toward Diedersdorf, always with the feeling that Ivan was breathing down the back of our necks. On the next hill Lieutenant Diesing directed us to the so-called 'Stein-Stellung'.[3] Here I came across a further eight men from my company, making thirteen men in all, the strongest company left in our combat team. Only one man in ten had survived the last 27 hours fit and well.

Late afternoon we received from Major Wandmaker, the new regimental commander, the collective order: 'All 76th back to Diedersdorf!'

I remember the depression that came over us as we moved back defeated and exhausted through the countryside. The overwhelming might thrown against us had broken our backbone. Our regiment had ceased to exist as a regiment. It was the first time that I had experienced such a loss of self-confidence among our troops, as we recognised our powerlessness against this steamroller from the east. I was reminded of a line from our regimental song: 'A Hanseatic regiment knows only victory – or death!'

Suddenly we found ourselves in an occupied anti-aircraft position. Two dug-in 88 mm guns, well camouflaged, thirty to fifty metres deep in the wood, with prepared avenues of fire. To our question: 'What are you waiting here for? We are the last of the infantry – Ivan will be here in thirty minutes!' came the answer: 'We still have five armour-piercing shells left per gun, which will get us eight tanks and then allow us to blow up our guns with the last two – then we will come!' About five to seven hundred metres further on the woods came to an end, and we arrived at our new positions another hundred metres on.

Here, every single soldier was personally briefed and given a specific combat task. In addition, Staff Sergeant Hellbrun was attached to me with several soldiers and we also got the support of three Jagdtigers from a Waffen-SS unit. In this connection, I must recall the unfortunate strength comparisons – what could three self-propelled guns do against the one hundred T-34 tanks we had had constantly in our view for the past two days? Despite the heavy losses we had inflicted on the Russians, reckoning on up to sixty or more shot-up and burning tanks per day, there were always new ones ready to come up against us. It was discouraging.[4]

At last, after two days, we were able to eat again. Everyone remained quietly in his corner. Shortly before dusk we suddenly heard the unpleasant howling sound of the anti-aircraft guns in front of us. This awakened a short and intense noise of gun fire and armour-piercing shells exploding at close range. As quickly as it had begun, the noise subsided again. How had it gone out there in front? To find out and re-establish contact with our anti-aircraft gunners, I sent a scout party through the woods. They reported back about ninety minutes later, with the news that there were seven burning T-34s in front of the woods opposite. A further twenty tanks had turned round and withdrawn out of firing range. Our anti-aircraft gunners were all fine and were calmly preparing their guns for demolition. That our men had not brought back the gunners with them immediately, or provided them with infantry fire cover until they could withdraw, proved to be a fatal tactical error next day.

For once we were not disturbed, the Russians also being quiet, and we assumed that nothing decisive would occur before sunrise. As I had been continuously on my feet for forty-five hours, I collapsed in my trench so exhausted that I slept like the dead. It was already light when I was cruelly awakened. I had slept through two heavy bombardments, so that my men thought I must have been fatally wounded. I had been so over-tired that even an artillery bombardment could not wake me. Harsh reality seized me once more.

All were in their firing positions, our nerves stretched to the limit. Suddenly we saw movement in the bushes at the edge of the woods. Figures emerged, and I could see how the Russians were preparing to feel their way forward. When they were about sixty to eighty metres away, I called out: 'Fire at will!'

Our carbines and machine guns fired at the attackers. After our first or second burst of fire we heard German voices, 'Comrades, don't shoot, we are German!'

Immediately our weapons stopped firing. Since I had been asleep, I could not have known that our anti-aircraft gunners had not returned during the night. Between the attacking Russians we could now see some German helmets. For seconds there was a paralysing horror on our side.

Our fire resumed individually, but by now it was too late. The Russian artillery laid a barrage on the railway embankment behind us, as their infantry broke into our trenches. The picture that now plays in front of my eyes, still haunts me in my sleep. Although I had been a soldier for three and a half years, of which seventeen months had been in action with a front-line unit, I had never experienced anything like this, nor believed it possible. Men were fighting with clubs and knives just as in the Middle Ages.

'I can't take any more of this!' I felt like shouting. When I stood up over the trench, a second of panic gripped me and I ran back to the wall of fire on the railway embankment. Subconsciously, I noticed that someone was following me. It must have been only seconds before we were about 50 metres from the railway embankment and crawling up it. Two terrifying explosions immediately behind us forced us against the embankment. Corporal Schröder asked me if I had been hit. Yes, a shot through the right lower leg and a hit in the left foot. For a moment I was unable to get up. Schröder himself must have been in the dead angle from the explosion, i.e. immediately next to it, and so was miraculously unwounded. He seized the initiative and quickly pulled me over the railway lines into cover on the far side.

As if ordered, there stood a motorcycle ready to go. So we drove across country in a northwesterly direction to a nearby wood, where Schröder tied me on in a makeshift fashion. Once ready, we were electrified by the sound of tracks of moving tanks. I could see tanks moving slowly toward us like an armada, snapping off the young trees of the little wood like matchsticks. Yet again, as on the previous day, our troops were being surrounded by tanks in a pincer movement and overrolled in a flanking action.

The condition of my unit and the naked fear of death gave me the strength to run. In order to survive, we had to reach the edge of the woods furthest from the tanks and cross the open field beyond. We went up a sloping meadow and had just reached the crest of the hill when we saw the heavy tanks driving out of the little wood. The Diedersdorf-Heinersdorf road, along which the remainder of our supply vehicles, some horse-drawn, were retreating, ran along the far side of the hill in dead ground to the Russians. With the last of my strength, I clambered up on to an open horse-drawn wagon, which took me to the Main Dressing Station in Heinersdorf.[5] The Russian tanks were firing from the edge of the wood, even though their shots could only reach the tops of the trees lining the road. Despite the splinters from bursting shells, nothing serious occurred.

Schröder left me at the Main Dressing Station with a heavy heart. I sat for one or two hours with a lump in my throat. I could hardly think, as the experience kept going around in my mind. Once I had been tended to and bandaged, I was laid on a stretcher outside; outside being an area the size of a football field, filled with with wounded soldiers laid out in rows on stretchers.

Like a flash of lightning from the sky, two Russian fighter-bombers suddenly attacked the Main Dressing Station at low level, mowing gaps in the rows of helpless men with their machine guns. They circled a couple of times repeating their murderous fire before flying off to seek new targets.

I could see how long the transport was taking to evacuate the wounded, there being only four vehicles available, so, with the driver's consent, I sat on the forward left mudguard of an ambulance with my back to the direction of travel and held fast on to the driving mirror. After a drive lasting over four hours, we were eventually delivered to a reserve hospital in Königs Wusterhausen.

Against all the rules and some well-meaning advice, I did not stay there, but made my way back by train to Hamburg. So, on 22 April, only three weeks after my departure, I found myself back home again. My sister did not recognise me when she opened the door. My mother came to the door with my father behind her. In his surprise he said: 'Are you a deserter?' When I replied: 'No, I have been wounded.' he said: 'In that case, you can come in!'

Tams became a sucessful businessman in Hamburg after the war.

1 The present Seelow Museum was originally established by the Government of the German Democratic Republic as a 'Memorial to the Liberation'.
2 Known as the 'Mistel', its target were the Soviet bridges.
3 The 'Stein-Stellung' was a prepared but unmanned, main defensive strip.
4 Presumably Panzerjäger Tiger Ausf B Jägdtigers of the SS Heavy Panzer Battalion 502, which had been lagered nearby. Heavily armoured and armed with an 88mm gun, these were in fact formidable fighting vehicles.
5 The Headquarters of the XIth SS Panzer Corps (see 'The Siege of Klessin') had been located here.

SEVEN

Marxdorf

ERICH WITTOR

Erich Wittor, squadron commander in the Armoured Reconnaissance Battalion 'Kurmark', was in divisional reserve at Falkenhagen, so he and his unit were not committed to action until 18 April 1945, when his experience appears to take over from that of Karl-Hermann Tams.

At battalion headquarters on 18 April 1945, I was given the task of defending the area southwest of Seelow with my squadron, where the enemy had broken through. We immediately drove via Lietzen to Neuentempel. I was checking out the area on the edge of some woods to the west and northwest, and giving instructions to my NCOs, when we came under shell fire. Without any cover whatsoever, without even our steel helmets, we lay defenceless on the open ground, trying to make ourselves as flat as flounders, only able to pray that we would not be hit, the explosions coming right on top of us. Stones, clumps of earth and twigs pattered down all round us. A few minutes seemed like eternity. At last the artillery stopped firing, and the first thing I did was to get out the steel helmets.

Then the squadron was deployed into defensive positions and started digging in. My command post was in an earthen dug-out with a roof of logs that only a direct hit could have penetrated.[1] By evening we were fully prepared for defence and could have held our positions. It became dark, and again artillery fire fell on our positions. Suddenly, from my dug-out I could hear the sound of tanks, and wanted to look out and see what this meant. I had already gone up five or six steps when a shell exploded close by, the blast driving me back down again. I felt numbed, unable to stand or feel anything.

Had something happened to me? I could neither feel nor hear anything. My senses came slowly back to life. A shell splinter as long as a little finger was sticking out of my left hip, jutting out like a needle, so that the medical sergeant was able to pull it out on the spot. I had been lucky. For safety, he later gave me an anti-tetanus injection. Fortunately, the sounds had come from some Tiger tanks coming to our support.

On the 19th we were ordered back to the area south of Marxdorf, which had already been penetrated by the Russians. The enemy had to be tackled with hard, hour-long fighting in the woods, in which my men fought bravely and willingly, the NCOs giving excellent examples to their men. Eventually we gained the edge of the woods south of Marxdorf and set ourselves up for defence.

Here my company sergeant major brought in a staff sergeant and a sergeant who had aroused his suspicions. I could not spend much time on them and had them sent back to the command post. They were wearing German uniforms with badges of rank and decorations, but none of us knew them, and what they had to say made us suspicious. Later I was told that they were members of the National Committee for a Free Germany and had been sent by the Russians to cause confusion and thus give the Russians the advantage. The fate of these two is not hard to guess. Even as prisoners of war, one cannot act against one's own country and work for the enemy, whatever the reasons. This was the first time that I had come across members of this committee.

The Königstiger tanks of the Waffen-SS had taken up position on the right flank of my squadron, and we were soon to discover how valuable they were.

Late afternoon some T-34 tanks began attacking Marxdorf from a patch of woodland to one side. With incredible accuracy the Tigers' 88 mm guns shot up tank after tank, each shell causing the T-34 hit to explode, mostly leaving only the glowing remains of what had been a fast-moving, attacking tank. There was not a single miss, and we were overjoyed with the outcome.

The excellent siting of our tanks did not give the Russians a chance to retaliate, and they were able to push forward into Marxdorf only at night.

With nightfall we were able to conduct a reconnaissance in Marxdorf, capturing some drunken Russians and also had the opportunity to use our Panzerfausts.

Next morning a grenadier battalion of the 'Nordland' prepared to launch an attack from immediately west of the village, and soon did so. We were able to observe the action from our positions quite clearly. The SS-Grenadiers advanced as if on exercise, cutting through as in our best times. Within a short while they had taken the village and driven the Russians out, displaying the fighting morale of our troops all over again, their spirit and steadfastness even now leading to success even when outnumbered two-to-one. Unfortunately, the overwhelming numbers and equipment of the other side were so great that this disparity could not for long be overcome by the tactical skills of our leaders, nor the courage and steadfastness of our troops. It was 20 April 1945.[2]

Erich Wittor was wounded during the last days of the war but managed to get through to the American lines across the Elbe at Tangermünde, where he was taken prisoner. The Americans had so many prisoners that they passed some on to the British and some to the Soviets. Wittor was fortunate enough to be passed on to the British, who released him at the end of August 1945. He joined the Bundeswehr as a lieutenant of Reconnaissance Troops in 1956 and went on in that branch to end his service in 1984 as the Deputy Commandant of the Bundeswehr's Armoured Training School in the rank of colonel.

1 This would have been already in existence as part of the 'Stein-Stellung', the second defensive belt, unmanned and relying on survivors from the first defensive belt to man it in due course.
2 Hitler's birthday.

EIGHT

Retreat from Seelow

DR. FRITZ-RUDI AVERDIECK

Rudi Averdieck was the radio sergeant of Panzergrenadier-Regiment 90 of the 20th Panzergrenadier Division that was deployed around Seelow awaiting the main Soviet offensive on Berlin. Averdieck had been conscripted in 1938 and had been with the same unit as a radio operator throughout the Polish, French and Russian campaigns.

The bombardment which started at 0700 hours on 14 April introduced the last phase of the war on the Eastern Front.[1] The initial enemy attacks were all beaten back, the 76th Regiment shooting up twelve tanks, and by midday some small breaches in our lines had been eliminated. However, our counter-attack failed in the face of the second Russian bombardment, which was reinforced by simultaneous heavy air attacks. The companies fled back, incurring heavy casualties. They then occupied the main battle line about 200 metres in front of the Annahof. The Soviets could be seen hitting our surviving wounded with spades. At dusk the enemy closed in and the Annahof came under fire from artillery, rockets and heavy weapons. We withdrew during the night and occupied the lines on the Seelow Heights above Werbig, in which we spent yet another quiet Sunday (15 April) under occasional disruptive fire. We had a magnificent view over the Oderbruch from these Heights, except when smoke from the explosions made everything hazy. I spent the night with my driver in a small, very fragile bunker.

On Monday, 16 April, we were awakened at 0400 hours by the Russian bombardment. Every time we tried to get out and run to the armoured personnel carrier (APC), flashes of lightning illuminated the darkness and dirt and shrapnel whistled around our ears. An enemy battery had taken our command post as its aiming mark. Luckily, it moved its fire back some 70 metres across the fields. This inferno continued until 0600 hours and then the aircraft appeared. A squadron of twin-engined bombers dropped a carpet of bombs over a wood behind us in which there were all sorts of artillery. However, our batteries fired only very seldom. The nakedly exposed Heights and roads were meanwhile being controlled from the air, our own air effort being exceptionally weak.

By midday, from the sounds of battle and rumours, the enemy were already past us on the left and right. The remains of the detachments deployed in front of us were caught in our positions. Our troops were running from their trenches towards us as the Russian infantry appeared and, before we knew it, the Ivans were already on our Heights. With hastily assembled forces they were driven back halfway down again and our new positions held for the night. Air activity and continual mortaring robbed us of any sleep that night and caused some deaths in the supply column.

At 0400 hours on 17 April our command post was moved back more centrally in our sector to Gusow railway station. We had hardly camouflaged the vehicle and moved into the cellar of the station when a tank alert was given. The tanks had come up the road without firing. At the same time the bomber squadron reappeared and started bombing a little to our rear. To add to our misfortunes, alarming reports were radioed from the battalions. The enemy was in the rear of the 1st and 2nd Battalions with tanks and infantry, and the 3rd Battalion was falling back. At 0900 hours there was another bombardment on our forward positions, knocking out the radio APC of the 1st Battalion, and the crew of the 3rd Battalion's radio APC were injured by wood splinters. The section leader, although the most seriously wounded, nevertheless drove the vehicle back to the supply column himself.

The regiment was now in such disorder, with no communications or physical contact, for instance, that we had to withdraw under cover of some self-propelled guns (SPGs) and tanks[2] to the next line of defence, the 'Stein-Stellung' near

Görlsdorf. It was none too soon, for we were already being fired at from the flank and we were showered with wood splinters in the copse where we stopped to assemble. When we arrived at midday with the remainder of the regiment at the 'Stein-Stellung' it was already under shellfire and the Russians were assembling tanks and infantry opposite. Of our 1st and 2nd Battalions only a few scattered groups had come back, and these were now re-organised into a weak battalion. The command post was set up on the reverse slopes of the defence position.

While the commanders were setting the sector boundaries, the enemy artillery and mortar fire steadily increased. Mortar bombs and salvoes of rockets crashed down around us and it was getting more and more uncomfortable. Helmut Melzer was killed by this fire as he tried to get through the woods on a bicycle to the supply lines to get a new radio.

Suddenly there was another alarm. Somehow the Russians had got through our lines and were behind us. There was a mad rush by the staff to get some soldiers together and recover our positions with a counterattack. Soon machine gun and tank fire was coming from every direction. At dusk we went into the attack with the support of some 20mm anti-aircraft guns and tanks, although these heavy vehicles could not manoeuvre much in the woods. We formed a blocking position on the corner of a wood with our APC. The fighting went on into the night but the old positions were not recovered.

As tanks drove into our flank from the left on the morning of 18 April, our APC and the remaining vehicles were sent back a kilometre to Worin. The small, deserted village looked so peaceful, but hardly had we set ourselves up in a house than a cannonade of tank fire broke out in our corner. As we were at a crossroads, we came under fire from heavy weapons and artillery fire, in which several soldiers sheltering in a barn several meters behind our APC were wounded. In those two days our signals platoon suffered 17 casualties. During the morning the companies withdrew to Worin and the command post found itself in the front line, the regimental commander himself becoming a casualty. The divisional headquarters were only a few hundred meters away in the same village. To add to our misfortunes we had a mixture of petrol and diesel oil in our fuel tank so that the APC would only move very slowly and the engine had to be kept turning over. Our young second lieutenant, who had only been with the regiment a few days, had a daring plan to drive the APC over open country to the command post, for as the route was downhill, should we fall into a hole we would quickly come out again! As we started off, we came under a real mortar barrage. The vehicle speeded up, backfiring several times, and we were expecting it to give up the ghost. After minutes that seemed to last for hours, we reached the cover of a sunken lane and followed it to behind a barn, where all kinds of vehicles had assembled, oddly enough failing to attract the attention of enemy aircraft.

The Russians were bombarding the supply routes that we would have to withdraw over later. As their tanks penetrated Worin I decided to leave the place with my lame APC and with luck creep over the hill to the edge of the woods to await further events. Splintering trees forced us to move back further into the wood. There was some heavy anti-aircraft artillery hidden in a commanding position on the edge of the woods. Everyone was to withdraw to positions in front of Müncheberg during the afternoon, but our division was to take up the rearguard once more. Convoys of vehicles rolled through the woods to Jahnsfelde to join the main road back to Müncheberg. However, a short while later the last convoy returned with the news that we were cut off. There were only about two kilometres of woodland track to the positions and tanks in our rear – Jahnsfelde was already occupied by the enemy – and we could hear machine gun fire from that direction. We knew that there had been fighting on either side of us for some time, and now there was no way out. As it emerged from the woods, the divisional radio vehicle, which had tried to make a breakout on its own, fell into Russian hands, along with three of its five-man crew. With our APC almost lame from its fuel problem, the situation was particularly uncomfortable, especially as there were none of our own positions behind us. We prepared for action and aimed our machine-gun in the direction from which we expected danger, at the same time preparing the vehicle for demolition.

Towards evening our companies withdrew from Worin to re-deploy to Müncheberg. Everyone assembled in the woods, infantry, armour and vehicles. The only possibility was to break through to our lines along a route unknown to the enemy. Our Regimental Commander, a lieutenant, organised those on foot, and our APC was put on tow by a Tiger. At dusk we took up positions along the edge of the woods. Firing behind us indicated that Ivan had followed us into the woods from Worin. As soon as it was dark enough, we broke out of the woods and encountered no resistance. We passed through the burning village of Jahnsfelde without incident and reached the main road to Müncheberg and then, a little later, our own lines, which we occupied immediately. Our APC was towed on into the town, where the fuel tank was emptied and refilled by our supply column.

19 April had hardly begun when I was woken from a few hours of death-like sleep by the headquarters staff with orders to prepare for an immediate move. As a result of enemy tanks breaking through our lines, we would have to pull back yet again. As there was enough fuel, the little APC whose crew had been wounded by wood splinters was re-manned and sent on in advance. We reached the new supply column location in a pine forest at noon and prepared our vehicle for action once more. We were in touch with the little APC, which reported being unable to get through to the regimental command post and that the situation was completely confused. Then I failed to get any further response to my transmissions. Later the crew returned on foot, their APC having suddenly been attacked by a T-34, which chased them and shot them up. Then we had to drive on straight away, having received urgent orders to move, as enemy armoured spearheads were only a kilometre from our position. Apparently the Russians were no longer meeting any resistance, our enormous supply columns being in full flight without any thought of putting up any resistance. The journey to Rüdersdorf in the Berlin-Erkner area lasted until 0300 hours. Close by was a horde of refugees that had been forced to leave their homes in the middle of the night with their pushcarts.

We remained in Rüdersdorf until noon on this new day, 20 April. As the regiment's fighting capacity was down to only 90 men, the supply column was combed through and a company of another 90 men established. Even the signals platoon was broken up and the radio operators deployed as riflemen. The supply company marched off well spread out under heavy Russian air activity. We followed them a little later in the APC with the commanders, two lieutenants. We were bombed on the way, as we were fully visible on the now completely deserted road. Near Hennickendorf we took cover in a wood close to the divisional headquarters. Low-flying aircraft passed over often without noticing us.

That evening we received the task with our 180 men, of which only the 90-man supply company were for the moment available, of blocking the gap between two lakes. At dusk we had to march to our new positions under a hail of explosives and incendiaries. Often we had to stop on the clogged roads, while the darkness became like something out of a fairy tale as a 'Christmas Tree'[3] lit up the area around as bright as day. We had to wait in our APC for a long time until the company arrived. Of the 90 men 30 had fallen out on the way, having apparently deserted. Of the other 90 survivors of the regiment there was no sign. With our weak force we then relieved an APC company with two tanks at its disposal. Shortly before, a Stalin tank had broken through the lines after shooting up a Panther, raced along the road about 100 metres from us and driven into an anti-tank barrier. A Panzerfaust hit it in a shower of sparks. As it tried to withdraw it was destroyed by a second Panther. An ammunition and fuel dump was burning nearby with crackles and explosions, sounding like a battle in progress. The air attacks broke off. We drove the APC off the road to the edge of a wood and camouflaged it well. Our location was several kilometres from Hennickendorf on a country road leading through pine forests and meadows. After the surprise attack by the Russian tank, which had sounded very noisy on the road, I fell asleep to the crackling of the ammunition dump. It was still dark when I awoke and the crackling was still going on, but it was something else that I could hear, the screeching and track noises of tanks on the road left and right of us. The Russians had meanwhile broken through again and our supply column heroes had taken to their heels. The way back along the road was cut off. The indecision of our lieutenants had nearly cost us our APC, as it soon would be light.

Trusting in our luck, we followed the edge of the woods across the fields, shovelling our way under machine gun fire out of a ditch that proved too wide, and managed to reach the first houses in Hennickendorf under the cover of a light morning mist with the sound of enemy tank engines in our ears. Several tanks and SPGs from our armoured unit were standing there in the open, engaging the Stalin tanks that had just appeared out of the woods in a duel that we watched as spectators. We could see quite clearly how the tracers bounced off the Stalin tanks and flew into the air. A little later one of our tanks was hit in the flank and burst into flames. The weather and rain prevented intervention from the air. As this was no longer our regiment's position, our divisional engineers having taken over, the two lieutenants decided to look for the supply column again. We received its location over the radio.

The defence of Berlin presented a strange picture, as we saw for ourselves on our way. It really consisted only of individual, independent combat groups. For instance, here and there we saw Hitler Youths in defensive positions. Strangely, too, we were shelled the whole way to Schöneiche. Everything gave us the feeling of inevitable defeat. 'Berlin remains German' was displayed on a board by the roadside, which meant that the city centre was already prepared for defence and full of SS. In Schöneiche we found the supply column troops comfortably quartered, something we could not easily forgive them. However, that afternoon we were under way again in an endlessly long column with hour-long halts caused by blockages, passing lovely villas and spring-bedecked suburban gardens, bathing pools and parks. The Russians had already reached Köpenick and were threatening to cut us off.[4] The fleeing supply column, in which there were also many civilian vehicles, came up against troops marching in the opposite direction. We went through Köpenick, across the Spree, and through Adlershof and Altglienicke to the suburb of Rudow, where we looked for quarters. The small combatant part of the division took up defensive positions in Adlershof.

No sooner had we been allocated quarters in Rudow than we were sent forward in our APC again. At my request my radio operator and myself were given permission to fall out for 24 hours and get some sleep for once. How often have I cursed myself since! However, first of all we could take a bath and sleep in a proper bed. We slept until noon the following day, Sunday

22 April. The weather was fine and so there were constant air attacks. The noise of battle grew ever nearer and clouds of smoke rose constantly to the south and east. I chatted until evening with the people in my billet, who had already prepared themselves mentally for Bolshevism, but when I went to look up my comrades next door, I found everyone, including the vehicles, gone. They had apparently left their quarters in such a hurry that they had forgotten to tell us. Not knowing exactly where they had gone, we set off hoping to catch them up. Just as it was getting dark we met our division's ammunition column, which took us along with them to Neukölln, but they also did not know where our supply column was, which was difficult to understand. Night found us in the streets with 'Lame Ducks'[5] dropping bombs and a Russian machine-gun firing nearby. Ivan had broken through again somehow.

As dawn broke on this Monday morning the local inhabitants began to appear on the streets and gave us hot coffee. Then we drove on with the ammunition column to Rudow, from where we marched to Adlershof to see if we could find either our APC or the regimental command post. The road was already under artillery fire, but women and young girls were still going about their shopping. No sooner had we gone round an anti-tank barrier that was under a railway bridge than a Second Lieutenant asked us where we were going and then wanted to conscript us into his defence team. Fortunately a motorcycle combination from our division appeared from the direction of Adlershof and so we jumped on and thundered away from his press gang.

The road was under very heavy fire as we returned to Rudow. We had now met up with some men from Panzergrenadier Regiment 76 that wanted to pick up an anti-aircraft gun and at the same time were also looking for the supply column. An attempt to find the divisional staff in Schöneweide proved fruitless, but we were lucky enough to meet up with our divisional engineers' horse-drawn supply column, into which we managed to integrate ourselves with some difficulty, so that at least we would be able to pass through the numerous patrols and military police barriers. We marched right through Berlin at high speed until our feet finally refused to obey orders any more. We went past Nollendorfplatz, the Zoo, the Memorial Church and then along the Kaiserdamm to Charlottenburg through areas well known to me. Several streets were barricaded off and were already under Russian shell fire. Many refugees went along with us looking for some means of escaping by train. The engineers stopped near the Funkturm, where orders were received that all the supply columns were to return to Berlin. We were told that Panzergrenadier Regiment 90's supply column was at Döberitz. We two radio operators were to remain until our supply column returned, and meanwhile were sent to a cold billet in Witzleben with some very unfriendly people. As we were given neither blankets nor food and were completely exhausted, we did not feel very welcome in this strange unit in which we knew no one.

Next morning, 24 April, with still no sign of our people and the firing from the direction of Spandau getting closer and closer, we tried to find a vehicle from our division on the Kaiserdamm that could eventually take us to Döberitz. We waited in vain. Then I decided upon a subterfuge. I went to the engineer company commander and told him that we had met an officer from our unit who had informed us that our supply column was now in Döberitz, so he gave us a marching order in writing and we set off down the Heerstrasse. The marching order enabled us to pass through the barriers and we got a lift on a truck for part of the way. There was already fighting in Spandau, and machine gun fire could be heard not far off. Shortly before Döberitz, like an angel to our rescue, our headquarter company commander appeared on a motorcycle. He told us that our APC was at the Reichssportfeld. He himself had gone to look for the supply column in Döberitz but had not found it. We were to turn back again and he would come and pick us up with a motorcycle combination. I was somewhat sceptical about this and set off on foot with my comrade for the Reichssportfeld, which was fortunate for us. On our way between Spandau and the Reichssportfeld, which we made with two rests, we kept our eyes open for the motorcycle, and were delighted when our APC suddenly appeared instead. We quickly jumped aboard. The vehicle was full of women, nurses, working girls and wounded as well as the crew and regimental staff. The street barriers were already closed in Spandau and Russian tanks had shot up several vehicles in front of us, so we had to turn and seek a way through further to the south. Columns of smoke around us showed roughly where the front line was. By using tracks and country roads we reached the neighbourhood of Potsdam, which was already surrounded by the Russians. We had to make detours several times and often to open anti-tank barriers to get through. Finally we realised that Berlin had been surrounded and that we would have to risk a break-out.

Near Ketzin, north-west of Potsdam, the lakes and bridges seemed to provide the most favourable opportunity for our purpose, and we met up with several SPGs from our own armoured unit. We prepared the vehicle for battle and set up sub-machine guns and assault rifles around the APC's coping. Then we burst into Ketzin. The enemy infantry did not bother with us, only a tank trying to shoot us up, but its shell hit a building 30 metres behind us. A little further to the west we came across some SS troops taking up defensive positions; we had broken out of the Berlin pocket. We came across several units from the division on our way, including our horse-drawn supply column.

The Russian pincers had thrust far ahead. To the south they were already in Brandenburg, and to the north in Nauen. There were columns of smoke all around. During the night we had to pass through a military police barrier in Kyritz, but then we were fortunate to find the collecting point for the remainder of the 20th Panzergrenadier Division, which was in a wood by the village of Wutzetz on the Rhin Canal near Friesack. But depression soon followed our joy at having escaped from the encirclement. 'What now?' was the question everyone was asking.

On 25 April we were re-organised as the Armoured Brigade of the 20th Panzergrenadier Division. The supply column was combed through again and again so that eventually we produced two infantry battalions, two artillery detachments, an armoured company with eight SPGs, one anti-aircraft and one infantry mortar company, all fully motorised. We were to be allocated as an independent brigade to a corps operating to the north. It was clear that not much could be expected of these supply column soldiers, more of whom were deserting daily. Nevertheless, we continued with our training, for which the corps allowed us a few days in which to prepare ourselves.

On 27 April we pulled out of the wood for Wutzetz and took up quarters in a former prison camp for Polish officers. At first the days were quiet, but later we were increasingly sought out by enemy aircraft, so that at times we were having to seek shelter in our little earthen bunkers every quarter of an hour. During repeated air attacks on 1 May my radio platoon leader and I, with no one to stop us, took cover in the asparagus fields. That evening Wutzetz was in flames and the Russians had penetrated Friesack. Our neighbours, who had similarly taken up defensive positions on the Rhin Canal, pulled out. At 2100 hours we also pulled out, taking all kinds of refugees along with us. There were enormous columns of vehicles on the road and 'Lame Ducks' were dropping flares. Our journey via Wusterhausen took us to a farm near Neustadt, where we settled down for the night, while the companies took up defensive positions. Rumours caused me to switch on my radio again at midnight. After some solemn, stately music came the announcement that the Führer had fallen in battle in Berlin that day. All our will to continue resisting the enemy now vanished.

During the night the Russians penetrated Neustadt. As we had no radio contact with the brigade staff, our orderly officer was sent to brigade to get instructions. There he found only the brigade orderly officer, who was about to leave. The latter advised him to drive to Segeberg, which was passed to our commander as an order. The brigade commander, Major Rostock, and his even worse deputy, Captain Kern, had abandoned us to drive home unimpeded in a small vehicle.

Following the dispersal of our infantry companies during the night-time confusion at Neustadt, we drove off with the motorised units at dawn on the 2nd May for Schwerin via Segeberg. Near Havelberg the route went off towards Perleberg, which was already occupied by the Russians, so we turned south-west and drove past Wittenberge, which was in sight of the Americans. Just before Ludwigslust our despatch rider returned with the news that American tanks were already in Schwerin and Ludwigslust. The Russians and Americans had already joined hands north of us, and it was only a few kilometres to the American spearheads. The officers conferred amongst themselves. The only choice before us lay between east and west. The decision was made after careful consideration. The commander then addressed us; he did not want to shed any more blood, but those who wanted to go on fighting should report to him.

After a distribution of rations we set off to the west once more. I had to leave my trusty APC behind for lack of fuel and drive on in our radio truck. We stopped again sometime later. In front of us was an Air Force convoy that had already sent an envoy to the Americans. Then a vehicle arrived with large white flags on it and an American officer inside. He took the pistols from our officers then waved us on. At 1830 hours we drove across the American lines into captivity. We gave up our weapons on the way. Most of us lost our watches too. Some of the Americans were drunk, apparently from looted schnapps. Liberated Poles were firing pistols and taking the farmers' cows from their stalls. It was mildly comforting to see that the people still waved to us. We spend the night on an airfield near Hagenow.

Next day we drove in our own vehicles via Hagenow to Sückau, near Neuhaus, where we assembled and camped with 7,000 men in a meadow. We were to remain there for the time being and pitch our tents. At midnight on 7/8 May Germany capitulated unconditionally.[6] The war was over.

We stayed in the meadow near Sückau until 17 May virtually unguarded and unenclosed. Then we marched singing by companies through the Mecklenburg villages to an ammunition dump near Lübtheen, abused and spat on from passing trucks carrying foreigners, while our own people wanted to give us flowers and refreshments, though the latter were denied us by our American escorts.

On 30 May we marched to Pritzier, where we were loaded into goods wagons in which we rode with open doors via Hagenow, Ratzeburg, Lübeck and Neustadt to Eutin. From there we marched to the Oldenburg-in-Holstein Reservation through an area well known to me, as I had spent my last holiday there before joining the Army. It was under its own German administration, which set up offices for our release. We set up a tented camp in a beautiful, leafy wood near the little village of Grubenhagen, half an hour from the Baltic resorts of Dahme and

Kellenhusen. After all the hard times we had been through we found recuperation on the beaches of the Baltic.[7]

After his brief experience as a prisoner of war, Averdieck obtained a doctorate in biology and for thirty years thereafter worked as a geologist and botanist in northern Germany and as an archaeologist at the University of Kiel. Retired since 1985, his current hobbies are botany, geology and the writing of the history of his old division.

1 This was the beginning of Marshal Zhukov's two-day 'Reconnaissance in Force' in preparation for the launching of 'Operation Berlin' on the 16th. An essential factor was to gain enough ground to establish routes through the minefields for the main attack.

2 The 245th SPG Brigade and some tanks of the 8th Panzer Battalion were operating in this area.

3 A kind of parachute flare that scattered smaller elements to produce an illuminated Christmas tree effect.

4 Elements of the 3rd Guards Tank Army of the rival 1st Ukrainian Front.

5 Soviet Po-2 biplanes.

6 The surrender signed by Colonel General Jodl at Rheims.

7 The way that the remains of the 20th Panzergrenadier Division were kept intact and isolated by the British before allowing the division to disband itself, lends colour to the Soviet allegation that the British were contemplating using German troops against the Red Army should the need arise.

141

NINE

At the Zoo Flak-Tower

Harry Schweizer

Harry Schweizer wrote to me after reading the German version of my book The Battle of Berlin 1945, *providing me with further details about the armament on the Zoo Flak-tower. Subsequently, upon my request, he provided me with this account of his experiences as a schoolboy Flak Auxiliary.*

On 1 January 1944, I was conscripted into the Auxiliary Flak along with others born in 1928. After basic training, I served on a 150 cm searchlight site near Blumberg outside Berlin. Our searchlight battery lay some two kilometres from Blumberg in the middle of a field near some woods. The battery consisted of four 150 cm searchlights and a separate 200 cm spotting searchlight and radar apparatus. We usually picked up our target from the 200 cm searchlight and followed it through. The personnel consisted of a sergeant, a corporal and several young flak auxiliaries, who all came from the same school. In the mornings we went to school by train to Berlin, but in the afternoons we were on duty at the battery. Often Russian prisoners of war were employed on construction work at the position. They slept in another barrack hut and got the same food as ourselves. In time we developed almost friendly relations with them, although we all had a great fear of the Russians, especially later at the Zoo Bunker.

Our school class was a colourful mixture of characters, mainly as a result of our different upbringings at home. We included some fanatical Nazis, but also some convinced Communists.

In July 1944 we were replaced on the searchlight battery by female flak auxiliaries and sent to join the flak artillery at the Zoo Bunker, where we were met by the NCOs. Our easy times were over! First we had to put our uniforms in order, sewing our Hitler Jugend armbands and badges back on, and then we were given some hard drill.

There were two big lifts in the centre of the tower and four cargo lifts at the corners. The central lifts were for passengers and were covered with reinforced glass. The NCOs took these lifts while making us run up the five stories wearing our gas masks, and that was only one of many exercises we were put through at the beginning to accustom ourselves to being on active serve. But things got better later on. The officers and NCOs were very decent toward us and we got on well.

On one occasion we were sitting in our barrack room on the fifth floor, having skipped an aircraft recognition class, and were listening to some lively music from an English station. Suddenly there was a break in the music, then came a drum beat and: 'Germany calling! Germany calling! Hier ist BBC London in deutsche Sprache!' At that moment the door opened and Second Lieutenant Skodowski stood in the room. He had heard everything but said nothing, only ordering us to report for duty. He did not betray us, which was just as well, for listening to foreign broadcasts was a heavily punishable offence.

The Zoo Bunker was the most comfortable of the three big flak-towers in Berlin. It was well equipped with the best available materials, whereas the interior fittings of the Friedrichshain and Humbolthain Bunkers had been skimped, only the military equipment being first rate. The Zoo Bunker's fighting equipment consisted of four twin 128 mm guns on the upper platform, and a gallery about five metres lower down with a 37 mm gun at each corner, and a twin barrelled 20 mm gun in the centre of each side flanked by solo 20 mm guns left and right. The twin 128s were fired optically (by line of sight) whenever the weather was clear enough, otherwise electronically by remote control. The settings came from the smaller flak bunker nearby, which only had light flak on its gallery for its defence, but was especially equipped with electronic devices. A long range 'Blaupunkt' radar was installed there and our firing settings came from a giant

'Würzburg' radar as far away as Hannover. That bunker also contained the control room for air situation reports and was responsible for issuing air raid warnings to the public.

Our training went along simultaneously with action with the heavy and light artillery pieces. We also received some basic training on radar and explosives. We suffered no casualties from air attacks, but comrades were killed by gun barrels exploding and recoils. The shells for the 128s relied on the radar readings for their fuse settings and were moved centrally on rubber rollers up to the breech. If there was the slightest film of oil on the rollers, the already primed shell would not move fast enough into the breech and would explode.

The smaller flak bunker was once hit by a bomb, but it turned out to be a dud and they were just shocked.

The 128s were used mainly for firing at the leading aircraft of a group, as these were believed to be the controllers of the raid and this would cause the others to lose direction. Salvoes were also fired, that is several twins firing together, when according to the radar's calculations, the circle of each explosion covered about 50 metres, giving the aircraft in a wide area little chance of survival.

When we were below on the gallery with the 37s or 20s driving off low flying aircraft, we would hear the din and have to grimace to compensate for the pressure changes that came with the firing of the 128s. We were not allowed to fasten the chin straps of our steel helmets so as to prevent injury from the blast.

Later when we fired the 128s at clusters of tanks as far out as Tegel, the barrels were down to zero degrees and the shock waves were enough to break the cement of the 70 cm high and 50 cm wide parapet of the gallery five metres below, exposing the steel rods beneath.

The 37s and 20s were seldom used against British and American aircraft as they flew above the range of those guns, and low flying aircraft seldom came within range. It was different when the Russians set their low flying aircraft against the tower. The magazines of the 37s were normally filled with eight rounds of tracer but, as the Russian machines were armoured, this was changed to red tracer and green armour-piercing shells. These aircraft attacked almost ceaselessly in

April to try and weaken the 128s, which were already firing at ground targets. The towers had considerable fire power and many aircraft were shot down. We had no protection like a shield on our guns and, when the wings of the attacking aircraft spurted fire at us and the shells whistled over our heads, it was not a nice feeling. The fire power of the three towers was quite noticeable and we could see that after the first salvo following units would turn away to get out of firing range.

When we watched the carpet bombing of the city from the tower, several times in the Lichtenberg direction where my parents lived, we thought that no one could possibly survive unharmed. I was especially pleased one day to get a short leave and to find that my parents were still well. The partition walls in the apartment were missing and the windows nailed over with cardboard, but that was normal in Berlin.

I visited my parents for the last time shortly before the Russians arrived in Lichtenberg. We could already observe their artillery fire. The people in the block told me that the war was lost and that I should put on civilian clothes and stay with my parents, but I had already seen several soldiers hanging from lampposts on the Unter den Linden with placards round their necks on which was written 'I was too much of a coward to defend my country'. Fear of being arrested by the SS and of dying in that way was greater than that of the front line. I still reckoned that I had a chance of surviving and preferred to return to the Zoo Bunker.

The fighting bunker had been built with an elastic foundation to take the shock of the discharge of the 128s. Two twin-128s firing alone would have been sufficient to break a rigid foundation. The bunker had its own water and power supplies along with an up-to-date and well-equipped hospital in which, among others, prominent people like Rudel, the famous Stuka pilot, could be cared for. Rudel had a 37 mm cannon mounted in his aircraft, but we had later versions of the gun on the tower and he often came up to the platform to see the weapons in action during our time there. Normally only the gun crews were allowed on to the platform, but our superiors made an exception in his case.

During the last days the hospital was completely overcrowded and the wounded were even lying in the passage ways, the orderlies and doctors only being able to attend emergency cases.

Our beds were removed from our accommodation for them and, as we had little time for sleep anyway, sacks of straw sufficed.

Apart from ourselves, some of the guns were manned by so-called 'SS-Cadets'. These were White Russians of our age who wore a yellow-blue armband with a lion's head in the centre. We got on quite well with them, but they were extreme fanatics with a great hatred of the Soviet Army. Any of them that fell into Russian hands would have been lucky to survive.

Even on the fifth storey the walls of the barrack accommodation were over two metres thick and there were 5 cm thick steel shutters hung on two hinges over the windows. Whenever there was an alert or we had to leave the room for a long period, these shutters had to be closed. When the Russians approached the bunker and started shooting with their anti-tank guns and other artillery at the walls and shutters, they eventually concentrated on the shutter hinges. The hinge outside the tailor's shop was destroyed and the shutter hung askew. A shell entered the room and killed two people, so the room was cleared and further hits there were to no avail. The passage ways behind the outer rooms were so designed that nothing could happen.

On 26 April 1945, volunteers were called for the tank destroyer teams and many of my age group, among them myself, volunteered. We were quickly instructed and equipped for our new role. There were four men in a team, one with a Panzerfaust, one with a glass bottle containing a milky fluid which, when mixed with the oxygen in the air would cause a tank engine to stop, and two escorts armed with sub-machine guns to fire at the enemy as soon as they bailed out. Apart from this a Volkswagen jeep was put at our disposal to give us mobility, but was then taken away again next day because of the shortage of fuel, and since we were only intended for deployment in the Zoo area.

Our second lieutenant had some trees chopped down between the Zoo Bunker and the Zoo Railway Station to provide us with a good field of fire, and also had some anti-tank barriers erected at the station. Our command post was located in the Aquarium.

The first member of our small team was wounded at the anti-tank barrier when a burning beam fell from a building on his thigh. He was immediately taken to the hospital and fully recovered later, as he told me after the war.

A unit had paraded in front of the barrier. Why the person in charge had so badly misjudged the situation, I cannot say, but suddenly Russian aircraft appeared like lightning and started dropping shrapnel bombs, and many of the soldiers were wounded. We rushed to their aid but had no stretchers to carry them on, so used table tops from a nearby abandoned restaurant. It was frightful. I helped carry a table top on which a soldier lay whose leg had been ripped up to the knee. He spoke quite normally to us without complaining, but the pain must have been greater than we could imagine.

The only occasion we went into action against a tank was catastrophic for both sides. We had to destroy a tank on the corner of Wichmannstrasse and Keithstrasse whose gunfire was dominating the street. We crept through ruins and cellars until we could see the tank from a cellar window each. The tank stood across the street from us and was firing steadily down Keithstrasse. A Russian with a slung sub-machine gun was standing in a doorway near the tank watching it fire. We debated whether we should shoot the soldier or the tank first, deciding upon the tank since the tank crew would be alert. Comrade Hitzinger fired at the tank with a Panzerfaust from his cellar window and hit it, but at the same time cried out with pain, as he had not taken the back blast into account and was burning all over. The Russian in the doorway had vanished. We attended to our comrade and put out the flames with our jackets, and then took him back to the hospital in the bunker. (He too survived.)

Now only two members of our team were left. We reported back to the Aquarium and were given the order to report to an SS unit that was involved in the street fighting in the Budapester Strasse. We reported there and were ordered to fire out of a doorway at a Russian machine gun post that was dug in on a corner and keeping the street under fire. We left the safety of the doorway for a few seconds and fired in the direction of the Russian machine gun post, but whether we hit anything, I do not know. My friend, Bernd Vandre, who was bigger than me and perhaps also somewhat heavier, reached the cover of the doorway too late and was wounded in the lungs. He was taken straight back to the bunker and tended to. (Incredibly, he survived and we met again after the war.)

Now I was the only one left, and when I reported back to the

SS unit I was sent to the Aquarium to get reinforcements. Eight elderly soldiers were detailed off to me at the Aquarium as reinforcements. When we came to a crossroads I asked a soldier lying on the other side of the street whether it was free from fire. He called back that everything was all right, so I ran across the street with three of the soldiers and got across safely. Then I beckoned the others to come cross quickly. They started off, but too slowly, for when they reached the middle of the street they were shot at and some of them were wounded, although they all got across. We took the wounded men to a nearby barber's shop below street level and gave them first aid. They were later taken to the hospital.

I had now had enough of this and, instead of reporting back to the SS unit, I returned to my proper unit in the Zoo Bunker.

Once more I was sent back into the Zoo gardens, this time with a soldier and orders to wait for the Russian tanks with a Panzerfaust in a slit trench. We laid the Panzerfaust down carefully some distance from our trench to avoid being blown up should it be hit by chance. It was already dark and no tanks came. Eventually we were relieved and returned to the Zoo Bunker.

When I unbuckled my pistol back in the barrack room, I saw that a shot had gone through the holster and smashed the spare magazine against the pistol. I had not noticed it happen and had been extremely lucky that the pistol had stopped me getting a shot in the stomach. That was on 30 April, and I remained in the bunker. The Russians were close by, packages of explosives were being thrown down on them from the gallery and being replied to with mortar fire. There were now about 25,000 people in the Zoo Bunker, including all kinds of servicemen, and it was a complete mix-up.

There was a female flak auxiliary working in the bunkers signals section, a very pretty blonde called Dora from East Prussia, with whom we were all in love, myself especially. It was nothing really serious, but as it is with one's first youthful love, I could think of hardly anything else. On 1 May 1945, the last day in the Zoo Bunker, an officer cadet of the Luftwaffe with whom I had become friends, Dora and myself spent most of the time together. He had been seconded to us as there was no fuel left for flying.

At about 2300 hours on the evening of 1 May an announcement came over the loudspeakers to prepare for a break-out from the tower. We quickly put our things together. There was not much, just a haversack, water bottle, weapon and ammunition, and an emergency ration of chocolate. We three waited together until several thousand had left the tower, not wanting to be among the first to leave, as we did not know what awaited us outside. Several of the older soldiers, some of them highly decorated, remained behind as they said it was all the same to them if they met their fate there or elsewhere.

As we mixed in the stream of people and emerged outside, it seemed to be quite peaceful with only the occasional shot nearby coming out of the dark night, and we were not fired at. We could not understand how we could get out of the bunker so easily. Somehow this stream of all kinds of servicemen, without any leadership, found its way to Spandau via the Olympic Stadium. Apart from a few shots at the Olympic Stadium, we reached a newly built part of Spandau without any interference from the enemy.

On the morning of 2 May, combat teams were formed to fight their way over the Charlotten Bridge through the Russians occupying Spandau to the Elbe River in the west. We joined one of these teams, as we were determined to get through to the Americans. Our propaganda had made us afraid of falling into Russian hands.

The Russians defended their position on the opposite side of the Charlotten Bridge, but we were able to get across with the help of tanks and other heavy weapons, and to reach the street leading to the west. The buildings on either side of the street were occupied by Russians and we were fired on from the rooftops. It was difficult to go on and eventually we had to seek shelter in the entrance to a building. We kept Dora between us to give her the maximum protection, and were very lucky, as several times shots from rifles or sub-machine guns sprayed the road surface close to us.

At midday we sought shelter in a cellar with some other soldiers all waiting for nightfall to go on. Wounded were crying out with pain in the yard behind the cellar and begging us to shoot them, but it was absolutely impossible to do anything for them without exposing oneself to heavy fire.

We waited until dark and then got as far as a residential area without attracting fire. Vehicles were racing along the streets with soldiers hanging on to them like bunches of grapes. We tried to get on a vehicle several times in order to get through to the west quicker, but it was just not possible. (Later on as a prisoner I had to march through Döberitz and saw these shot-up and burnt-out vehicles with their many dead soldiers.)

Between us and the residential area was a big open space that we had to cross if we were going to get any further. We started crawling across it on our stomachs, but shots came toward us from the buildings up ahead, so we crept back again. We could see that we no longer had a chance of getting through, so we threw our weapons away and waited for things to happen. Dora put on a Red Cross armband in the hope of fooling the Russians. I gave her my parents' address, as she had no one in Berlin to whom she could turn. After my time in captivity I learned from my parents that she had been to see them and had been given shoes and clothing, but that nothing more had been heard of her. During the first part of my captivity I could not get her out of my mind. I was always thinking of her. Such is young love.

On the morning of 3 May some civilians came into our cellar and begged us to give ourselves up. They were afraid that if soldiers were found in the building they would suffer for it. We said goodbye to Dora and left the cellar. A big Russian with a pistol in his hand took us. We had to walk ahead of him with our hands up. Whenever we passed dead Russian soldiers on the street he would say something in Russian that we did not understand. We were terribly frightened that he was going to shoot us. With my hands up, my 'Mauthe' watch that I had been given by my parents for my confirmation in 1944 was soon gone. In my fear, I did not care. I was also wearing a silver signet ring with a death's head on it of a type that was all the rage with us youngsters. He took the ring, but fortunately did not associate me with the SS because of it. We were taken to a cellar that already contained some captured German soldiers. Frightening rumours were making the rounds, whoever had this or that uniform would be shot straight away, etcetera, but nothing happened. After a short while an officer appeared and climbed on to a table. He said that the war was over, Hitler dead, and we would now just be registered and then sent home. However, it did not work out that way and we began our period of captivity.

Taken prisoner by the Soviets, Schweizer was too frail in body to be of any useful work potential to them, and so was released in November 1945. He trained as a mason before qualifying as an architect and engineer in 1952.

Fifteen years later he was entrusted by the East German government with the planning and supervision of construction of a steel rolling mill in North Vietnam. From there he went to work on a project in Czechoslovakia before returning to North Vietnam to construct a glass works. Later he worked on similar projects in Algeria, the Congo, Cuba and East Germany, retiring in 1991. He now lives on the Baltic coast.

TEN

Halbe

HARRY ZVI GLASER

This is part of the quite extraordinary tale of Harry Zvi Glaser, whom I met in 1996 at an annual reunion of survivors of the break-out of the German 9th Army at Halbe, in which some 40,000 troops and accompanying refugees were killed. Most of those present were former Waffen-SS, but Harry had been on the other side, a corporal in the Red Army. A short, slim, bronzed figure armed with a large camera, Harry was happily conversing in imperfect German with his hosts. This was his second visit and clearly he was an honoured guest.

Yet Harry was a Latvian Jew who had fled his countrymen's persecution ahead of the Nazi invasion and worked as a teenage coalminer in Kazakhstan before volunteering for the Red Army. With the eradication of the German forces in East Prussia, Harry's 129th Division held an inspiring ceremonial parade at which it received the Order of the Red Banner. Then, after a short rest, the division joined Marshal Zhukov's 1st Byelorussian Front east of the Oder River opposite Frankfurt/Oder. For two weeks they rested and rehearsed the battle tactics for the forthcoming operation, for which their parent 3rd Army was in reserve. On 26 April, the division reached the outskirts of Berlin.

The platoon was put on a Studebaker truck. Harry set the squad's machine gun on top of the driver's cab and they drove into the German capital. Then a Panzerfaust hit the truck, luckily only on the left wheel. Gunfire opened on the platoon. Harry provided covering fire with the machine gun as his squad jumped off and took cover in the nearest building. A tank came up in support and, after a dozen shots into the building, the squad were able to clear it. One German was dead, two wounded, one of them a woman in Luftwaffe uniform. Even bleeding she looked fanatical, more so than the men. Harry was wounded a second time, but bandaged himself and stayed with his men.

Next day the spearheads fighting their way forward from the south and east met near Tempelhof Airport. The day after, the neighbouring army's leading unit thrust towards the city centre, aiming for the Reichstag and Reichs Chancellery, Hitler's last redoubt. The Führer gave his last desperate orders to cut Berlin's encirclement. Harry's unit was ordered to pull out and turn south to counter this attempt. The 35 kilometer forced march down the Berlin-Dresden autobahn that night was more of a trot than a walk. Twice they were met by enemy fire and suffered several casualties, but pressed on to join the northern flank of the encircling Soviet forces around the remains of General Busse's German 9th Army, which was part of the army group that Hitler was depending upon for his relief.

At dawn Harry led his squad into their last battle. The village of Halbe, 40 kilometers southeast of Berlin, appeared to be deserted with any civilians remaining in hiding. The squad deployed on the eastern edge of the village overlooking a vast neglected pasture. A Maxim machine gun was brought up to reinforce the riflemen. Harry placed it on his right flank and, after issuing orders to his men, went to search the farmhouse to their rear. In the cellar he discovered the frightened inhabitants. 'Stay indoors, don't leave the house under any circumstances until you get fresh instructions!' he told the astonished inhabitants in fluent German. 'Ja, jawohl, Herr Offizier!' they responded in chorus. Harry's eyes scanned the shelf on the wall and spotted a row of cans of preserved meat. 'Please take it!' said an old man, the only male in the family. Harry picked up two of the cans, locked the door and went back to the trenches, stepping over a few corpses of German soldiers.

He was just in time. His soldiers were holding a German, a 15 year-old who had been riding a bicycle with a Panzerfaust on his shoulder. Reaching the squad, he realized that he had come to the wrong address, turned around and fell off his bicycle. There was no need to disarm him; the boy looked pathetic and scared to death. On being asked how he came to be there, the boy said: 'Three days ago we were assembled in a school in east Berlin to meet Goebbels. The Reichs Minister spoke to us, promising that we would win the war, we would just have to answer the Führer's call to help out until the new weapons arrive.' Harry felt sorry for the boy. He helped him straighten his wheel out and sent him home to his mother.

He wiped the dust from his binoculars and went on observing the area. 'Not a single sign of life, it's too quiet!' he said to himself. At this instant an image appeared, moving across the field. Harry adjusted his lens and saw a woman with a baby in her arms running towards the village. Just as suddenly, she disappeared. 'What the hell is she doing there?' he asked himself as he went to distribute the two cans of meat to his hungry riflemen. Then the runner arrived with a call for Harry to report to the battalion command post.

The battalion commander and his staff were on the south side of the street dividing Halbe in two, and were looking south across the pasture to the woods. White flags were waving among the trees, indicating a wish to surrender. Harry stood to one side waiting to report his situation and state of readiness. The battalion commander turned to him: 'Corporal, you speak German, don't you?' Harry nodded and the captain continued: 'You see the white flags? It's less than a kilometer. If you want to earn the 'Red Banner'[1], go clarify the situation and bring back some delegates with you for their surrender.' Harry began crossing the pasture. After going about two hundred yards he stopped. The white flags had disappeared. He looked back. The command group was no longer there either. Several gun shots sounded from the woods. Harry looked towards the Germans again, but there was no sign of life.

Fifty years later he learned by chance what those flags had been, which also explained the commander's remark about the high decoration, for he must have known how risky the task was. A group of German soldiers, known as Seydlitz-Troops and claiming to represent the National Komitee Freies Deutschland, for various reasons were working with the Soviets against Hitler. Many of them had had experience on the Eastern Front and had no wish to go on fighting Hitler's war. Meanwhile the Soviet intelligence service had organized special task forces for parachuting behind the German lines, operating a complex spy and diversion system. Encouraged by the Soviets, the Seydlitz-Troops grew in numbers with the retreat of the German Army on the Eastern Front, encouraging whole groups to desert, and thus sabotaging the Nazi war effort. As soon as they were discovered by the SS or other convinced Nazis, they would be shot. Thus the Fifth Column worked on both sides. The white flags Harry had seen were being waved by a group of Seydlitz-Troops attempting to arrange the surrender of the main body to the Russians, but they were spotted and most of them killed by the SS.

Harry realized that he was in danger of falling into a trap, and went back to his squad. The next moment the runner appeared: 'German tanks are moving towards the village with infantry following them.' The pasture immediately became alive as the German assault began. Letting them advance 200 meters, the squad opened fire, mowing down many of the attacking infantry, and the rest rolled back. The situation was worse to the squad's rear on the main street of the village, where German tanks were rolling forward, machine guns firing from their turrets, and followed by infantry assault groups, among them black-uniformed SS with sub-machine guns. Now they were fast approaching Harry's lines and two men had already been wounded. The squad was firing non-stop at the attackers, the Maxim disappeared and a third man fell, dead. The Germans kept coming on endlessly and the fighting was fierce. The supporting light 45 mm gun on the sidewalk could not stop the German tanks. A shell from the leading heavy 'Tiger' tank hit the gun, killing or wounding all the crew. The squad tried to withdraw, but it was too late, the main street was already overrun. Then, as if by Divine intervention, a sudden dusk fell, which enabled them to reach the backyards, crawling with their wounded until they got out of Halbe and back to their main forces.

Twilight found the devastated battalion in retreat, having lost many of its combatants, including the commander. Many wounded were left behind, most of whom were found by the Germans during the night and shot. At this point, with a desperate effort, the Germans succeeded in breaking out of their encirclement. As Harry would learn fifty years later, their aim was to avoid Russian captivity, rather than to save the Führer and the already encircled Berlin garrison.

During the following day the battalion recovered, received reinforcements and prepared to retake the village. The field kitchen arrived and set up on the ground. The corpses of enemy soldiers and horses were all around, but the smell of burnt flesh could not keep the troops from their meal. The mail came and with it a three month-old field postcard from Jaka for Harry: 'Dear Brother, I am finally back in Riga. I found Aunt Jenny. She told me the sad news: Mother was shot at the beginning of 1944, just before the liberation of the city, while trying to escape the last selection (for execution).' The blood rose to Harry's head. He put the postcard into his breast pocket for safety.

A contingent of Katyusha multiple-barrelled rocket launchers arrived and took up firing positions. The T-34 tanks were also ready. The night passed without much emotion; they knew it would be 'hot' next day.

It began early in the morning. The Katyushas softened up the Germans for ten minutes, then the infantry went in to clean out whatever tried to resist. Harry's squad piled itself on to the leading tank, which moved towards the forest where the remains of the pocket were concentrated. The tank stopped a hundred metres short of the woods to avoid being hit by Panzerfausts, and the squad jumped off and ran into the woods. A few gunshots were all the resistance that was encountered from the remaining German soldiers. One was shot, the others dropped their weapons and raised their hands. Further on a whole mass of Germans stood up with raised hands, obeying the order for the prisoners to assemble in groups. At the same time the rest of the platoon captured a colonel who was a highly decorated tank commander.[2]

Next day it was all over. Sixty thousand Germans from this pocket surrendered. An estimated forty thousand, including the civilians sheltering with the remains of the 9th Army, had been killed in the encirclement and break-out.

Later Harry was awarded the Order of Glory, the second highest ranking medal for valor, but received no explicit citation with it, so he could not attribute it to any particular event.

Harry served on in the Soviet Army after the war, attaining the rank of sergeant major. He left to become a newspaper photographer back in Riga. Later he was one of the first of the younger generation to obtain a visa allowing him to emigrate to Israel, where he continued to work as a photographer, got married, raised a family and divorced. Years later he was invited to visit his grandchildren in America and decided to stay on, becoming an American citizen. During a state visit by President Yeltsin he eventually received his award of the Order of Glory from him at a ceremony held at the White House.

1 The second highest decoration after the Order of Lenin.
2 Exactly fifty years later on this battlefield, sixty-nine year-old Harry would meet his former enemies, the 'Halbe Gruppe,' and among them the eighty-four year-old Panzer leader Hans von Luck, commander of the 125th Panzer Regiment of the 21st Panzer Division.

ELEVEN

The Surrender of the 'Phantom Division'

TONY LE TISSIER

This story came to my attention at a luncheon of the 94th US Infantry Division Veterans' Association at Perl, Germany, in September 1999, when related by Professor Schaeffer-Kehnert, a former artillery officer with the 11th Panzer Division that had opposed them in the fighting for the Orscholtz Switch of the Siegfried Line. This account is gleaned from the official history of the 11th Panzer Division and an article by Brigadier General William W. Molla in the magazine of the 21st US Infantry Division's Veterans Association.

Its predecessor in the 1940 French campaign having been dubbed the 'Phantom Brigade' by the British, the 11th Panzer Division took over the title with pride, calling itself the 'Gespenterdivision', which the Americans then translated as the 'Ghost Division'.

On 15 April 1945, by which time the 11th Panzer Division had been obliged to withdraw to the line of the Weisser Elster either side of the town of Greiz, its respected commander Lieutenant General von Wietersheim belatedly handed over command of the division to Major General von Buttlar in accordance with orders received several days previously to take over command of the XXXXIst Panzer Corps east of Berlin. Aware that the route to the north was already blocked, General von Wietersheim decided to stay with the division until the end of the war. He therefore reported sick to the divisional medical unit with a feigned stomach complaint and remained close to the Rear Command Post, where he kept in touch with the divisional Ia (Chief of Staff).

That same day the division took delivery of twenty Hetzer tank-destroyers from a factory in nearby Plauen, thereby increasing its armoured strength at a time when the manpower establishment was more than filled, as stragglers and parentless units seemed to be drawn to the cohesive organisation of the division as if by a magnet.

However, the division happened to be in imminent danger of being surrounded as the Americans broke through the neighbouring units on either flank. Some hard fighting developed that day during which one of the panzer-grenadier battalions destroyed fifteen American tanks in close combat.

During the night orders were received by radio to break out to the south, so the division formed up into a long column and drove off with headlights blazing. The Americans did not intervene and the division was able to reach the western edge of the Erzgebirge Mountains and form a northwest front between Eibenstock and Klingenthal, where conditions remained peaceful.

Then on about 23 April the division received orders from Army Group G to link up with the LXXXVth Corps at Passau. The rumour spread that it would be joining SS units in the defence of the so-called 'Alpine Redoubt'. The division set off and eventually reached the area of Taus in the Bohemian Forest, 45 kilometres southwest of Pilsen. A new front was then formed facing southwest along the German-Czech border between Forst am Wald and Zwiesel. As this was happening, Patton's 3rd Army was passing across the divisional front toward the Alps, occupying the last part of southern Germany.

Meanwhile some more fuel had become available, and so the newly reconstituted 111th Panzer-Grenadier Regiment and divisional support units under Major General von Buttlar were able to push forward to the Wallern area, about 40 kilometres northeast of Passau, in accordance with orders received to block the American advance on Linz, leaving the main body behind to follow as best it might.

General von Wietersheim thereupon returned to duty, taking over command of the main body on his own responsibility. The main body then moved a short distance toward Klattau and Neuern. Poor radio conditions in this mountainous area led to a complete breakdown in communications between these two elements now 100 kilometres apart, and they were only to meet up again in captivity.

Then on 2 May the expected order arrived from Field Marshal Schörner for the division to join the Eastern Front in Czechoslovakia. All guns and armoured vehicles immobilised through lack of fuel were to be destroyed and their crews set off on foot as infantry.

At a conference of unit commanders and senior staff officers, it was agreed that to comply with these orders would only lead to the needless destruction of the division and inevitable captivity in Soviet hands. The Alpine Front had already surrendered and other formations around them were disappearing or disbanding themselves without orders. It was therefore unanimously agreed to surrender to the Americans if honourable terms could be met.

On the morning of 4 May General von Wietersheim sent two of his staff officers, Major Voigtmann and Lieutenant Knorr, with an interpreter under a white flag to the headquarters of the 90th US Infantry Division on the German-Czechoslovakian border at Neumarkt with a letter that read: 'The development of the military and political situation makes it desirable for me to avoid further losses on both sides. I have therefore ordered the Major, and the bearer of this note, to negotiate with you the cessation of hostilities.'

The honourable terms requested were beyond the competence of the commander of the 90th Division, General Earnest, to agree so he referred them on to General Patton, who approved them with the comment that the 11th Panzer was the 'fairest and bravest' German division that his 3rd Army had fought! General Bradley also approved the terms, adding that the division should arrive in proper order, 'with its kitchens'.

The terms enabled officers to retain their sidearms and the men to continue to be armed until clear of Czechoslovakia. The division was then to form a camp at Kötzting until able to disband.

Also involved in the surrender negotiations was Colonel Charles H. Reed of the 2nd Cavalry Group, which had been an opponent of the 11th Panzer in Lorraine, when a good rapport between foes had been formed to the extent of even exchanging seriously wounded prisoners during lulls in the fighting. Now he was responsible for preventing Soviet representatives from intervening in this matter.

The various units of the division paraded for a last 'hurrah!' for the fatherland before marching across the border into captivity.

Fresh clothing and supplies had been drawn from depots in Czechoslovakia and these were now evenly distributed among the troops, as were the divisional funds, professional soldiers getting a little more than the others as their transition to civilian life would be harder for them.

Meanwhile General von Buttlar canvassed his task force near Wallern for opinions whether to continue with their task or join the main group in American captivity at Kötzting. The majority opted for the latter, so at 0700 hours on 7 May General von Buttlar contacted the 101st US Infantry Regiment of the 26th Yankee Infantry Division at Andreasburg. However, it was to be another week before von Buttlar's task force rejoined the main body of the division at Kötzting after the delivery by American tankers of 135,000 litres of fuel for their vehicles.

The story is not over, for at Kötzting the main event of the year was the Whitsun mounted carnival, a major attraction for the old cavalry hands of the 11th Panzer Division and 2nd Cavalry Group alike.

It so happened that the famous stud of 400 Lippizaner horses had been evacuated to the German Army Stud Farm at Hostau, where they had been joined by a Russian stud of 200 horses. On 26 April, with the Red Army only 60 kilometres away, elements of the 2nd Cavalry Group reached the Czechoslovakian border, where they stopped in accordance with the terms of the Yalta Agreement. This placed them nearer to the stud than the Russians. By means of a letter written by a Luftwaffe colonel in American captivity, it was suggested to Lieutenant Colonel Rudofsky, commander of the stud farm, that it might be possible to bring the horses across the border into American custody. Rudofsky sent his chief veterinary surgeon, Dr. Lessing, to negotiate and on the evening of the 26th he met Colonel Reed in a farmhouse on the border. The Americans suggested that the horses be brought out on foot, but this was impractical as there were too few grooms and also many of the mares were about to produce or already had newly-born foals at their heels. Dr. Lessing returned to Hostau accompanied by Captain Stewart of the 2nd Cavalry Group, to see what could be done.

Meanwhile an officer had arrived in Hostau to organise its defence. At first he refused to meet the Americans, but after long discussions, not least with the relevant Corps commander, he was persuaded that resistance would be pointless, and that it would be a good idea to get the horses back into Bavaria. The next day the Americans arrived and took over the entire stud establishment without having to fire a shot.

On 15 May the bulk of the herd set off, partly on foot and partly in trucks acquired from a captured artillery school. The Americans blocked all the main crossroads so that the horses passed through safely via Furth im Wald to prepared quarters in the little village of Schwarzenberg. Out of the whole herd only three young colts were lost when stopped by armed Czechs near the border. Again the Americans had successfully prevented the Soviets from intervening.

The first discharge certificate from the 11th Panzer Division went to the man leading the mounted procession in the Kötzting carnival.

Apart from the Generals and General Staff Officers, who came under a special detention category, all members of the division were soon released in accordance with the instructions given. Those going to the western part of Germany were provided transport to near their homes, while those from eastern Germany that did not accompany them found accommodation locally.

TWELVE

The Band of the
Leibstandarte-SS Adolf Hitler

WILLI ROGMANN (5 APR 1923–18 FEB 1997)

A builder by trade, Willi Rogmann volunteered to do his military service as a policeman, but found himself transferred into the 'Leibstandarte-SS Adolf Hitler' when it suffered heavy casualties in the invasion of Poland in 1939, for both the police and the Waffen-SS came under Himmler's aegis. He served in the same company for four years as their smallest man, first in Greece and then in Russia, ending up a SS-Oberscharführer (sergeant major) and winning the Iron Cross Second and First Class, the German Cross in Gold (see Citation at rear) and the Gold Close Combat Clasp. After being wounded for the eighth time in the fighting near Caen, and subsequent convalescence, Willi Rogmann was posted to the Guard Battalion in Berlin, where he served in the Guard Platoon on duty within the Reichs Chancellery until those duties were taken over by the SD Security Service of the SS.

Cheeky, outspoken and opinionated, he held strong views on the ineptness of some of his superiors and was seldom afraid to voice them.

THE LAST BIRTHDAY PARADE

At 0300 hours on 16 April 1945, the Soviets began their major offensive on Berlin with what was to be a four-day battle before they broke through the last of the German defences masking their Oderbruch bridgehead only eighty kilometres east of the city.

Of all this we knew little in Berlin, where duty in our barracks at Lichterfelde went on as normal, as if it was of no consequence. However, it was another matter with our Training & Replacement Battalion in Spreenhagen, 25 kilometres southeast of Berlin. Part of our twelve company-strong battalion had already been sent off to the Eastern front as Regiment 'Falke' under the 9th Army, and the rest were preparing to march to Berlin to join Combat Team 'Mohnke' in the defence of the Governmental Quarter. This battalion under SS-Captain Schäfer was supposed to fight as part of the Regiment 'Anhalt'.

I myself was sent home by SS-Major Kaschulla, the commanding officer of the Guard Battalion, on a sham duty journey ostensibly to collect some orthopædic boots, as if they were still available. In reality I was being sent home for good. Quietly I understood that Kaschulla had given me the opportunity to decide for myself whether to return to Berlin or not. At this point the front in the west had been shattered and was quickly falling back, and I, as an experienced front line soldier, could count on five fingers the number of days until my home would be overrun. By the time I was supposed to return to Berlin on 4 April, if I did not propose deserting or simply staying at home, in just three days the front had reached Hannover. However, as a conscientious, duty-bound soldier, I took the last train for Berlin and what seemed like certain death.

I could not say anything of this to my wife and relatives. Unlike myself, they all still believed in final victory, hard as it is to credit now. If I had expressed my opinions to them they would have reported me to the local Party official. However, he could not have locked me up, as he would have done with a civilian, for I came under military jurisdiction. No, the Party official would have sent a report to my unit, which would have landed on SS-Major Kaschulla's desk. He would have put me on report, closed the door behind us so that his adjutant could not hear, for he was a sharp one, and would have told me off for being so outspoken, torn up the report and thrown it into the waste paper basket.

But I had even been outspoken with our Führer when I had had the opportunity to do so, and he had asked me to. This happened as follows. From February 1945, I was in charge of the Inner Guard at the Reichs Chancellery, a permanent duty as I was not allowed to return to the front as I would have preferred because of my golden close-combat badge, for the regiment was my home. One night the sentry at the bottom of the steps rang me, signalling that something special was happening. When I rushed down to him he told me that the Führer was wandering around.

Then I saw him in the half darkness (caused by the blackout) coming toward me. He went past me toward the Mosaic Hall. I stood there like a pillar of salt, as we were not allowed to salute him or draw attention to ourselves. Then he beckoned me to follow him. Shortly before a dud bomb had broken through the Mosaic Hall down to the cellar, leaving behind a hole in the ceiling and floor about three or four metres across. He stood in front of it looking at it gloomily and turning to me, said: 'Now they want to crush us.' Naturally I did not reply, as it was not for me to do so.

Then he asked me directly what I as a front line soldier, as he could see from my many decorations, made of the way the war was going. I was taken aback and said: 'My Führer, you have many more competent advisors.'

'Yes,' he said, 'certainly, but they all lie to me. I want to know from you, the front line soldiers.'

'What do you want to hear then,' I said, 'a propaganda speech or the naked truth?'

'Naturally the last,' he said.

Then I told him: 'If you haven't got a good ace up your sleeve, then the war is long since lost.'

'How does this effect the fighting morale?' he wanted to know.

'With the Waffen-SS hardly at all,' was my reply. 'We fight on even when we know that all is lost. But with the Wehrmacht it is devastating.'

'Can you give me examples?' he wanted to know.

'That I can.'

Then he sighed deeply and left.

When I went back to barracks after this episode on 4 April, I was told that the commanding officer wanted to see me immediately. When I reported to him, he told me that my Reichs

Chancellery duties were finished. There were no more visitors and the SD (the SS security service under Criminal Director Hoegl) had taken over. I was told the same by my deputy and landsman, Karl Berg, when he returned to barracks. As I had to have something to do, SS-Major Kaschulla put a convoy of trucks and men at my disposal, and with them I drove to the Elbe River every day.

At first we drove to an underground petrol depot at Ferchland. Then I went further north along the eastern bank of the Elbe to where there were some moored barges containing special supplies for the U-Boats. There were some police units guarding the Elbe, and I could hear their stomachs grumbling, but from fear of fire from the Americans, who had taken up positions on the other bank. When we arrived, they did not want to let us get at the goodies, which was hardly to my liking. I promised them that they would get a share.

I went ahead with a torch and determined what should be stuffed into the mail bags. The loveliest things that we had not seen for years were stored here for our submariners, who had little hope of returning, and nothing but the best sufficed for them.

So we set off back in the early morning with our rich booty, and the policemen were also very happy. Nevertheless an incident occurred that could have ended badly. One of my men came up on deck with an armload of champagne bottles, shouting with glee. I had found some sekt beforehand and we were all a bit drunk. I kicked him in the shin and he dropped the bottles in surprise. Soon some heavy machine gun fire came from across the river and we had to take cover quickly. The stupid chap had not realised that voices carry easily over the water at night. Of course we could not do any more that night and had to return with half empty trucks.

On the way back I managed to shoot two deer in a wood near Brandenburg. Then a boy suddenly appeared on the roadside and stopped us. 'Sergeant Major, do you need some schnapps and wine?' Of course we did. He indicated a manor house on a hill top, where there was plenty for us.

It turned out that a major in the paratroops was in charge of the store there. When he asked for a requisitioning order, I had to let it go, but when I reported to my commanding officer, the situation soon changed. The adjutant had to make out a requisitioning order, and it was on a large scale, authorising me to acquire schnapps and wine for 1,000 men. Now the major issued us as much as we could carry. Naturally I kept aside 200 bottles for my personal use.

This resulted in my having no lack of friends back in barracks. A whole row of my superiors wanted to drink 'Bruderschaft' (brotherhood) with me. The sergeant major of the 1st Guard Company wanted to be my friend and invited me to the house near the barracks that he looked after and lived in with his girlfriend. He even invited me to move in with them and bring female company, but I declined, as I believed this period of happiness would only last a few days more.

And that is what happened. We came to 20 April and, to honour our Führer's birthday, a proper parade was to be held in the barracks once more. Even I was expected to take part. I marched past the saluting base in the first rank of the 1st Company with a drawn rifle to the ringing music. SS-Brigadier Mohnke took the parade with some other senior officers.

After the parade things became hectic in the barracks. The sirens howled a long note: 'Tank Alert!' Marshal Koniev's 3rd Guards Tank Army under General Rybalko had thrust up from the south toward Berlin and was suddenly threatening the city. There was only one serious obstacle in his path, the Teltow Canal. He was soon able to establish several bridgeheads and threaten the southern part of Berlin in which our barracks were located. As the Guard Battalion was expected to man the innermost defences, it could not be sent into action against Koniev's troops, so the whole battalion had to fall in and be reorganised as a combatant battalion, and not before time!

The commander of the 1st Guard Company, in whose headquarters I lived, had asked me to stay out of this, as he wanted me to act as a sort of adjutant to him, so to say 'extra to establishment', as such an appointment did not officially exist. He had confidence in me as he had hardly any combat experience himself. His experience had been a brief period at the front, an Iron Cross 2nd Class, and a posting to an officer cadet school, and since then he had never returned to the front but had made his career here.

For me it was of no consequence where or how I would fight, and I had agreed. While the battalion adjutant did the detailing, I kept in the background, but once he had finished, he noticed me. I told him what the commander of the 1st Guard Company had told me, and the latter ran up when he saw I needed support. When he heard what I had to say, there came a strong denial. I reminded the adjutant of the Führer-Order that prevented him from assigning me to combat duty. The adjutant agreed but called upon my sense of duty. He had still to set up a mortar platoon and needed a commander for it.

As I had not done this before and knew nothing about mortars, I declined. But he rejected this and said: 'The way you are, you should be able to do it easily, and the other commanders,' looking at the company commanders, 'have no experience of leadership in combat. You will learn quickly and probably do better than most.'

When I asked him what men I would get, he pointed to the band, who, when they saw my long face, looked grinning into space, and my heart sank. But with hindsight, they were to show themselves absolutely contrary to what I expected. They never let me down and were with me to the very end.

We then drew six 8 cm mortars with all their equipment, such as telephones, cable, etcetera, and ammunition. In doing so I discovered that my three sergeants knew something about them. I myself knew how to fire them, for I had often done so with captured weapons, but I had no specialised knowledge.

There, in a corner of the armoury, I saw a pile of sub-machine guns of a kind that I had never seen before. To my question, the armourer replied that they had been dropped out of British aircraft to arm foreign partisans. They had fallen into our hands and were just waiting here for someone to take them. I examined them and saw that they were quite primitive in appearance with differing hand grips, and none more than 25 cm in length.[1] Then I thought that if it came to partisan warfare, these would be just right for us.

While our men took the weapons and equipment back to their quarters, I went down to the underground firing range with my sergeants and fired these things. I discovered that they fired even with dirt in their moving parts, and that our ammunition fitted.

Now I could put aside my Italian sub-machine gun that I had brought back from Italy because the German sub-machine guns jammed so often.

There was even an MG 42[2] in the armoury that we took. When I gave the armourer a gift of a couple of bottles of wine, he positively hummed with pleasure.

We divided up into three sections, each of a sergeant and twelve men. My Headquarters Section was led by a corporal and consisted of two runners, the linesmen-to-be and the machine gun section. We were in all about fifty men strong.

Then I told my men that they could collect cigarettes and tobacco from me, as I had reserved a considerable amount for myself. Also food and drink were available to them from my supplies. These were taken with murmurs of pleasure, and soon they were celebrating in their quarters as they had not done for years. I had taken the hearts of my men by storm.

Now I must describe my last Hitler's birthday celebrations, which I held in the two rooms I shared with SS-Sergeant Karl Berg, my deputy at the Reichs Chancellery. He had a stiff leg from a wound acquired during the preparation for Operation 'Citadel', the big tank battle.[3] He had come to us as a Luftwaffe replacement, being a sergeant in a Luftwaffe field division, and so was taken on as an SS-Sergeant. I tried to persuade him to become my fourth sergeant. (He had hidden himself during the battalion reorganisation and so not been detailed.) But he was not interested and only wanted to get on one of the vehicles leaving Berlin, which he succeeded in doing. I met him on a tram in Magdeburg after the war, and he told me that he had been taken to Hamburg, where he obtained his release from the Waffen-SS and joined the local police force, thus avoiding being taken a prisoner of war when the British arrived.

But back to my celebration. Tables and chairs were set out and everyone who came was made welcome. Meanwhile the barrack square was filling with vehicles from all kinds of units, all filling up with the petrol that I had brought back, so as to get away on the last route still open, Reichsstrasse 6.

Everyone of these 'heroes', when one spoke to them, had important reasons for leaving, but the word really was: 'Get out of the Berlin trap, and don't get caught by the Russians!' Several offered to take me along with them. These rear area types did not want to stay behind and fight beside the Führer and die, to remain loyal until death, as they had sworn. But I had to tell them that it was out of the question for me; I did not want to break my oath. But there were other cases.

I was told that my former company commander, SS-Major Ernst Kleinert, who had lost a leg in Russia and now had an artificial limb, and had nevertheless commanded the 'March' Company at Hartmannsdorf/Spreenhagen, was on the square with his staff car, accompanied by his wife and child. I quickly wrapped up some food for him and hurried to say goodbye. He was not leaving on his own accord but had orders from Mohnke to take the 'Leibstandarte' wounded out of Berlin in buses, which he managed to do, taking them to a polder in Schleswig-Holstein. However, despite some of them being very seriously wounded, they all became prisoners of war and some were held for a long time under primitive and degrading conditions, permanently hungry, so that their artificial limbs no longer fitted.

The most senior guest at my party was SS-Brigadier Meyer ('Sippenmeyer') from the SS Sippenhauptamt.[4] His driver, an SS-sergeant major, knew one of my sergeants and had asked if his chief could come. He want to see again how real soldiers celebrated the Führer's birthday. Now he sat next to me, the host. He too needed to get to Hamburg urgently. While he was still sober, he exuded powerful confidence in victory and explained to me the defensive strategy of our leadership with regard to Fortress Berlin, where, he said, he would take the teeth out of the Russians.

It was not clear to me why he wanted to leave Berlin instead of participating in the great triumph here, but as a mere sergeant major it was not for me to ask a general such a question!

He went on to explain to me in detail the defensive rings around and in Berlin. The last inner defensive ring, which interested us particularly as we had to defend it, was called 'Zitadelle' and was commanded by SS-Brigadier Mohnke, who came directly under Hitler. It comprised the inner city with the Reichs Chancellery, the Reichstag, the ministries and main governmental offices.

So that was how I came to be briefed on our Highest Command's defence concept by SS-Brigadier Meyer. However, in my lowly capacity, I could not use this extensive knowledge, as a platoon commander is only interested in his position and what is to the left and right of him should he have to make contact.

The party was quite jolly, if you can use that word to describe my men's gallows humour. They got drunk, knowing full well what lay before them. Thanks to my new comrades from the band, I had music in the house, and several played industriously for the last time in their lives.

'Sippenmeyer' became drunk and his slurred speech was quite different to his arrogant talking before. This intrigued me more as he whispered into my ear tales of treason by Himmler and Göring. He went on stuttering: 'There is only the Führer now, only the Führer.' So they had already baled out, but I said to myself: 'And what can we dummies do about it? We will share our Führer's fate.'

But even the best parties come to an end, as did mine. The next day we went into the city centre by tram, so low had the 'Leibstandarte' sunk. And then on by foot, one cannot describe it as marching, to Voss-Strasse and across to the Reichs Chancellery.

I gave the female tram driver a few goodies. I had had to leave most of my treasures behind and just hoped that the Russians would choke on them. Of course we had to leave most of our private possessions behind, as in every case of going into action. The fighting soldier has enough to carry as it is, but this was always the way.

So our whole battalion went by tram, for the vast amount of fuel that I had brought from Ferchland on the Elbe had been given to the Hamburg exodus, as a result of which the tanks of the 'Nordland'[5] when they joined us later had no fuel with which to manoeuvre and had to be employed as static fire points.

As no one seemed interested in us here, I left my platoon on the Reichs Chancellery steps and went to look for accommodation with my section sergeants. The cellars under the Reichs Chancellery, where we looked first, were already occupied, not by combatants ready to take over the defence here, but by officials' families waiting transport to take them away. This made me furious, for how could one fight here with women and children in the way?

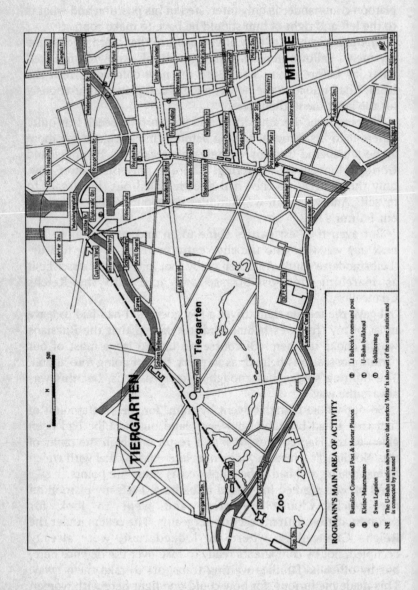

ROGMANN'S MAIN AREA OF ACTIVITY

- ⊗ Battalion Command Post & Mortar Platoon
- ⊗ Kleine-Mauerstrasse
- ⊗ Swiss Legation
- ⊗ Lt Babcek's command post
- ⊗ U-Bahn bulkhead
- ⊗ Schützensteg

NE The U-Bahn station shown above that marked 'Mitte' is also part of the same station and is connected by a tunnel

So we went up to the ground floor, where there was an unusual to-ing and fro-ing of important-looking people, but again no real combatants. Here again all the rooms were occupied.

Then I looked into the Führer's study. This was empty. No one had dared move in here. I thought to myself: 'Well the Führer will not be working here any more, and my men are not accustomed to living in the open air, and they need accommodation, for the weather is fresh and rainy outside.'

The big windows had been blown out in the last air raid and no one had replaced them, as they would only be damaged again in the nightly raids, but at least one had a roof over one's head. So I had my men come in, and they managed to fit in with all of their equipment.

Then I searched the big desk and found a box of cigars for visitors, as the Führer smoked as little as I did in those days. There was also a bottle of good Cognac. I sampled it and finished the bottle, not bothering to look for glasses. Then I curled up on the wonderful carpet and slept. A soldier never knows what the next hour will bring. (According to a Soviet general, it later took fifteen men to remove the carpet so as to take it back to Moscow.)

I was rudely woken up during the night. Once I had pushed away the torch shining into my face, (there was no electric light because of the blackout) I saw an SD patrol standing in front of me and talking about shooting me as the senior rank present for desecrating the 'Almighty's' study. The Führer's study was no doss house, etcetera. I tried to explain to them that I was fully aware of the significance of the room from my previous job in the Reichs Chancellery. We did not want to stay here but would go wherever we were ordered to fight, and that would happen sooner than they, whom one could see wore no decorations and had never been in action, could think.

My men, who had found some more Cognac and were full of bravado, crowded round us and said aggressively that there were only two possible ways of getting us out of here, either to find us better accommodation or to kill us. Neither of the SD 'heroes' were in a position to do anything. As they had nothing left to say, I suggested to them that they might like to join us as ammunition carriers, for it would be a shame if the war were to end without them even getting a sniff of powder. I would have a word about this with their chief, Criminal Director Hoegl, I suggested. They were fit enough, I said, having felt their arm muscles. But they did not want to know, and left us muttering threats. But how can one threaten a person already facing certain death?

So we settled down to sleep again. Then early in the morning SS-Lieutenant Puttkamer (a relative of Hitler's naval adjutant) came in and introduced himself as my company commander. He started giving me a telling off for the way I had treated the SD patrol during the night. I rejected this sharply and said: 'Unlike myself, you already knew yesterday what your appointment was to be and that you would be responsible for a company. Since you did not show yourself, I had to use my initiative. In case you are unaware of your responsibilities as the commander of a troop, you should know that it is no umbrella that can be left lying about anywhere.'

Thus I made it quite clear between us at the start. As he wore only the Iron Cross Second Class, it was quite obvious to me that he had not been exposed to real fighting before. Perhaps he had been adequately protected by his big-shot relative from having to go to the front, and so had also got a role like this, for there was no such thing as a mortar company in combat. Normally the platoon would be split up in direct support of either the regimental or battalion commander.

He took us down into the cellars, which had meanwhile emptied noticeably, the officials' families having left during the night. The rooms he showed me were near Mohnke's command post on Hermann-Göring-Strasse. They filled me with confidence as soon as I saw them, for they were constructed out of reinforced concrete and the partition walls of similar construction supported the ceiling. As an experienced builder, I saw this all with one glance. It would take an enormous shell to break through.

Our company commander occupied a small room down here with his heavily pregnant wife. 'Good God,' I thought, 'is he crazy?' He had stupidly taken a room with a window next to the outside wall, where the cellar was only one and a half metres below ground. The first shell to explode on the pavement would send splinters straight in. Naturally, I did not tell this superfluous warrior what I thought.

His wife was feeling permanently ill, which was not surprising in her condition, but she had to go on telling everyone about it, while he stood by saying nothing. With her too I had to draw a line, which made me look a unfeeling clot. He even had to sit beside her to comfort her when the shelling started.

After this exchange of words, I moved with my headquarters section into a small room and the rest settled down around. Our predecessors, like ourselves, had left their personal things behind. To my surprise there were a pair of highly polished officer's jackboots and some passable breeches to go with them. I had not seen such beautiful boots for years, since my father, a master shoemaker, had made me such a pair. In one of them was a holster for a small pistol, a 6.35 Walther, and in the other was a sheath for a stiletto with a needle point and razor-sharp blade. I tried them on and they fitted perfectly. Then I tried walking a few steps in them, which took me out into the cellar passageway. A young woman came toward me with an Alsatian puppy. The puppy leant against one of the shining boots and pissed inside. I kicked him away, which did not please the young woman.

She scolded me and got a sharp response back. Then I noticed that my old company comrade Heinz Jurkewitz, who was now with the Führer bodyguard, was standing behind her, making violent hand signals to me that I could not understand.

I shouted at her: 'Get your dog out of here and leave us alone!' Whereupon she put the puppy on the lead and went off with him without a word.

'For goodness sake, Willi,' Heinz said to me, 'what have you done? Do you know who that was?'

'No, I didn't know.'

'That was Fräulein Braun!'

'It could have been Fräulein Schwarz as far as I am concerned,' I said. 'What about it?'

Then he had to tell me confidentially who Fräulein Braun was, and that he had been assigned to her as her bodyguard.

With this explanation I should make it clear that even I who had been on duty in the Reichs Chancellery knew nothing of the existence of this woman. It was a taboo subject and no one talked about it. We were trained to be discreet. Nevertheless, she had been here in the Führerbunker at the Reichs Chancellery since 15 April and had come, against the Führer's will, to share his fate. She usually lived at the Führer's mountain retreat in Berchtesgaden. The puppy came from Blondi, the Führer's Alsatian, and he had given it to Fräulein Braun so that she had something to remind her of him, since he could not come because of the war. When it was time to die, the pup would die too.

Of course I took this hard and asked Heinz to ask my forgiveness for my ignorance, as I had no access to the Führerbunker myself.

After this fiasco I took off the boots and breeches. Like their owner, I had no need for these special boots.

Then the company commander ordered us to go into the Tiergarten and practise with the mortars. This was certainly rather late, but necessary, for the mortars had lain unused in the barracks and now had to augment the fighting strength of two regiments.

So we moved into the Tiergarten and practised setting up and so on. The company commander stood there saying nothing. Whether he knew more about these things than I did, I cannot say. It is best in such circumstances to let the sergeants get on with it, so I left them to it.

The 1st Platoon was commanded by a senior officer cadet[6] I knew from the barracks. This was the last time either I or the company commander was to see him. He was on duty in the barracks as Duty NCO every other day, and strutted around like a peacock, which was enough to set me off teasing him. He still did not have the necessary front decorations to go to officer school, and must therefore have had a powerful patron, as otherwise this would not have been possible. When such similar 'experts' came to the front and were set above me, although just a lowly sergeant major, they did not have it easy.

I had no intention of being sent with my men into an uncertain mission. Even my men, without my having said anything, would simply turn away if he tried to give orders over my head. For them it did not matter how many stars a superior had. They looked at it from the standpoint of what their chances of survival were with that superior, and I would rather go myself than send anyone into a dangerous mission.

So here this gentleman had no protector any more and at last had to show what he was made of.

While we were exercising, some heavy shells burst unexpectedly several hundred yards away, for the first time in the city centre. As I had heard no discharge, it was immediately apparent to me they were from a long range battery firing off a map, and were of no great concern to an experienced soldier.

So, without haste, I had my platoon move by sections into two concrete garages that stood nearby. These would not have stood up to a direct hit, of course, but that would have been highly unlikely. In order to show my men how dangerously I treated the situation I, a non-smoker, lit a cigarette and passed round the packet and started cracking jokes, and soon the first witticisms were being passed around among my men. So everyone remained calm, which was the main thing.

But the senior officer cadet, who was unfamiliar with such shelling, cried out: 'All is lost, save yourselves!' The company commander stood as still as a marble statue, not taking it in.

I immediately took over command of this wildly scattering mob and ordered them to lie down. Then I took them into cover by sections. The firing soon stopped and we had no casualties.

These were the kind of commanders that lead men to destruction for no reason at all, and it boded ill for the future.

As I read in Soviet military literature after the war, the shelling had been purely a propaganda gesture in order to be able to report to Stalin that: 'The lion's den now lies under heavy destructive fire.' I even saw pictures of the guns, primitive things with a range of about 18 kilometres mounted on self-propelled tracks.

I did not wait for the company commander's orders, but took my troops back to the Reichs Chancellery, not without throwing a look of contempt at these two 'heroes', who already had their heads together.

SS-Lieutenant August Krönke was waiting for me at the Reichs Chancellery. He was adjutant to the 'Anhalt' Regiment's 2nd Battalion, commanded by SS-Captain Schäfer, to which my platoon belonged, according to my instructions, thus removing me from Puttkamer's direct command.

First Krönke had to show me the location of the battalion's

positions. The battalion was already deployed and wherever possible I was shown round by the company commander responsible. But as Schäfer never held a company commanders' conference, which I too would have had to attend, I never got to know them all. The battalion was fully committed, and there were no reserves. I just had to go along the streets behind the buildings in which our companies were deployed. I made a provisional sketch of the front and later was able to copy everything out on graph paper for my forward observers. I myself would remain primarily at the base position and send out my sergeants as observers, as they knew more about the business.

The battalion boundary on the left was the right wing of Belle-Alliance-Platz (Mehringplatz), from where it followed the Landwehr Canal to the Tiergarten, then cut across the Tiergarten to the Spree River. It then followed the Spree through the Diplomatic Quarter as far as the Kronprinzen Bridge. The Reichstag was our boundary with SS-Captain Thomas Mrugalla's 1st Battalion. The right flank at the Reichstag was under the command of SS-Lieutenant Babick, whose heroic fight at the Reichstag I will report on later.

In the Tiergarten we could only manage a two-man foxhole every fifty metres, but here were also the tanks of the 'Hermann von Salza' battalion of the SS Panzergrenadier Division 'Nordland' under SS-Lieutenant Colonel Peter Kausch, a very brave man and holder of the Oak Leaves to the Iron Cross.[7]

There was also the mighty Zoo flak-tower, whose area was defended by Volkssturm and Hitler Youth units. This flak-tower later evolved into a strong bastion in the defence, although the flak-towers had not been designed for this purpose. With its massive concrete walls and its height, it was almost unassailable and could not be taken by the Soviets. Nevertheless, the thousands of civilians in this bunker had a terrible time.

We returned to the battalion command post on the lowest level of the Potsdamer Platz S-Bahn station, where I was introduced to the battalion commander, SS-Captain Schäfer. Schäfer's command post was in a platform guard's office, where he remained until the end. Opposite his office were several S-Bahn carriages full of supplies under the control of a quartermaster.

I was invited to eat. The commander's batman prepared sandwiches all day long for him and his visitors. With this went either tea or ersatz coffee, and the supplies lasted until the end.

Schäfer instructed me to leave my men in reserve at the Reichs Chancellery. He would call us when he needed us.

When I got back, my men were busy unloading trucks that were driving into the inner yard one after the other with ammunition and supplies from the outer districts. The Reichs Chancellery was being transformed into a vast underground supply depot.

My men had to do this out of self-preservation. No one invited them to eat or take them on ration strength. I could not approach my company commander on such a triviality. As my men told me, he just sat there comforting his wife as the shells exploded outside.

I may be over-critical, but a unit commander cannot take his wife to war with him, and here the war was becoming ever more intense, even in the Reichs Chancellery, so I can rightly accuse him of failing lamentably in his responsibilities.

Consequently, my men had to steal their daily bread by the sweat of their brows. To my shame I must admit in helping them by asking the storekeeper stupid questions while they carried off the stolen items to their quarters. Let the readers think what they like, the full stomachs of my men were more important to me than morals and propriety. Hunger hurts and the food that we had brought with us from the barracks had run out. The storekeeper, who had no hunger, could not understand this. He was a typical quartermaster and such people only respond to written orders for the issue of anything. To find such an order would have only led to unnecessary work and anger, which is why I emphasise this point. Once my men had removed enough, we took time off. No one bothered about the storekeeper's complaints.

As we did not know what was in the boxes, we opened them with our bayonets and stuffed ourselves full of the choicer items. Without asking me, someone had the idea of taking some food across to the Puttkamer family, and soon we had another drama. I had to take a lecture on morals and propriety, to which I listened without saying a word. No, I would not do it again, I promised.

I did not believe that the Puttkamers with their connections would have to go hungry, but they never thought of giving anything to the soldiers.

Our comrades in the Senior Officer Cadet's platoon were also hungry, but that was nothing to do with me. I do not know what happened to them later but with the commander they had, it could only have been catastrophic.

Meanwhile a serious incident occurred within our regimental area. Major General Mummert, the commander of the Panzer Division 'Müncheberg', with or without the knowledge of our regimental commander SS-Colonel Anhalt, and I never discovered which, as the latter only gave out instructions on rare occasions, ordered our 1st Battalion from its allocated positions into operational reserve at Alexanderplatz. As a result of this a gap opened on our right flank that Schäfer would have been unable to fill with his battalion. That there were no serious consequences is a wonder. I did not understand it.

Next day, 24 April, the situation changed as follows. General Weidling, commander of the LVIth Panzer Corps, which consisted of the 9th Parachute Division, the 18th and 20th Panzergrenadier Divisions, the Panzer Division 'Müncheberg' and the SS-Panzergrenadier Division 'Nordland', was appointed Battle Commandant of Berlin by Hitler. He replaced General Reymann and came directly under Hitler. General Mummert became commander of the LVIth Panzer Corps.

THE JANNOWITZ BRIDGE

Our going into action happened fully otherwise than had been intended. As only one mortar platoon had been allocated to the Regiment 'Anhalt', each of the battalions wanted it for themselves. The other platoon went to Mohnke's second regiment, which consisted mainly of Berlin-based SS office staff. Strangely enough, Mohnke could not even remember the commander's name when he returned from captivity, and I did not know it either. These office staff seemed only interested in the defence of their own office buildings, as I was to discover later with the Ministry of the Interior.

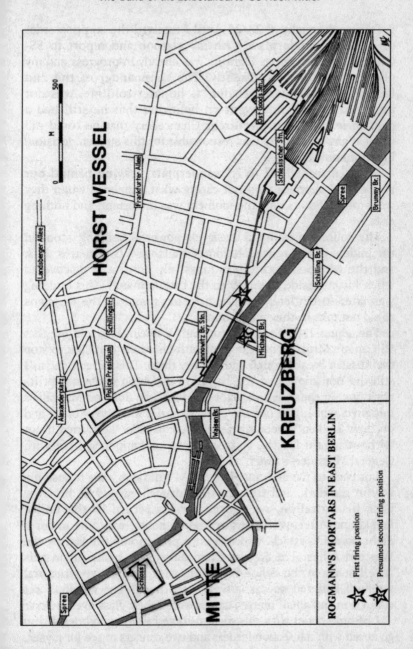

ROGMANN'S MORTARS IN EAST BERLIN

☆ First firing position

☆ Presumed second firing position

During the night of 23/24 April I received the surprise order to go to Alexanderplatz with my platoon and report to SS-Captain Mrugalla there. Fighting was already in progress and my platoon was needed urgently. The commander of the 2nd Battalion, SS-Captain Schäfer, as he later told me, was not informed of this, and went on believing that he still had a platoon in reserve at the Reichs Chancellery that he could call upon at any time. Who was responsible for this sudden decision, I do not know either.

So we marched off to Alexanderplatz, leaving behind our stolen food supplies, and not caring what happened when they were found. For us only the moment was important, and nothing else.

The Police Presidium, a massively powerful building, stood in the middle of the square. Its outer walls were two metres thick and the whole structure was massively built, as I discovered when I went inside to report to the battalion staff. This building was later to be defended like a fortress, and as the Russians could not take it, they went round it.

The adjutant, SS-Second Lieutenant Wilhelm Fey, told me that SS-Captain Mrugalla had gone off with his whole battalion to stop the Russian breakthrough and destroy them. This puzzled me as I still did not know that the battalion had been taken out of its positions. At the time I thought this had been done on Mrugalla's initiative, which was not the case. Mrugalla was a very brave and obedient soldier. Whenever he received an order, he carried it out without regard for the consequences, as happened here with General Mummert's order.

But back to me and my platoon. As I did not want to lose my way in the dark, and thought that Mrugalla would be bringing back his battalion, we waited for his return in the Police Presidium. After we had waited some hours, we came under a night bombing attack, which was to prove to be the last by the Western Allies. The Reichs Chancellery was badly hit in this raid, but we in the Police Presidium with its massive structural strength suffered no casualties, even though the windows set about one and a half metres up showered their glass everywhere.

I became bored with this unaccustomed waiting and decided to go ahead with my section leaders and two runners to see for myself, leaving the platoon behind in the Presidium. It was still dark, but a few streets further east at Schillingstrasse I saw something the like of which I had never seen throughout the whole war. SS-Captain Mrugalla was leading his whole battalion as a reconnaissance party. In the middle of the street were two Panther tanks that General Mummert had lent him, for we had none of our own. The men were advancing three paces apart on either side of the street alongside the buildings, which were still not ruins, with the battalion commander and his staff behind the tanks in the middle.

I can still see the scene decades after as if it were yesterday, it was so unusual. They were moving like a funeral procession, going from street to street looking for an enemy that was not there. As I was moving faster than their funereal pace, I soon caught up with the battalion commander and reported to him.

'Where is your mortar platoon then?' he asked. 'It could be needed urgently any minute.'

I replied: 'You don't think for a moment that I would have my men take part in this buffoonery, do you? I have never seen anything so ridiculous in all my life! What is going on?'

This naturally came as a shock to him, but I was always one to speak my mind, and what I saw here was beyond comprehension.

He stopped still, as did his whole battalion, including the tanks. Everyone wanted to see what this exchange was about. So I told him that I did not know whether it was his idea or General Mummert's, but who was going to occupy his section of the defences while he led his battalion into a trap that would destroy them all?

Meanwhile it had become light and as I, like the others, was wearing no camouflage jacket, he could see my decorations. Perhaps he started having doubts about his enterprise, but how could he have known what to do? He was only a senior administration official and, as I later discovered, dean of a school of administration in Arolsen. His men too all came from SS administrative posts. As his company commanders gathered round, I saw that none of them wore a worthwhile decoration, so there was no one that could have advised him in such matters.

He said to me: 'But I have left a strong standing patrol behind me at the Spree bridges!'

'You are a useless shit!' I said to him cheekily, 'When the Russians come they will overpower them in minutes.'

'What would you do in my case then?' he asked.

'Break off this business immediately and occupy the positions allocated to you by the regimental commander.'

'But how will I carry out my task of locating the Russians?'

To my mind the Russians did not need locating, but I said: 'I will take that on with my mortar platoon.'

'You will do it with only a few men?' he asked doubtfully.

'Just march your men back and I will soon let you know how far off the Russians are.'

He agreed that I should take over the role, which was not all that agreeable to me. We each took a Panzerfaust as he gave the order to go back.

Then two Hitler Youth leaders that had overheard the conversation came after us and asked if they could come along with us. We stopped again and I asked these two fourteen year-olds whether they would not prefer to help their mothers with the washing up, which upset them. They told me that they commanded a fifty-strong Hitler Youth unit and were looking for a unit to join on to, and that after our discussion with Mrugalla's battalion that did not appear to be the right one. However, I still did not want any children coming along with me, and so sent them to await my return at the Police Praesidium.

We went on marching eastward. A few streets further on I came to a barricade manned by two Waffen-SS sentries, both completely drunk. No information could be obtained from them in their state and they would obviously fall easy prey to the Russians for they were incapable of understanding anything.

So we went on further and must have gone quite a distance before we suddenly saw two Stalin tanks standing side by side blocking the street. We crouched down and fired Panzerfausts at them but, as I feared, they failed to penetrate the frontal armour and we could not tackle them from the side, so this only served to wake them up. Then we came under fire from sub-machine guns from two windows, which we soon silenced with Panzerfausts.

We beat a hasty retreat and had just got round the street corner as the tank guns opened up. I made a note of the name of the street so that Mrugalla would not have to look for himself, but in fact we were on the wrong course, as I later discovered.

The main Russian attack was coming from the Schlesischer Station and so went past us. Why the Russians attacked from there I later learnt from Soviet military literature. General Bokov, the political commissar to the 5th Shock Army, whose commander Colonel General Berzarin was appointed City Commandant that day, wrote that the army had captured, together with its ammunition, some heavy German siege artillery of the Thor type in Silesia that had been used in the siege of Sevastopol. These mortars were mounted on railway wagons adjusted to the Russian gauge and, according to Bokov, a track had been adjusted to this gauge as far as the Schlesischer Station and they started firing their bombs into the centre of Berlin on 25 April.[8]

When we got back to the Police Praesidium and I reported back to Mrugalla, he was already preparing to move out his battalion, having received new orders to defend the Schlesischer Station. He gave me the order to set up my mortar platoon – I would know better where than he – in support of his battalion. He gave me a company of Volkssturm in support as he knew how much mortars could fire, and they could collect mortar bombs from the Reichs Chancellery so that I could provide a proper barrage, as he put it. I accepted gratefully, as we only had one set of ammunition with us.

The Hitler Youth boys were also there, asking to go into action. As I now knew that Mrugalla would not think of establishing a proper screen behind which I could operate, I was in desperate need of infantry cover and so reluctantly took on the Hitler Youths. These boys were well equipped with automatic carbines, goodness knows who had arranged that. In comparison, the Volkssturm only had captured French and Italian rifles with hardly any ammunition for them.

So now I moved along between the raised stretch of S-Bahn track and the Spree with my headquarters section, the Volkssturm commander and the runners, as well as the two Hitler Youth leaders, toward the Schlesischer Station.

At the Jannowitz Bridge S-Bahn Station the track was about ten metres up on an almost vertical structure of hewn sandstone blocks. Just beyond the Jannowitz Bridge I found the place I was looking for. The massive S-Bahn elevation was hollow like a kind of casemate with some concrete steps leading down inside. I wanted to set up here in a dead angle of the casemate, where the artillery could not reach me, only high trajectory fire, for which the Russians had more than enough stuff. Their 120 mm mortars, for instance, against which my 80 mm mortars were nothing.

I summoned my platoon, and the Volkssturm men knew where to find me with the ammunition.

My platoon arrived and started setting up. With one of my section sergeants who was assigned as forward observer, the signallers and the Hitler Youths that had arrived meanwhile, we went along the tracks to the Jannowitz Bridge Station. I looked for a good location for the Hitler Youth to set up a defensive position. I found one but, as I was to discover, not as good as our mortar position.

With the forward observer, the signallers and four Hitler Youths, who wanted to protect the observer, we went some distance toward the Schlesischer Station. I found a tall building from where the observer would have a good overall view. The signallers paid out the telephone cable and I went back to my position.

We soon had communication and the forward observer started calling for fire, although he still did not have a proper target. He reported that the Russians were sticking up a red flag every time they took a tall building, but that most of these flags were promptly being shot down again. Then the Volkssturm came over the bridge behind us and delivered about five hundred mortar bombs. Now we had what we needed and could start.

Then the forward observer called. The enemy were advancing in a dense group supported by tanks. We began peppering them and when one thinks that with practice a mortar can have as many as ten bombs in the air at one time, one can get some idea of the fire-power of these six mortars.

A mortar bomb normally makes a hole about two hands wide upon impact, but on a roadway it makes no hole but breaks up into tiny splinters that riddle human targets like a sieve, and there must have been fearful casualties among that dense mob of advancing Russians.

When the Volkssturm came with a second load and saw our barrage they quickly put their bombs into the casemate and vanished. This was quite right, for it was a hot place to be. Then the forward observer called for us to stop. There was no longer a target. The surviving Russians had fled for cover.

My men now thought that they had earned a rest before the next engagement, and I agreed with them. They had acquitted themselves very well in their first action, and I dug out some tobacco for them. Nevertheless, I told them not to stand around in the open but to take cover in the casemates, thinking that we could expect some retaliation for what we had done. But that it would be so bad, I had no idea.

So I was standing outside alone with one of my NCOs when I heard a noise that I recognised as the discharge of numerous artillery pieces and the dull thump of heavy mortars. I quickly grabbed a mortar and took it under cover. The NCO promptly followed suit as the storm burst over us.

We raced down into the casemates and not a second too soon. Then it hit. Our eardrums were nearly displaced with the din of bursting shells. I had never experienced anything like it. How long the barrage lasted, I cannot say. It could have been seconds or hours. We sat or lay there with the anxious feeling that it would never end, unable to communicate with each other because of the din, each man isolated within himself.

When at last we could go outside again, the sudden silence came like a pain to our ears, and the sky had darkened with the fumes from the exploding shells still hanging in the air.

I first looked at our mortars. Only the two that we had taken inside remained serviceable, the rest being nothing but torn and twisted metal, and that after only our first time in action. Our communications were also lost, the telephone cable having been shot through in several places.

I had the two surviving mortars set up roughly and shot off the remaining ammunition blindly. I did not want to stay here, but to withdraw over the Spree, so sent a runner to recall the forward observer, if he was still alive. I went forward myself to see how the boys were and how they had got on under fire.

When I reached the Hitler Youth position, it was a shattering sight. One could say that there was not a single stone left standing on another. Everything had been churned over several times by the artillery fire and the boys shredded into small pieces. I looked on with the tears running down my face.

I reproached myself for having accepted the boys' offer, when I should have remained firm and sent them away. But my self-reproach came too late, as they too firmly believed that they could do something for their country. Their mothers would wait in vain for their return. I could not inform them of their sons' fate, for I did not even know any of their names.

Now the forward observer returned with his four Hitler Youth volunteers. The barrage had passed right over them, leaving them unhurt. They too started crying when they saw what had happened to their comrades, but when I hoped that they had had enough, they said to me, still crying: 'Sergeant Major, this makes us even harder. We want to stay with you until the last!' What can one say to a boy like that? They were twelve to fifteen year-olds. Today's youngsters would never believe what their predecessors had to put up with.

When we went back, my platoon was already across the bridge behind us on the other side of the Spree. The bridge was still intact and there was no sign of Mrugalla's standing patrol. As I now established, the bridge had not even been prepared for demolition. Here too the leadership had left everything to chance. Colonel Lobeck[9] probably did not want to blow the bridge, for like every bridge it carried essential services such as water, gas and electricity for the civilian population, who would be deprived of these things if the bridge were blown.

My two remaining mortars had been set up behind a vast building. As the bridge was unsecured, I used those of my men now without mortars to form a thin protective screen, to which I also sent the machine gun section and the four remaining Hitler Youths with their good automatic carbines. They would not run away when things got hot, of that I was sure.

I sent the forward observer up on to the roof of the building. I did not have the heart to send him back over the Spree after our last fiasco. He now fired on sight, being able to see over the top of the S-Bahn embankment.

Then I went into the cellars of the building to see whether we could shelter here should it hail down on us again. My hair stood on end when I saw what was being stored there unguarded. Big rockets were lying in their wooded crates such as I had never seen before. They resembled Stalin Organs but were much bigger. It struck me that the cases must also serve as their launchers, but I had no idea how they worked. I became angry that our leadership should have left these dangerous things lying around unguarded and unused. What if the Russians occupied this area, would they not use them against us? They certainly had no regard for the civilian population. The rockets were not primed of course, but there were some boxes stacked in one corner with what looked like detonators packed in wood shavings. So everything was there except someone who knew how to use them.

When I got back into the daylight, I beckoned my NCOs over and the forward observer down from the roof. I told them briefly what I had found in the cellar and ordered an immediate change of location to get away from this place with its dangerous devices.

Somewhat closer to the Schlesischer Station we found what we were looking for. A stranger came toward us. From his uniform, I took him to be a Wehrmacht official. I stopped him and asked him who he was walking alone through this area. He identified himself as an ammunition technician working for Colonel Lobeck. 'So,' I thought, 'he can explain something.'

I took him down into the vast cellars, watching him closely. He showed no surprise when he saw the cases. I suggested that he must be the storekeeper, but he denied it.

'Can you show me how these things work?' I said.

He said: 'I am an explosives expert and already had a proper training in it during peacetime and have attended courses ever since, so I know all about the latest products. I can of course show you how these work.'

'Then help me to get them into position and fire them when necessary.'

He said: 'I don't think so. I have officer's rank and only take orders from Colonel Lobeck.'

'We can soon change that,' I told him. 'Lobeck is far off, but I am here with full executive powers. My Hitler Youths are trigger happy and, having just lost their comrades, are in the right state of mind. One gesture from me and you will be looking down their gun muzzles. But you can at least show me how these things work, and when you have helped me to secure the bridge, you can go wherever you like.'

'Blowing a bridge without direct orders from Colonel Lobeck is out of the question as far as I am concerned. I wouldn't do it even if you stood me against the wall.'

'I too have no orders to do it, nor do I know our leadership's intentions. I will only secure it so that we are not overrun by Russian tanks,' I told him.

This made him more amenable. I summoned my comrades and we carried out two of the rockets and laid them in the middle of the bridge. Of course this was not the correct procedure, but I had no intention of getting involved in sapper tasks. If these things should blow up, I thought, they will not leave one stone standing on another. Under cover of my comrades, he prepared a fuse for me and secured it fast. He must have known something of his trade, for General Bokov describes in his book on the conquest of Berlin how their engineers had to work all day to dismantle this particular security device. In fact we did not blow the bridge, nor did our successors, and when I went there after the war I found it still intact.

I then took my NCOs and had him explain to them exactly how they worked, and how one primed them. As this chap took the right pieces out of the right corner without having to look for them, even the batteries that were needed to provide a weak electrical current to detonate the rockets, I said to my NCOs in his presence: 'Isn't it strange that this prophet knows where everything is without having to look for it?' They laughed hollowly. One suggested throwing him into the Spree to feed the fish. When this 'hero' saw my NCOs looking at him angrily, he began to stutter fearfully. So I said to him: 'Get lost before I change my mind!'

We then carried out one of the rockets, which took eight men, and set it up against the wall of the embankment, ready for firing. Having discussed it with my men, I wanted to carry out a trial shot. The forward observer climbed back up to the roof, as this was the tallest building far and wide.

I ignited the rocket while my men took cover. It howled off like a fiery comet and fell in our old target area, as our forward observer reported when he came down again. Now we could see the cloud of dust from ground level. The Russians would have wondered where this monster came from.

Naturally I took care not to set off any more of these monsters. We had enough experience of the Russians not to let them trace them back to us.

However, as far as the bridge was concerned, I would not have hesitated to blow it for a minute if immediate danger threatened. I had no intention of letting ourselves be overrun by tanks.

Then my Hitler Youths came up with the idea of going forward again to recover and bury their comrades. Some sympathetic Volkssturm men accompanied them and I sent my machine gun section to provide them with cover, but I did not go myself as I knew what the outcome would be. How could one find earth to bury the remains in that rubble waste?

And that is exactly what happened. They returned unsuccessful, having only been able to recover a few identity cards and personal possessions from the dead children. The Volkssturm men, many of whom had not seen active service, had never seen anything so terrible and were deeply shocked. Several had nervous breakdowns, but the youngsters became even harder and led them away.

I told the Volkssturm commander to leave a couple of runners behind and take his men to the Reichs Chancellery and wait my call. Should I eventually require more mortar bombs or just need their help, I would let him know. I certainly did not want to use them for defence with their quaint rifles and sparse ammunition.

I then had a whole batch of rockets carried out and set up along the walled river embankment ready for firing. They were set almost vertically so as to aim at the street on the opposite embankment. This meant them exploding only 150 metres from us, so I had the shot-up remains of our telephone cable, which we had reconnected together, used as extensions of the ignition cables. Then I had everyone, including the defensive screen, take cover some distance back and lie in wait for whatever was to come. Although it was quiet where we were, thunder and lightning continued to come from the Schlesischer Station area.

I was surprised not to have received any messages or new orders from Mrugalla. At first he had cried out for heavy weapons and now he seemed to have forgotten us. I think that he had already withdrawn a little toward Alexanderplatz. As I later discovered, he had meanwhile been injured in the arm, but remained with his troops like a good soldier.

We had to wait quite a long time before it came to shooting again. It was evening and already beginning to go dark when a dozen Russian tanks came along the street on the far bank from the east, having gone round the Schlesischer Station, and headed toward Alexanderplatz. This was the moment we had been hoping and waiting for.

Unsuspectingly, for no one was firing at them from the flanks, they slowly rolled forward into the trap. When I thought that they had reached the right point, I fired the rockets, which howled down on their targets, striking them and turning it into a frightful fiasco for the Russians. Some of the splinters even came across the Spree. Several tanks must have received direct hits, as they split apart like soap boxes, increasing the overall effect. One tipped over into the Spree and the water gurgled over it. Some that had been driving next to the exploding tanks either simply tipped over or were slammed against the S-Bahn structure as if they were toys. All had been knocked out. A few crewmen bailed out and tried to escape crouched down and crawling out of the field of fire. We let them get away so that they could report back what had happened to them.

An unusual silence fell. We withdrew and took cover in the cellars, as I was afraid that the storm would descend upon us again, but nothing happened. I can only assume that the Russian forward observers had been unable to identify where the rockets came from. That we had had the audacity to fire at such short range probably did not occur to them.

When we realised that we were not going to be punished, we carried out some more rockets but set them up at another location aimed at the station area. There one could shoot wherever one wanted and be sure of hitting a Russian target, but I was cautious about firing them, for at night the after glow that the rockets trailed behind them was visible for miles.

How the Reichs Chancellery discovered that we were firing these rockets, I have no idea, but suddenly a convoy of trucks drove directly up to us in the night. Accompanying them was

SS-Second Lieutenant Triebes, who brought orders for us to load as many rockets and their equipment as possible and take them to Potsdamer Platz. He had also brought the Volkssturm along with him.

IN ACTION AT POTSDAMER PLATZ

We loaded as quickly as possible, our mortars and ammunition too. Then we climbed aboard the trucks and the Volkssturm followed behind on foot.

Thank goodness we had not come under fire while loading, or we would have been blown to smithereens. A sergeant and some men remained behind and detonated the rockets that we had previously set up as soon as we had gone some distance, and they were able to catch up with us before the Soviets retaliated.

The rockets and our equipment were unloaded at Potsdamer Platz and taken below ground to the upper level of the S-Bahn station. The Volkssturm men that had followed us and then helped to unload I ordered to occupy two S-Bahn carriages on the lower level, where I reserved a carriage for my men and the last four of our Hitler Youths. I myself was hardly to use the accommodation at all, as much work awaited me.

Four Red Cross nurses appeared and offered to tend our wounded in the forthcoming fighting, an offer I gladly accepted.

Then I had trouble with our four remaining Hitler Youths. As I had no task for them for the moment, they stood outside our S-Bahn carriage, which was near the entrance to the Potsdamer Strasse tunnel and starting accosting 'stragglers', having simply adopted the role of military police.

While the real military police were handing these 'stragglers' over to us to feed into our front positions, these young policemen were briefly asking: 'Where are you going? Where do you come from?' Whoever was unable to give a thoroughly satisfactory explanation was being shot out of hand.

We had no intention of doing such a thing. When I say 'we', I refer to my battalion commander, who was in charge here. As was his way, he was doing nothing about the coming and going of the numerous 'stragglers', who could only be described as 'stragglers' because they did not want to fight any more. These people lived in the tunnels and only emerged when driven out by hunger or thirst, when they would try to meet their needs in the S-Bahn stations.

Now when one of my men stormed up to me and angrily reported what these military police were up to, I went down with my NCOs. We disarmed them and gave them a dressing down. What could we do with these kids? Shoot them? Of course I could understand that it galled them that most of the soldiers no longer wanted to fight. I felt the same. But they did not have the motto on their belt buckles like us.[10] So I chased the four boys away and shouted after them: 'Don't let me see you here again!'

They looked at me as if they could not understand me or the world any more. But it was no use, for our paths crossed again the next day. Having come from an area already occupied by the Russians, they did not know where to go, and promised to behave, but I had to stress to them that my orders were sacred and must be carried out instantly and zealously. I did not give them their weapons back, but there were plenty lying around that those tired of war had thrown away, so they were soon able to rearm themselves.

However, what pleased me was that we were immediately taken on the ration strength, including my supply train, which had not previously been the case. Until now we had only been on stand-by or fighting. What kind of leaders were these that never thought that their men had to be looked after! While I helped myself shamelessly to the battalion commander's standing table of sandwiches, my men carried their share into their S-Bahn carriage.

Now the real military police started combing through the tunnels and bringing the 'stragglers' to us to be fed into our front line trenches.

Then the battalion commander came to me and said: 'You only have two mortars now, apart from the rockets, of which you have not fired one. You are hardly overloaded.'

Not knowing what SS-Captain Schäfer wanted of me, I said: 'Then send me forward, and if you are short of a company commander, I will gladly take over, even a platoon will do for me. That would suit me much better than this job here.'

'Oh no!' said Schäfer, 'since your rocket action at the Jannowitz Bridge you have become a well known and respected person. I would be in trouble if I took you away from your post, which was not what I meant. Apart from this, between ourselves, the adjutant has brought back from the Reichs Chancellery the news that you are to get the Knight's Cross for that action, and also be promoted for your bravery.'

'And what happens then?' I wanted to know. 'Come on, spill the beans! Every day I have to take the stragglers rounded up by the military police forward to the various company commanders. Even though there are officers going about without proper jobs, a sergeant major has to be detailed as Duty Officer!'

Schäfer thought about this and then said: 'If it hots up outside, these administrative types will be formed into a shock troop, something they have never done before. There are none among them that can replace you, so I will continue to pass on the stragglers to you to fill the holes in the front line.'

So I handed over the command to my senior NCO and set off with the stragglers.

THE DEATH OF SS-COLONEL ANHALT

Early on 25 April our regimental commander came to Potsdamer Platz wanting to speak to SS-Captain Schäfer. With him was his liaison officer, SS-Second Lieutenant Triebes and his driver, SS-Corporal Masbender. They left their staff car up on the square.

When he saw our rockets stacked around and some we were setting up ready for action, he came up to me. I reported to him and he began talking to me about our Alexanderplatz-Schlessischer Station operation, congratulating me. I did not approve of the Mrugalla's battalion operation and told him so. When it came to the Russians and the unguarded bridges in the city centre, I said that heads should roll. He gave no indication of how much he knew of Mrugalla's action or of whether he approved, for a regimental commander does not have to explain his thoughts and plans to a mere platoon commander, but I could see that I had caught his attention.

He was impatient and ordered me to accompany him

immediately to Alexanderplatz to clarify my accusations. This set my ears burning for having opened my mouth so freely. When commanders argue among themselves, sergeant majors are likely to end up crushed between the millstones. However, I had to follow Anhalt, who did not even go down to see Schäfer, for everything was quiet here. I gave my deputy a wave to indicate that I was going off with Anhalt and hastened after him. I sat down in the rear seat next to SS-Second Lieutenant Triebes.

What neither I nor my regimental commander realised was that the Russians now had the heavy siege artillery ready to fire on the city centre. They would not need many targets, as they could not miss in the city centre. Each shot would be a direct hit, whether on German soldiers or innocent civilians. The buildings would collapse like houses of cards, the roofs of the S-Bahn and U-Bahn tunnels would be broken and numerous people killed by these super shells.

Meanwhile we drove via Hermann-Göring-Strasse, past the Brandenburg Gate, which was barricaded up so that we could not pass through, and stopped in Kleine Mauerstrasse between the Unter den Linden and Behrenstrasse, as Anhalt did not want to travel so openly to Alexanderplatz when the shells started landing. I too was happier on foot and going through tunnels, as it had become very risky. So I left them and went ahead to warn Mrugalla of our arrival.

When we got to the Police Presidium, the adjutant sent off a runner to get Mrugalla. As the others failed to appear, I went back to see what had happened to them.

I found Anhalt lying at the place where I had left him. A large shell splinter had penetrated his lungs from behind, killing him. His escort seemed to have disappeared.

Instinctively, I removed his papers, decorations, etc. and went off to get a stretcher and assistance, as one cannot leave an SS-Colonel lying around like a simple soldier. So I ran back under shell fire to the Police Presidium and got two men and a stretcher, but when I returned both Anhalt and his staff car had gone.

I returned to the Police Presidium and reported to SS-Captain Mrugalla, who had arrived in the meantime, and told him that now one of the two battalion commanders would have to take over command of the regiment. I also gave him Anhalt's effects.

There was nothing else for me to do there, so I set off back, but via the Villa Goebbels in order to clarify the matter of Anhalt's death.

I discovered that Anhalt had already been buried in the garden. The two escorts had already left, presumably to the Reichs Chancellery to collect SS-Major Wahl, who was now our regimental commander.

Wahl had a completely different background to the two battalion commanders, for he had been a unit commander and holder of the Knight's Cross in the 5th SS-Panzer Division 'Viking', but I did not know him myself. However, it was through this change in commanding officers that my promotion and award of the Knight's Cross fell through, not that it bothered me.

As I was returning to my troops via Leipziger Strasse, a mortar bomb, whose approach I had not heard, exploded in front of me on the roadway. A fragment hit me in the throat, blocking my airpipe so that I could hardly breathe. I crawled, for I did not have enough air to walk, back to our field hospital in the Hotel Adlon. There everything was overcrowded with the wounded lying on top of instead of alongside each other. The splinter was removed, my throat bandaged up and luckily I was also given an anti-tetanus injection. I left quickly, depressed by so much misery.

When I returned to Potsdamer Platz, the work went on. The Potsdamer Strasse entrance had received a direct hit from a heavy shell, which had destroyed the concrete steps and exposed the earth below, making it ideal for setting up our mortars. We could now fire our high trajectory weapons safe from all but a direct hit.

The battalion commander came along and said that we should start using our rockets. that was why we had brought them. 'But where?' I asked him, for it was stupid demanding something like this. There was no concentration of enemy tanks to aim at such as we had had at the Schlesischer Station. There were only the weasly enemy scouts around that were becoming ever more cheeky as they wriggled their way through our thinly manned positions. Every runner emerging into the open was being shot at, as happened to me when I was returning from taking out stragglers to the forward positions. I was a dead shot and picked off a small group of scouts with my captured sub-machine gun. I asked a survivor: 'What interests you here?' and got a surprising reply. These Russians had the mad idea of capturing Hitler, whom in their innocence they believed was hidden somewhere around here. They had come to collect him and fly him back to Stalin, who would award them with a medal and send them home on leave. We could only laugh at this simplicity, as if the bodyguards would allow anyone to get near to Hitler. They would rather let themselves be hacked to pieces first.

But others too had silly ideas. Grand Admiral Dönitz, for instance, sent some specially selected sailors to Berlin to guard Hitler. When they landed at Gatow they were immediately brought to the Reichs Chancellery, but what could Mohnke do with them? There were enough guards there already, apart from the SD. So Mohnke sent them to the Reichstag to fill the gap that the Russians fortunately had not discovered. Unfortunately these sailors were not adequately equipped for combat, having come from an honour guard and a radar school, for it was thought that they would be only used as an honour guard at the Reichs Chancellery. However, despite the senior ranks of the naval officers accompanying them, they subordinated themselves to SS-Lieutenant Babick, who had had combat experience under Joachim Peiper, even though he had nothing higher than an Iron Cross First Class.[11]

I had now sent out two of my NCOs as forward observers, one covering the area Hallisches Tor-Möckern Bridge, the other the area Potsdamer Bridge-Lützowplatz. They both came back at night when there was nothing further to see. But they too could not offer any targets for the rockets, and we could not use these weapons for shooting at sparrows.

However, the pressure from the Reichs Chancellery continued to increase, and I had to do something to please my superiors, sitting in their bombproof cellars with no consideration for the civilian population. The rockets would only destroy their homes, burying them under the rubble. No, I would not do that. If I was not hitting the enemy, I had to find a target where I would not do any damage.

So I went into the Tiergarten where the tanks of the 'Nordland' under the command of the brave SS-Lieutenant Colonel Peter Kausch were located. When I explained my problem to him he clapped me on the shoulder and said: 'You are quite right. Those gentlemen are shitting themselves.' He pulled out his tanks and I fired two rockets into the vacated area. None of my superiors noticed, as they were not going to stick their heads outside. Following my report, all these gentlemen were content and left me in peace.

As I was curious how things were going, I used my wound as an excuse to visit the Reichs Chancellery almost every day, although I had our own nurses do the bandaging. There were about 1,500 wounded lying in the cellars almost on top of each other. The doctors bustled about tending to them with carbide lamps as only the Führerbunker had its own electricity supply. At least there was enough to eat, as well as sufficient supplies of other kinds. We could also get mortar bombs from there, but the shells for the artillery were almost finished, and once Gatow Airfield had fallen there were no more. Consequently the German artillery fire became ever weaker.

With regard to artillery, a one-armed army lieutenant approached me. He had two 105 mm guns but had lost contact with his unit, and was looking for another unit to attach himself to. With my battalion commander's permission, we combined forces. He still had some ammunition for his guns, which he had brought with him. We put them under cover down below with us. If a super shell burst through the roof now, we would all be blown to smithereens. These Wehrmacht soldiers stuck with us to the end and we worked well together, including our forward observers.

The military police now wanted me to send my Volkssturm men forward into action. Despite my protests, they said: 'No one can afford to sit around doing nothing any more. Send them into action somewhere.'

I suggested they comb out the Reichs Chancellery, where there were plenty of Party officials doing nothing, but they protested that that was not their job. These obnoxious types, whom every front line soldier hated, went off grumbling, but I realised that I would have to find something useful for my Volkssturm men to do.

I had asked the women that had established themselves on the station platforms with their children how we could help them. They said that they were hungry, for no one supplied them with anything, but that the worst thing was thirst. There was no water available down below as the system was out of order, and they were going crazy with thirst.

So we collected all the containers we could and set off to search for water. There were still some street water pumps in Berlin that had not been been used for years but were relatively intact. When we found one at last, the water carrying role began. Once I told my men that we would carry on doing this, there was no more wrangling about water. Of course, anyone attempting to use the water for washing would have been lynched, and men under 60 had to fend for themselves, but the Volkssturm men remained undisturbed in their task, for the women would have beaten up the military police mercilessly if they had intervened.

In the meantime the Russians had moved forward up to the Landwehr Canal on one side of the Tiergarten and up to the Spree on the other. Now we had targets enough, except in the Tiergarten where our own forces lay, and especially round the Zoo bunker, whose anti-aircraft guns were now engaged in the land battle.

On 27 April I took another group of stragglers up to Belle-Alliance-Platz (Mehringplatz), but found no one there to hand them over to, so I appointed the senior serving soldier in charge of the mob, which is all you could call them, set them on guard and went back. I could see that they would run when the first Russian appeared, but I hoped that there would still be some of our comrades around in the ruins that would take them on. The companies were now a complete mixture of different kinds of combatants. Often the stragglers made their way back, only to be rounded up and sent forward again like cattle to the slaughter. Among them I recognised some familiar faces, but I played dumb and pretended not to notice.

On my way back I made a detour to check on my forward observer, who was located on top of a tall building, but when I got there the building had gone. A super shell must have demolished it. I thought that he must have had a quick death and could not have suffered much.

It so happened that another group of stragglers had been rounded up for me to deliver to the same area. By some fluke, I was taking them past the pile of rubble under which my comrade was buried, when we heard groans. I stormed into the rubble, assisted by the others, and found the unconscious comrade about two metres down. We carried him back to Potsdamer Platz, where we handed him over to our nurses, who kept him with them rather than take him to the field hospital. 'We will soon have him back on his feet,' they said, 'and he will be among familiar faces.' And they were quite right. I took my group of stragglers back to the assigned area, and by the time I had returned he had regained consciousness. The shell had struck like lightning and he could remember nothing about it, but all he had suffered was a bruised head and some other contusions. He had been extremely lucky.

On 28 April I went across to the Reichs Chancellery again, overtly to liaise, but in fact trying to get some idea of the overall situation. As I was about to enter the gate off Hermann-Göring-Strasse, I bumped into my old company comrade, Bruno Weinke. Some years before Bruno had been promoted over me, but he was then transferred to the Führer Escort where there were no promotions, so I now outranked him, and there he was standing on sentry duty like an ordinary soldier. He engaged me in discussion about the war situation, which he said he knew about first-hand, for the walls of the Führerbunker were not so thick that nothing got through. Backstairs gossip, I thought, but listened, not wanting to be rude. He told me of Hitler's plan for the decisive battle of Berlin that would bring about a major change in the war. General Busse, who was southeast of Berlin with his 9th Army, had been ordered to break through the enveloping arms of Marshal Koniev's 1st Ukrainian Front, thus cutting through his lines of communication and causing chaos, and then push through to Berlin.

(What no one here knew was that Busse's young, inexperienced soldiers lying quiet and still in the Halbe woods were currently being shot up like rabbits by Koniev's tanks and that the remainder, mainly armoured units, were not breaking through to Berlin but to General Wenck's 12th Army.)

The Führer had great hopes in Wenck's 12th Army, he said.

Since it had been pulled back from the line of the Elbe, assembled and directed on Berlin, its armoured spearheads had reached Treuenbrietzen and tank gunfire had been heard in Potsdam. I said to Bruno: 'I hear the news but I lack the faith. I got to know those divisions on the Elbe and they consist merely of emergency units. They may have proud names but I do not believe they have anything beyond that. I have met these troops and I simply do not believe that they can get us out of this mess.'

Then Bruno went on about SS-General Steiner and his IIIrd Germanic SS-Panzer Corps. I had more confidence in an SS-general. In accordance with Hitler's orders, he was supposed to be attacking down from the north in the Oranienburg-Eberswalde area to our relief. But I no longer believed in miracles, so I left Weinke at his post and went on my way.

Gatow Airfield was lost on 27 April, despite a desperate defence. This was a bitter blow for the defence of the capital, as most of the ammunition was being flown in through there. An attempt was next made to use part of the East-West-Axis as an airstrip, but this only lasted a short while. Some of the incoming transport aircraft were shot down by enemy fighters and others crashed into shell holes.

THE BATTLE FOR THE MOLTKE BRIDGE

The main Soviet attack was directed at the Reichstag, which we could not understand as it had been in ruins since the fire of 1933. The assault was conducted by Colonel General V.I. Kutznetsov's 3rd Shock Army's 79th Rifle Corps, commanded by Major General S.I. Perevertkin, and led to the Moltke Bridge.

As the situation heated up, our companies deployed near the bridge called for reinforcement, for they were spread out in two-man holes fifty metres apart.

We had not fired in this area until then, but now I had to send a forward observer to direct fire. The area around the bridge was to be brought under fire upon demand. My battalion commander suggested I withdraw an observer from the Potsdamer Bridge, which I did, but I still had the big problem of having to take our stragglers forward several times a day, which was getting on my

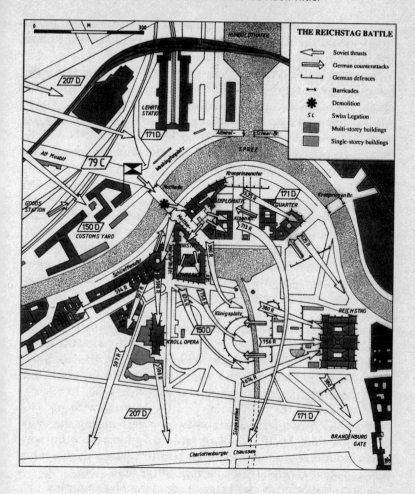

nerves. So I convinced the battalion commander that the fire direction would be so difficult there that I should do it myself, and that the NCO I had withdrawn should remain at base. My battalion commander did not like this, but I told him that I could not go on dividing my responsibilities. He should look for someone among the unemployed eaters walking around to take over the stragglers from me. Why, for instance, did we need a Duty Officer on our level? We could keep order ourselves. And my men should remain here, ready to form an instant storm troop should the Russians break through. (I did not want them used up, but kept back for the final battle.)

Whether he liked it or not, he must have taken me seriously, for there were no reserves left to deal with such a situation except ourselves. So he left and made no more objections.

I was important in this situation, because I was apparently the only one who could handle the rockets. The buck had been passed to me and my comrades. Goodness knows what had happened to the real owners.

When Kurt Abicht, the battery sergeant major, saw what I was up to, he decided to come along with me as a forward observer. We had become friends in the meantime, which happens quickly under such circumstances; one soon sees what the other is made of. He had absolutely no problems in his relationship with his battery commander, but had been feeling hemmed in and wanted to get out. He was also experienced, about the same age as myself and with the same way of speaking his mind in front of superiors.

The gunners had a radio, but it was needed by their forward observer, who had been sharing a nest close to the Potsdamer Bridge with the observer I had withdrawn. They had used the radio together, but now he would direct fire for both our resources with it, while Kurt would use my field cable.

So we set off for the Ministry of the Interior with my HQ Section NCO, two signallers and two runners during the early evening of 28 April. We were able to go part of the way underground by tunnel, but then had to make a dash across Königsplatz in daylight while paying out the field cable.

At the Ministry of the Interior, an extensive complex like a road block in front of the Moltke Bridge, a police colonel was in charge with his command post in a bunker in the cellars. This man straight away wanted to give me orders and we had a heated argument. I told him that my only interest in his building was as a good viewpoint over the bridge. I wanted to know why he had not sent some of his men to reinforce our positions at the bridge, but he would not be moved. This question caused him to howl with rage and brought a hollow laugh from Kurt and my men.

So we left and went across to the Diplomatic Quarter that filled the bend in the Spree. The embassies should have been left in peace, but neither side had time for that.

We found ourselves inside the deserted Swiss Legation, which had been burning for days and had a bombproof cellar that had been deepened and reinforced with concrete. With the steel door closed behind us, we soon warmed up. Outside it was still relatively cold at night, but here the heat from the fires came through the thick concrete walls.

Once we had warmed ourselves up, we looked for a building with a view of the bridge and the Customs Offices behind on the left. As it was quite dark at the time, I cannot say which building it was. Once the field cable was ready, we fired the first rocket, which landed across on Washingtonplatz to the right of the bridge. I gave the corrections, which could only be done roughly, as previously explained.

Then Kurt fired his guns, taking the bridge as his target. His battery commander had gone with a liaison officer from our battalion to the Reichs Chancellery to ask for shells. As the liaison officer sent by our battalion commander confirmed that he was firing from only two hundred metres, he got what he wanted.

My Volkssturm men then carried the shells across at night. It was relatively quiet at night as our opponents had other things to do and even their snipers disappeared.

Now we fired our mortars at the bridge as well, which was easier than with rockets. If I am not mistaken, this was at their maximum range. Hardly a shot came back from the other side, which made me suspect that they were up to something. Whenever a rocket hit Washingtonplatz there was such turmoil and running about, it was as if we had disturbed a hornets' nest. I later discovered that their artillery was fully deployed there in the open without any cover whatsoever. We heard more than we saw, because only the odd fire lit the scene.

The Spree was about fifty metres wide at this point with embankments walled with hewn stone rising about three metres above the level of the water. The bridge was also of hewn stone and had four arches spanning the Spree. Although the bridge was massively constructed it had already been badly damaged.

There were barricades built at either end of the bridge, but the one on the enemy side had been bulldozed aside.

As the enemy planned a surprise attack, this was not announced by an opening barrage that would have alerted us. The infantry attack began suddenly. According to Russian accounts this was made by a battalion each from the 150th and 171st Rifle Divisions, which stormed across the bridge toward us.

The machine guns of our two companies, which had been reinforced in the meantime by sailors, hacked away with steady fire. On their first attempt the infantry stuck on the barbed wired barricade at our end of the bridge. I was directing mortar fire to hail down on the bridge and my friend Kurt was using his guns to send shells ricocheting along it. They tried to withdraw, but none got away, for as they withdrew they were hit several times by the fine splinters from the mortar bombs and Kurt's ricochets ripping across the bridge, throwing bodies into the river with their blast.

Meanwhile a whole battery of rockets had been set up on Potsdamer Platz and I had them directed on Washintongplatz and the Customs Yard. I later learnt that General Perevertkin had his forward command post there, where he could observe the attack at close hand, but there is no mention of the effects of the rockets in the books. I only hope that they scared the pants off him and his divisional commanders.

Now bulldozer tanks rolled on to the bridge, scraping the dead and injured aside and then pushing aside the barricade at our end. Kurt's ricochets soon turned them into scrap. Anti-tank guns had joined in from our side as well as the 'Nordland's' tanks from the Tiergarten. Then the heavy anti-aircraft guns on the Zoo flak-tower also opened fire once they could see a little from the fires on the bridge, and a vast heap of scrap metal formed, blocking the way for the new tanks rolling forward.

Fresh infantry stormed the bridge and were able to form a small bridgehead on our side. Now the officials from the Ministry of the Interior went into action, frantically pouring fire from their windows with their old MG 34s.[12] They defended their building like a fortress, for they knew what their fate would be as 'Himmler's people', and were bypassed at first.

The Diplomatic Quarter was barely defended, for we wanted

to respect the neutrality of the embassies as much as possible, something which did not bother the Soviets. This was now stormed by the 171st Rifle Division. It was like the breaching of a dam; there was no holding them back. Russian artillery of all calibres was laying down a barrage on us that left a clear path for their infantry in the centre. We could hardly lift our heads to fight them off. Now I could see that their artillery was not just on Washingtonplatz but also deployed on the Customs Yard with self-propelled guns behind, all firing without cover. However, once it became light, this was not so good for them. Guns of all sizes opened up on them from the Zoo Flak-tower. I had not seen the heavy anti-aircraft guns in action before. They did not simply hit a tank, but blew it apart, especially when catching it in the flank as was the case here.

The piles of scrap metal grew higher, especially on the far bank, but this did not deter the enemy, who simply brought fresh tank regiments in from his reserve like a cardsharper pulling aces from his sleeve.

But now we started to counterattack, and on both sides of the river. From our side we saw some close-quarter fighting suddenly start up among the guns, so the troops on our side attacked too. The Russian infantry in their small bridgehead thus came under fire from both sides, so most of them just kept their heads down, as I charged forward with my men.

Green Verey lights were fired to warn the Zoo Flak-tower to stop firing. Normally this would have meant the opposite, but fortunately the flak-tower gunners understood straight away and held their fire.

But how was it that German troops had so suddenly appeared on the other side of the river? They were in fact men of the Colonel Harry Herrmann's 9th Parachute Division that had been defending the Lehrter Station and had been cut off in the goods station area. The Russians had overlooked them in their haste to cross the Spree and get to the Reichstag. Now they were using the opportunity to take the Russians by surprise from behind, putting many of the gun crews to flight and creating chaos before charging across the bridge to us.

A demolition team was quickly assembled to blow the bridge at last but, because of the haste and the Russian fire, they succeeded only in causing half of one span of the bridge to fall in the water. To try again was too dangerous as the Russians immediately seized the bridge again, the generals driving their men on. We could hear their hysterical cries from where we were.

Unfortunately the success of the counter-attack soon came to nothing, as we had been unable to drive the Russians out of the Diplomatic Quarter. There were too many of them. Also by this time they were filled with an immense sense of victory, knowing just as we did that this was their final battle of the war.

Now the fighting turned on the Ministry of the Interior, or 'Himmler's House' as the Russians called it, which the occupants defended virtually to the last man.

Then a runner arrived from the battalion commander with instructions for me to report back to Potsdamer Platz immediately. By this time our field cable had been shot through in several places and was useless. I was not unhappy to be called away, as I did not fancy having to fight alongside such a strange and unfriendly unit as that of the Ministry of the Interior. My friend Kurt Abicht thought the same, but I offered to lay a new field cable for him if he remained as our forward observer. However, I took back with me Alfred, my HQ Section leader, and the two runners. I got on with Alfred best of all my NCOs and liked to have him with me. He had no respect for anyone or anything and provided a witty Berliner commentary on events.

Back below in the depths of the Potsdamer Platz S-Bahn Station we received a warm welcome not only from our comrades, but also from the battalion commander himself. Here too things had heated up, and it seemed that he was afraid the Russians would burst in at any moment. Apart from my men, he had no one he could use in a close combat role. The civilians could easily panic and hinder or even prevent a defence, and should that occur, I would be the one who knew best what to do.

I was therefore to remain here, first constructing barricades on the upper level behind which we could entrench ourselves and conduct an all-round defence. Should the Russians break in, they would have to be dealt with quickly. We did not know from which entrance the Russians were likely to appear, so we had to have an all-round defence.

Meanwhile, above on the square, a vast scrap yard had formed of burnt-out abandoned vehicles and shot-up equipment strewn everywhere.

My attention now turned to our sector from Belle-Alliance-Platz to the Potsdamer Bridge. The situation at the bridge was still as previously described with an aerial mine suspended from either side and the bridge unblown. The bridge was stormed by the 79th Guards Rifle Division, supported by tanks of the 11th Tank Corps. Sappers had first to neutralise the mines, which cost them heavy casualties from our machine guns. We also fired our mortars and rockets as directed by our forward observer in the immediate vicinity, whose radio worked perfectly.

The Russians later made a big thing of the story that a child crying for its mother was rescued by the standard bearer of the 220th Guards Rifle Regiment at the risk of his own life, but the forward observer reported nothing of this and I think that it was just another one of their propaganda stories.[13]

The enemy infantry first advance under cover of a smokescreen, which enabled them to establish a small bridgehead. Then the tanks tried a new trick that our comrades fell for. The first tanks were shot up by the 'Nordland' tanks firing from the Tiergarten, where they were immobilised for lack of fuel. The Soviet tanks had protected themselves with sheet metal and other items against Panzerfausts, so one of them threw sacking over these projections and soaked it with fuel then set it alight to make the tank appear as if it had been hit, which enabled it to get across and take up position without being fired at.

Simultaneously the infantry of the 39th Guards Rifle Division swam across the canal and got up the embankment, while the 12th Motorised Rifle Brigade did the same thing at the Möckern Bridge U-Bahn Station and were suddenly on our side of the canal. Our defending troops were taken by surprise, but counterattacked vigorously and drove some of the Russians back into the canal. Unfortunately not everywhere, only where we had energetic leaders.

Further to the east at the Hallesche Tor the Russians were able to get some tanks across by means of pontoons, but as soon as they got their tracks on to firm ground tank destroyer units engaged and destroyed most of them.

The Russians could no longer use their aircraft against us as the lines were too close, barely two metres separating the antagonists in some places. In some buildings the Russians fought from the lower stories with Germans above them, and I would have to clear the lower stories myself before handing over my stragglers. My British sub-machine gun proved excellent for this close quarter fighting. At a range of thirty metres it was the best weapon going. Hardly any prisoners were taken under these circumstances.

Every reinforcement was gladly received by my comrades, who also welcomed the food and ammunition we brought with us. It was not so easy replacing defective machine guns. We had established an armourer's workshop in one of the S-Bahn carriages, but it was usually only possible to assemble one effective machine gun out of two defective ones.

The night of 28 April heavy fighting took place around Leipziger Strasse and Prinz-Albrecht-Strasse, where the Gestapo HQ was strongly defended. The Russians tried to break through here and succeeded briefly but the Gestapo counterattacked and regained their building. I always gave this area a wide berth to avoid these gentlemen laying their hands on me, and now they were having to fight for their lives.

29 April came and we were having to hold on to our positions and conduct counterattacks, all to little effect. We only knew through rumours of the big political decisions being made in the Reichs Chancellery, so I went across to see what I could find out. The battalion commander and his staff came with me. He too was not informed of what was going on, being too junior, but SS-Brigadier Mohnke was well informed, having had two meetings with Hitler that day. He told Hitler that the Russians were already at Potsdamer Platz and in the tunnels under Voss-Strasse, but that was not true, for the area around was still firmly in our hands.

The Russians finished their assault on the Ministry of the Interior at about 0400 hours on 30 April. I had had to send a forward observer back there, for the battalion commander had forbidden me to go myself. I had told my NCOs on no account to let themselves become cut off in the Ministry of the Interior. If the Russians found their field cable they would cut it and render it useless. So they went to the Swiss Legation building and stayed there until forced out by the 171st Rifle Division clearing the western half of the Diplomatic Quarter.

We had now used up the last of our mortar bombs and there were no more available, so I sent a runner to recall my men. I also recalled the observer from our left flank for the same reason. Now that we were 'unemployed', I used my NCOs for taking forward stragglers, and from the reports they brought me on their return I gained the following picture. The Russians had occupied both sides of Leipziger Strasse and had also occupied the Anhalter Station. The pressure was increasing as they closed in from all sides. The Zoo Bunker and its surrounding area was cut off from us and formed its own 'pocket'. Several stragglers from there got through the Russian positions to us at night and reported that barricades in the area manned by Hitler Youth and Volkssturm had been attacked by the Russians using 45mm guns at point blank range and then the Russians had forced civilians out of their cellars to clear them under German fire. Now that things had hotted up at the Zoo bunker, some of the civilians sheltering there had been driven out, thousands suddenly emerging into the open looking for cover and protection, and had come under fire from the Russians as they left the bunker.[14] Some of them got through to us and reported how terrible conditions were inside the bunker. There was hardly any air to breathe, the guns were constantly firing, and the screams of people breaking down under the strain made it unbearable. In contrast to the Zoo bunker they found the conditions in our tunnels quite pleasant. Even though there was not much room, they could still walk about and move around a bit. We had to supply these newcomers with water too, but there they had only received a mouthful from time to time.

THE BATTLE FOR THE REICHSTAG

This was a real battle in itself. I cannot describe it from my own experience but only from that of surviving combatants and also Russian reports, although the latter should be treated with great caution.

The commander of the defence at the Reichstag was SS-Lieutenant Babick of our battalion, who came from the same 2nd Regiment of the 'Leibstandarte Adolf Hitler' as I did, where he had previously commanded the 11th Company of our 3rd Battalion. After hospitalisation he had taken over the Potential Leaders Company at Spreenhagen in February 1945. I am not sure, but I think it was that company that he had at the Reichstag. The company was about 100 strong and he received no more support from our battalion commander. To this can be added the 250 sailors that had been flown in though, as previously mentioned, these men were not properly equipped for combat. We called them 'The Dönitz Contribution' and the accompanying naval officers acted as his platoon and section leaders. Then came the company of paratroopers from the 9th Parachute Division, plus the approximately 100 Volkssturm stragglers that I brought him. So in all Babick had a force of no more than 550 combatants at his disposal, as opposed to the 5,000 attributed to him by the Russians.

An all-round defence was established and Babick set up his command post in a cellar behind the Reichstag, from where there were several underground tunnels leading to other buildings. The Reichstag itself had been walled up after the 1933 fire, presumably to prevent further arson attempts.

The Russian attack began with a massive artillery barrage. As the attacking infantry of the 150th Rifle Division wheeled left out of the Ministry of the Interior building, it came under strong flanking fire from the fortified Kroll Opera House, the 'Nordland' tanks in the Tiergarten and Zoo Flak-tower. The attack had been launched immediately after securing the Ministry of the Interior, by which time the division had been reduced to only two regiments, without time for either rest or reconnaissance, and it soon foundered. Meanwhile the 171st Rifle Division had launched an attack on the eastern half of the Diplomatic Quarter across Alsenstrasse with an equal lack of success and at a heavy cost.

The corps commander, realising he would have to clear the Kroll Opera House, called in his reserve 207th Rifle Division, which had first to clear the lightly defended Schlieffenufer block alongside the Spree in order to get at the Opera House. The

Russians were under tremendous pressure as Stalin wanted the Red Flag hoisted on top of the Reichstag in time for the May Day celebrations. Additional artillery, tanks and rocket launchers were brought across to reinforce the Ministry of the Interior building in preparation for the next attack.

The second Soviet attack stalled on the line of a cutting for a U-Bahn tunnel that ran across Königsplatz to the Diplomatic Quarter and was not shown on the Russians' maps. This abandoned worksite was flooded and its depth and steep sides made it an ideal anti-tank obstacle, which had naturally been incorporated into the defensive system.

Although the 171st Rifle Division managed to secure the eastern half of the Diplomatic Quarter as far as the Kronprinzen Bridge, the 150th Rifle Division stuck fast on the line of the ditch under heavy fire from the Reichstag, so it was decided to await the cover of darkness for the final assault.

With nightfall at about 1800 hours, the Russian tanks became invisible to the Zoo Flak-tower and were able to get round the flooded ditch to give support to the infantry storming the building. The infantry used mortars firing horizontally to blast a small hole in the bricked-up doorway and, supported by the fire from the supporting tanks and self-propelled guns, were able to enter the building itself, where merciless close-quarter fighting broke out, gradually spreading over the various stories of this vast building. But it was very dark inside, which placed the newcomers at a serious disadvantage to the defenders who knew their way around.

The military council of the 3rd Shock Army had issued a special Flag No. 5 for this historical occasion and sent it forward under an escort of Communist Party members. Two sergeants were able to slip through and find a way up to the roof and hoist the flag. The official account and the photographs and filming taken next day to commemorate the event for posterity, showed them holding the flag against one of the pepperpot-like ornaments on the rear parapet of the building overlooking the Brandenburg Gate, with the claim that this had occurred seventy minutes before May Day. The two sergeants were awarded the golden stars of 'Hero of the Soviet Union' for their deed. However, it later transpired that the first Red Flag to be hoisted over the Reichstag was in fact raised by an artillery captain on a statue above the front entrance well before midnight, whereas the sergeants had been two hours into May Day and had used an equestrian statue over the rear entrance as their prop. The photographer then made them change location because of the lack of background establishing the site, resulting in the famous picture that was published round the world. The captain received only the 'Order of the Red Banner' for his pains.

Fighting continued inside the building all day on 1 May and until 1300 hours on 2 May, when General Weidling's order to surrender reached the survivors, who had by then been cut off from us for over thirty-six hours. Meanwhile, Soviet flame-throwers had started a fire within the building whose choking smoke made conditions even worse.

The attacking 79th Rifle Corps later claimed to have taken 2,000 prisoners and counted 2,500 German dead in these assaults on the Reichstag, Diplomatic Quarter, Schlieffenufer, Moltke Bridge and Kroll Opera House, but these figures are wildly exaggerated, as I have shown. Their own war memorial built close to the site significantly contains the bodies of 2,200 soldiers presumably killed in this same action.

THE BREAK-OUT FROM FRIEDRICHSTRASSE

The one-armed lieutenant, followed by Kurt Abicht and his men, came down to see me. He said that both his guns were now useless scrap and he thought that we were finished. My mortars were also useless for lack of bombs, and our rockets had long since been used up. We were now just simple infantrymen. We still had our machine gun with six hundred rounds and plenty of ammunition for our sub-machine guns, but that was all.

Losses among my own men had been thankfully few. This may have been because I preferred to do things myself rather than endanger others, but I cannot be sure. One of the sergeants had been wounded when he was buried under debris, but he could move around easily enough and was back on light duties.

As usual I went up to our barricades on the upper level on the night of 1/2 May. We still had not organised a shock troop, as we had been ordered from above, but fortunately we were spared this, and now we had been reinforced in our positions by the one-armed lieutenant and his men. Though they were not armed for close combat like ourselves, we now numbered about sixty in all. Claiming that he was no infantryman, the lieutenant handed over command to me.

I converted a former ticket office cabin into a quiet corner for myself and settled down there to doze. Suddenly a runner appeared with orders for the lieutenant and myself to report to the battalion commander. The lieutenant took along his battery sergeant major Kurt Abicht, and I took two of my Hitler Youths as runners. As usual they were as keen as mustard.

When we got to the command post on the lower level we found the battalion commander and his staff sitting there in the former platform guard's office with faces that looked pale and distraught in the candlelight. Schäfer said to his adjutant: 'Right, SS-Lieutenant Krönke, we are all here, you can begin.'

When I asked about the missing company commanders, Schäfer said; 'We don't need them at the moment. SS-Lieutenant Krönke has just returned from an order group with SS-Brigadier Mohnke at the Reichs Chancellery.'

Krönke read out what he said were the Führer's last orders. We were thanked for our loyalty to the Führer and released from our oath to him. We were then informed about the new government that was to be formed, of which still in Berlin were Dr Josef Goebbels, the new Reichs Chancellor, and Martin Bormann, the Party Minister. Anyone could now go if they so wished.

However, SS-Brigadier Mohnke had cancelled the latter statement with written orders for a break-out of all Waffen-SS troops under his command to go north from Friedrichstrasse. General Weidling's Army troops would break out to the west to join up with General Wenck's forces. SS-General Steiner would thrust toward us with his divisions and take us on to join our friends the Americans.

(This sounded odd to me, for I had never heard of such 'friends' before. Only six months before these 'friends' had killed my parents with a direct hit by a bomb on their country home.) Mohnke would lead the break-out from Friedrichstrasse himself, according to these orders.

It was only then that it sunk in that Hitler had already been dead thirty hours. It had been kept secret, the adjutant told us, so that the front would not collapse. Goebbels had wanted to negotiate a ceasefire with the Soviets. When I asked about Goebbels, I was told that he had had SS-Colonel Rattenhuber shoot his wife and himself.

I then asked about Martin Bormann, and was told that Bormann was now the highest ranking party official in Berlin and had nominated Mohnke to lead the break-out.

Now Schäfer issued his orders. We were to go through the S-Bahn tunnels as far as was possible, which would be partly under enemy lines. As the tunnels did not run directly to Friedrichstrasse S-Bahn Station, we would climb up a certain emergency exit and continue above ground to the station, where we would wait for Mohnke to issue further orders.

I now asked about our companies up forward. 'They will follow on later, but will first have to cover our withdrawal,' Schäfer said. 'You and the lieutenant can come with us, but your men will have to stay and cover our rear, or the Russians will get us from behind.'

I did not like the idea of leaving without my men, and neither did the lieutenant, so I said to the battalion commander: 'You alone are answerable for your companies, but I will not go one step from here without my men.'

The lieutenant said the same.

I went on: 'So I will stay here until you have gone. No Russians will get you from behind.'

'Oh no!' said Schäfer, 'I need you for your close combat experience in the break-out!'

'And with whom am I going to break out, if not with my men?' I asked. 'With a crowd like this, virtually unknown to me, it will not work. They would run round me like a flock of sheep!'

'I had not thought of it like that,' said Schäfer. 'As far as I am concerned, do as you like. As usual you have the last word!'

I then gave orders to my Hitler Youths, who were standing there with their mouths wide open at this discussion. One of them was told to blow up the two remaining mortars immediately with hand grenades and to return as quickly as possible with the gunners. The lieutenant nodded his approval.

The other one was told to go to our S-Bahn carriages and, if any of our men were there, to get them out with some excuse and send them back here. I used this ruse to avoid having the women and Volkssturm joining us in the break-out.

Kurt Abicht explained to these Volkssturm men what we intended doing. They should discard their armbands and caps and become proper civilians again. I also persuaded my Hitler Youths to go back home. At least they would be held in their mothers' arms once more, even if the mothers of those that had been killed cursed me.

Then I thrust aside the quartermaster standing distraught outside his S-Bahn wagon loaded with supplies and forced my way in. I sought and found boxes of 'Schokolada' and threw them on to the platform, where some burst open, sending the cans rolling around. I looked for some schnapps and found some cases of 'Aqua-Witt', a brand sometimes issued to the common soldier as part of his rations, and placed two of them on the platform. Meanwhile my men had gathered round wondering what was happening. 'Don't ask too many questions,' I said. 'Take as much 'Schokolada' as you can, as it will be the only nourishment you get during the next few days. Then everyone take a bottle of schnapps, but only one! You can all take one gulp, but keep the rest in case someone is wounded, when it will help ease the pain.'

They eagerly did what I said, as did the gunners. Then we set off. I led with my men. The torch batteries had all been exhausted, so I held a burning tallow candle in my hand.

We found the right emergency exit from the tunnel and we climbed up into the open air without having taken a step in the wrong direction. We then went across to Friedrichstrasse Station, where thousands of people had gathered. Instead of just Waffen-SS as had been planned, there were soldiers of all arms of the service standing around waiting for the breakthrough to start, even women. Some were secretaries from government offices with their chiefs, but there were also officers with their wives on their arms, which would handicap them in any fighting.

I am not sure of the exact time, but it must have been about midnight and everything was quiet at the Weidendammer Bridge except for the murmuring of the crowd. Our battalion had formed a circle and were discussing the situation. I kept apart, even though they wanted my opinion. There was no point. I had never been in such a situation before and my fighting experience was of no value here. The one-armed lieutenant was bored with it all. He did not feel himself bound to Mohnke's orders, and said to me: 'We will find our own way out. Good luck to you.'

I wished him and his men the same, and they left. I saw him again twelve years later, for they did not get through and had to tread the bitter road to Siberia, where they spent the next five years.

It was all too quiet for my liking, and that made me suspicious. Why was it taking so long? Time was not on our side, I thought. I took my HQ Section leader by the arm and we went up Friedrichstrasse. I had learnt not to do things without first making a reconnaissance, and here nobody was getting ready. We got as far as Chausseestrasse, about 780 metres up Friedrichstrasse without coming under fire. Had I been free to do so, I would have taken my men and gone there and then, and with Alfred's local knowledge we probably would have got through without heavy casualties, but it was not my choice, I had to obey orders. The Russians did not appear to have noticed us and there could only have been some of their scouts in the neighbourhood.

So we returned to our startpoint, where the discussion was still going on. I pulled the battalion commander out of the group and told him what I had observed. 'Yes, yes,' he said: 'I have already realised that this is the weakest point where we will break through.'

The biggest mistake here, however, was hanging around waiting for the leadership. The Russian scouts must have realised what was happening and passed the word. Friedrichstrasse seems to have been the boundary between the 3rd and 5th Shock Armies. Apparently their scouts must have established contact here and the gap was not closed until after midnight.

Gradually the comrades from the outlying companies joined us. Whether they had been informed by runners, or just noticed that the battalion staff had gone, I cannot say, but one company commander knocked Schäfer down under circumstances I was not party to. The Reichs Chancellery people also began turning up at intervals, and from some comrades from the Führer Escort that I knew, I learnt something of what had gone on.

Dismay and panic had broken out among the many wounded that could not come along and had no weapons left to shoot themselves with. Where one had been hidden, it was passed around until the ammunition ran out. Others begged the doctors, Professors Werner Haase and Günther Schenk to give them fatal injections, but they had none to give. Even the bandages were having to be washed and used several times over.

After Goebbels's ADC, Schwägermann, had set fire to the bodies of Goebbels and his wife, he had sprinkled petrol over everything in the Führerbunker and set it alight so that the Russians would not find anything worthwhile. This again caused panic as people thought the fire was due to sabotage, and the smoke made conditions in the bunker even worse.

Apparently Mohnke himself had decided the composition of the groups that would leave the Reichs Chancellery at regular intervals. There had been no mention of a combined break-out, the situation we now had here. Whether this was intentional, or through misunderstanding, I have never been able to clarify.

While we were waiting for Mohnke, he was already long gone with his group, which consisted of about fifteen people, whose names I was later given by SS-Captain Heinrich Mundt. Those that I can remember were: SS-Major Günsche (Hitler's ADC), SS-Captain Klingmeier (Mohnke's Adjutant), who had previously commanded the Training & Field Replacement Battalion of the 'Leibstandarte' at Spreenhagen, SS-Captain Mundt, previously divisional quartermaster of the 'Leibstandarte', Professor Dr Schenk, Ambassador Hewel (Foreign Office representative at the Reichs Chancellery), SS-Lieutenant Stehr (Mohnke's liaison officer), Vice Admiral Voss (Naval representative at the Reichs Chancellery), Frau Junge and Frau Christian (Hitler's secretaries), Frau Krüger (Bormann's secretary) and Frau Manzialy (Hitler's cook), plus a few officers from Mohnke's staff and SS-Major Wahl, our new regimental commander, but I cannot be sure.

The inclusion of four women in this group shows that Mohnke had no intention of leading the break-out from the front. Apparently he had promised Hitler to bring the women out safely, and in this he was successful with three of them who got through to the west, but the very pretty Frau Manzialy vanished without trace.

As I learnt later, Mohnke's group had taken the following route. They first sprinted across the open Wilhelmplatz to the Kaiserhof U-Bahn Station, along the tunnel to Mitte U-Bahn Station, from where they took the northbound tunnel under Friedrichstrasse, but when they reached the level of the Spree they found their way blocked by a closed bulkhead door guarded by two railwaymen, whose duty was to close the door after the last train had passed through at night. Although no trains had run for over a week, the doors were still closed and they refused to open them. Stupidly Mohnke accepted this and turned back to Friedrichstrasse U-Bahn Station and went along the embankment until they came to a footbridge. When one of the escort made to turn toward the station where we were waiting, Mohnke said to him: 'No, not by Friedrichstrasse, all hell will break loose there soon!' How right he was!

Mohnke's group removed the barbed wire blocking the footbridge and crossed the river. They then tried to find their way toward the Lehrter Station, but when they reached Invalidenstrasse, where SS-Captain Mundt left them, they took a wrong turning and went up Chausseestrasse as far as the Maikäfer Barracks, where they encountered some difficulties but were able to get away, finally reaching the Patzenhofer Brewery where they rested.

Meanwhile, we were all waiting in vain for Mohnke. I went around the crowd and met some people I had not seen for years, but it was no time to chat, we were all too concerned with what might await us.

Then at last there was some movement. A lone King Tiger tank rolled up noisily with a defective track. I crossed the Spree and stopped a short distance behind the barricade there, whose right hand side was open. Then a self-propelled gun and an armoured personnel carrier drew up side by side behind it. Next five armoured personnel carriers drew up and lined up behind the others. In the second one I could see a figure in a cap and overcoat whom in the darkness I took to be Mohnke. I was further convinced it was him when SS-Captain Schäfer ran up to the vehicle and spoke with him, but I was some thirty metres away and could not hear what was said.

As I thought Schäfer would be leading his battalion out at the head of his men, I lined up behind the vehicles with my men. Then Schäfer ran back, banged on the door of the last vehicle and cllmbed in with his adjutant, SS-Lieutenant Krönke. Then Schäfer called out: 'Rogmann! Do you need an invitation? Climb in!'

I went up to the vehicle and said to him: 'You don't think I am going to drive off with you and leave my men behind, do you?'

He started to say something, but I interrupted him with: 'You can cross me off the list!'

The door slammed shut.

The officer I had taken for Mohnke was in fact SS-Major Ternedde, commander of the 'Norge' Regiment of the 'Nordland', and all the vehicles were from that division.

It was not only that I did not want to leave my men behind, but also because of my natural infantryman's reluctance to ride in those 'mobile coffins'. Even if my men had not been there, I would not have gone with him willingly. Breaking through with those vehicles in street fighting is a really risky business that is only lessened when they are surrounded and protected by infantry, as it is so easy to toss grenades into them from above and turn them into mass graves.

The armoured vehicles started moving forward and we formed up across the street beyond the barricade. The first rank consisted of machine gunners with their weapons on slings, all carrying fifty-round drum magazines. Apart from my machine gunner, I and my men followed in the second rank.

The armoured vehicles speeded up. We followed in quick time, but could not keep up and soon lost contact. We then came under infantry fire from the windows of the buildings on the right of the street and all the machine gunners returned the fire, spraying the front of the buildings. The din caused by a hundred machine guns firing simultaneously was enough to burst one's eardrums. Now tanks opened up on us from either side.

My men, who had all taken a second swig from their bottles before setting off, were in the mood to face death. I had not taken a second drink, knowing the feeling of indifference that strong alcohol brings, for in this kind of situation I had to be able to think for these inexperienced men and be able to react like lightning.

There was no sense of leadership in this mob. There were no

responsible officers. My men only obeyed me because they knew me and trusted me. They had only to catch my eye and signal, for shouting was no good in this din, to follow my orders. Literally thousands of people were thrusting blindly forward behind us. I had never seen such a primitive form of attack, being used to an empty battlefield in modern warfare. This was utter nonsense.

They were not just Waffen-SS behind us, and not just soldiers, but officers with their wives, even my former company commander SS-Lieutenant von Puttkamer with his heavily pregnant wife.

Meanwhile we had reached the level of Ziegelstrasse on our right, which was now full of Russian tanks that must have been alerted to our impending breakout by their scouts. With our incomprehensibly long wait we had given them plenty of time to form up, although the tank had been able to slip through, if a bit damaged. But the self-propelled gun and one of the armoured personnel carriers had been shot up as the other armoured vehicles passed though, as I saw no other wrecks around.

The Russians fired into our packed ranks as we stumbled forward without regard for our dead and wounded. My group was now in the lead. Then we came under fire from tanks in Johannisstrasse on our right, and the effect of high explosive shells bursting in our ranks was simply terrible. The advance came to a halt and thousands of people started streaming back. I had never seen such a fiasco.

However, we did not go with them. It was obvious that there would be another attempt, so we vanished like lightning into the buildings on our left, where we were safe. As we had been out in front, no one could prevent us stepping aside as we did. We were in front because in an attack that is the safest place to be, as experienced front line soldiers know.

So far my own men had suffered no casualties and were still sticking together. We waited for the inevitable second attempt, which was preceded by an armoured personnel carrier firing on all sides as it raced toward us, but it was only hastening to its fate, for it stopped and burst into flames, blocking the street for the other armoured vehicles following.

As those on foot reached us, we jumped out to resume the

lead. The street now lay full of dead and wounded, the armoured vehicles racing over them. While under cover in the buildings, we had met up with some experienced men from the 'Nordland' and even some parachutists. Enemy tanks appeared in front of us again and we tried to creep up under their fire to knock them out in order to get past, but fresh tanks appeared behind them from the right and sprayed those in front with machine gun fire, the ricochets causing heavy casualties among us. Practically the whole of my platoon was hit by this fire, which broke up the attack, sending the masses streaming back again.

We pulled our wounded into the cover of the buildings and bandaged them up as best we could. I used my bottle of schnapps to pour courage into them. I realised that the whole business was hopeless. The Russians had been reinforced and when another crowd moved up they were slaughtered before my eyes.

We did not take any further part in this massacre. I worked out that the leadership had driven off, abandoning us, so I owed them no further allegiance and must save my own life and those of my few remaining unwounded men. We had to leave our wounded behind, which made my heart bleed, for it was for the first time in this war. So I said farewell to them, encouraging them by saying that the opposing Russians were also front line troops and would not do anything to them. I told them to remove their SS runes and make themselves unidentifiable as Waffen-SS, to get rid of all their documents and paybooks, and then they would be taken to hospital and treated as normal Wehrmacht soldiers.

Only two unwounded men remained, Alfred, my HQ Section leader, and a runner. During a pause in the firing we crept back to the Weidendammer Bridge together. I cannot describe the horror that lay on the street and increased with every attack.

With my remaining men I found the Schlütersteg and crossed the Spree without coming under fire, for the Russians were concentrating their efforts on Friedrichstrasse. We eventually reached the Lehrter Station, where one could see signs of the fighting that had taken place there, but no Russians. Once we got beyond the Nordhafen we headed north. My HQ Section leader knew his Berlin well and gave me good directions, but I still think that I could have found my way without his local knowledge. Wherever possible we went through cellars by means of the holes in the walls that had been knocked through as an air raid precaution, so that people could escape if their house was hit. This way we could go the whole length of some streets.

Eventually we came to a police building, possibly the police hospital, as there were policemen on guard at the windows. So we gradually made progress. It was now daylight and at any moment a Russian patrol could emerge from a doorway or yard entrance, so I removed my medals and insignia, as did my comrades, making ourselves unrecognisable as Waffen-SS. We met up with some German soldiers, making their way one by one in the same direction as ourselves.

Then we came across SS-Captain Mundt, who was alone. He was our divisional quartermaster with an office in the Lichterfelde barracks. It was a post he had held since 1934 and so he had never been in combat. Having once helped him with a job, he had always stopped to talk to me ever since. It was he who now told me what had happened to the Mohnke group, of which he had been a member. After they had crossed the Schlütersteg, firing had broken out in Friedrichstrasse after our first break-out attempt, whereupon Mohnke had commented: 'Now they have caught it!'

This comment had caused Mundt to leave the group and make his own way out. I told him that the senseless break-out attempt on Friedrichstrasse had cost my men their lives and that I felt responsible. I told him: 'The Führer is dead and my oath to him over. In future I will pick my own superiors, whether they wear generals' uniforms or not.'

Mundt did not respond, but went on his own way while we carried on to the north. We did not encounter any enemy and it must have been about 1600 hours when we arrived at the Patzenhofer Brewery premises in Prinzenstrasse, where thousands of men were standing around in groups talking and clearly waiting for something. I thought that they were waiting for orders for the next break-out attempt to the north. I mixed in among them looking for anyone I knew, but found no one and the individual groups were distrustful of outsiders and stopped talking whenever an outsider approached. This made me suspicious in turn and I continued my search with my two comrades. I then noticed a large bunker in the middle of the brewery yard with concrete steps leading down below. I handed my sub-machine gun to my men and went down the steps to a curtain, behind which I could hear voices, including Russian ones. I brushed back the curtain and went into a dimly lit large room full of officers, mainly Waffen-SS.

Mohnke was standing in the middle of the room talking to two Russian officers, one apparently a general and the other acting as an interpreter translating all that was being said. I heard Mohnke say: 'Let us sum up. At 1800 hours we hand over the city; the men go into honourable captivity and have to work; the officers will only have to work voluntarily; the staff officers retain their decorations and sidearms and of course their orderlies.'

The interpreter nodded eagerly, whereupon I stepped forward and said: 'And you believe that, Brigadier?'

Mohnke came up to me and said: 'Don't speak unless asked when generals are talking!'

We then had a strong exchange of words in front of the Russians that I will not go into. I stormed out of the room in a rage, threatening to warn the comrades above, as we did not want to end up in the Siberian lead mines. I heard Mohnke call out to two of his officers: 'Bring him back or he will spoil everything!'

But they were unable to stop me and my comrades helped me send them back down the steps into the bunker. Then another officer came after me, it was SS-Captain Mundt, and I said to him angrily: 'What do you want, then?'

He had been present but I had not noticed him. 'Oh, Rogmann,' he said, 'what a fool I have been thinking there was going to be another break-out. You don't know how right you are!'

'Oh yes I do!' I said.

Mundt went on: "No one dared say anything against it and then you burst in and stirred things up. I do not want to surrender and go into captivity either. Please take me with you on another route that will hopefully bring us to freedom!"

When I agreed, my two comrades put their heads together and started whispering to one another. Then they pulled me aside and said: 'Willi, just look at him! He can dress in anything he likes but he will still look like a Prussian officer, even at a distance!'

They were right, of course, but how could I leave him behind? I decided to take him, even if his presence might endanger us. Mundt understood what was happening and said: 'Rogmann, I would rather die than go to Siberia!'

'Of course I will take you with me,' was my reply, 'but I am in charge and you will have to do what you are told without any argument.'

He agreed, but now had to do things our way. I took his officers' hat from his head and flung it away, for it was easily recognisable at a distance, and then his shoulder straps and cut off his runes and stars with my knife. Of course his boots and tailor-made uniform still showed what he was, but we could not do anything about that for the moment. He removed his officers' belt and stuffed his pistol into his hip pocket.

In direct contrast, I was filthy, unkempt and unshaven, with a thick stubble on my face and my pockets bulging. I was wearing my trousers outside my boots and looked an absolute tramp, but in these circumstances, where the Russians were equally dirty, this was perfectly acceptable.

Then one of my comrades said: 'Now we are a foursome, and that is too many to get through. Don't take it wrong, but we prefer to make our own way.'

I sympathised, for they would have fewer difficulties without Mundt. Also Alfred was a Berliner and would soon find them shelter. So I thanked them for the loyalty they had shown and we hugged each other and said our farewells, thinking that it would be for ever. So off I went with Mundt, our first objective being to find civilian clothes.

I did not have to warn the other comrades. The place had thinned out considerably. Of the thousands that had been there standing around before only a few hundred remained and soon there would be even less. They were enthusiastically throwing their weapons on to a pile, on which I threw the sub-machine gun that I had liked so much, after removing the breech block so that no one else could use it.

We had reached Bornholmer Strasse and were crossing an open square when we were suddenly surrounded by a dozen armed foreigners, whose nationality I did not catch. They demanded we put our hands up and surrender.

I played dumb in order to allay their suspicions, with the idea of making a break for it, and this worked. The gang drifted off, looking for other targets, but two of them remained with us and started searching us. This infuriated Mundt. who picked his opponent up by the scruff of his neck and then kicked him hard. I had to join in too and felled my opponent with a hand chop to the throat. He fell without a sound and I grappled in my message pouch for my hidden 7.65 Mauser pistol.

Now we were attacked by the other foreigners, who had seen what had happened. There must have been a dozen of them dancing around us with knives. Mundt threw aside his lifeless opponent and pulled out the pistol from his hip pocket. We stood back to back for all-round defence. Time was not on our side, so I opened fire, as did Mundt. At this range every shot was a hit and soon they were either lying on the ground or in flight.

Then we suddenly had to deal with a far better armed enemy. There were several of them armed with rifles firing at us from only fifty metres away. We returned the fire but, while fifty yards is nothing for a rifle, it is too much for a pistol.

I emptied my magazine and had to change it, as did Mundt, so for a moment we were defenceless. The enemy, who had been dodging about with every shot we fired, noticed this and kept on firing. Two of them must have aimed at Mundt for he was hit twice in the head and fell down dead.

Having changed magazines, I rushed forward to close the range and so got the advantage of my faster firing weapon. I zigzagged as I ran, but they hit me twice, one a graze to the head and another to my lower left arm, which in my anger I only noted as a light blow. But then my enemies suddenly scattered in front of me and I heard sub-machine gun fire coming from behind me.

I had no time to look round to see who had fired, but raced into a doorway on my right. When my other enemies saw me appear, they tried to stop me, but I quickly pulled my second pistol out of my boot top and shot my way through with both hands. I found myself in a long passageway and, quickly looking back, saw a large group of armed Russians coming round a street corner.

I ran down the passage and came to a door at the far end with a key in it. I opened the door, pulled out the key and locked the door from the other side. Then I stood by the doorway listening to my pursuers creeping up. They began to break down the door. There was a crush of them there, so I fired through it a few times with my 7.65 pistol. Howls of pain announced that several of them had been hit, more than one with each round.

It was time to leave. I went across the backyard, climbed the wall into the next yard and so on. I could hear my pursuers some distance behind as they kept shouting. Eventually I came to an old disused cemetery, which gave plenty of cover with its clumps of bushes and big gravestones. I crouched down behind them as my pursuers passed quite close. I did not want to stay here long, as I was still without civilian clothes. When I checked my pistol, I saw that I had only two rounds left, too few for action. I rummaged through my message pouch, which I had stupidly been reluctant to part with, and emptied my pockets. Those contents that would have identified me, such as my paybook and decorations, I stuffed into my message pouch and buried in a hole that I dug with my hands behind a gravestone.

I crept through the cemetery and saw some multi-storied apartment blocks in the distance that looked undamaged. They were occupied and hardly any fighting had taken place in this area while the occupants sat in their cellars. I jumped over the cemetery wall, entered one of the buildings from the rear, and then went up to the second floor and knocked on a door. It opened and a voice came from inside, where two women, mother and daughter, were peacefully sorting out some bed linen. I told them that I needed some civilian clothing to change into. 'But why?' the mother asked naively. 'The Russians won't do anything to you, just look out into the street. You can see them leading German prisoners away peacefully.'

I offered the mother some valuables I had with me and said: 'I only want some old clothes such as your husband does not wear any more.'

So she got me some trousers and a jacket from a cupboard. The jacket was a bit too big and the trousers a bit too short, but these suited me fine. I wanted to look like a foreigner, best of all a Pole, since I spoke a bit of Russian and could pass as a Pole speaking it badly.

But I was not quite finished with these two women. I did not want to change my special boots, but I needed something on my head for, like all soldiers, I felt only half dressed without a hat. When I asked her for one, the woman said: 'I have only one hat and that's my husband's best thing.'

'All right,' I said, 'give it here.'

But before she did so, she spotted my wedding ring and said that the Russians would take it off me if they saw it, which was true, finger and all probably. These avaricious women had made me angry so I decided to leave them a 'present' that would not please them. I quickly pushed my little pistol behind the kitchen cupboard, thinking that it would do me more harm than good as a civilian. However, I kept the two egg grenades that I still had, and stuffed my knife into my boot.

So I said goodbye to the two women and went down to the street. Two Russians standing in the doorway looked at me curiously. I went straight into the attack, accosting them in Russian with: 'Instead of gawping at me, give me something to smoke.'

So they gave me a piece of newspaper and some of their strong Machorka tobacco. Although a non-smoker, I knew how to roll a cigarette Russian style, and the Russians' confidence in me grew as they watched. I then asked them for a light and drew in some smoke. I told them that I had just been visiting my girlfriend, whom I had only been able to see secretly before. As I was about to leave one of them joked that I must have been in my underpants for the last few hours, so we parted on friendly terms.

The street was now empty of victors and their prisoners. I thrust my hands into my pockets and strolled along. I had only gone a little way when I heard a voice from behind me. 'Willi! Wait a moment!'

I thought that nobody knew me here, but the call was repeated and a hand grabbed my arm. I told them in Russian to leave me alone, but then the familiar voice said: 'Willi, don't you speak German any more?'

The two people looking at me, who themselves looked like tramps, were Alfred and his comrade, both now in civilian clothes and no better dressed than myself. We moved aside to avoid drawing attention.

According to Alfred, after we had gone our separate ways, they felt sorry about leaving me alone with Mundt, as they did not think it would turn out well. So they had followed us, but first had to change clothes behind a wall. Both had been carrying haversacks with a civilian jacket and trousers, thinking from the beginning that they would need them at some stage. So they hid their uniforms but in this process lost sight of us. They only found us again when we became involved in the fire fight.

For Mundt they were a minute too late, but firing their sub-machine guns saved me by stopping the Russians. They had then hidden themselves until they could follow the sounds of the chase, which is how they had caught up with me again. Needless to say, we were all delighted to meet up.

Alfred then suggested that we should all go to his home not far away, where he lived with his young wife. I advised against it as he had been seen there in uniform countless times and could easily be betrayed to the Russians, but he insisted that he had no enemies that would do this. I was still sceptical, but it was getting dark and we had better get off the streets, as there was bound to be a curfew. So we set off.

There was a lot of movement on the street. Now that people were no longer confined to their cellars, they were moving around pushing handcarts and carrying parcels. They were also looting the shops, most of which appeared to have no owners present to stop them. The Russians as the occupying power seemed unconcerned and were doing nothing to prevent the looting.

When Alfred announced that his was the next street ahead, I asked him to keep twenty paces behind us and cover our rear in an emergency. He laughed at my cautiousness, but agreed. Looking round the street corner, we saw that it had five-storey buildings on one side, the other being bounded by the two metre brick wall of an industrial site. Parked along the right hand side of the street was a convoy of three-axled American Studebaker trucks, in which ammunition cases could be seen through the partly opened canopies. The trucks were parked closely together with only about two metres between them.

The Russians were so unconcerned that they had made open camp fires alongside about every third truck and were squatting around roasting their delicacies.

Just as Alfred was pointing out which was his apartment, a woman appeared leaning out of the window, her arms held by

Russians. She saw us and cried out in distress: 'Alfred, come quickly! The Russians . . .'

We heard no more as she was pulled back into the room.

We had arranged that we would remain below to cover him, but the other comrade could not be held back and stormed in with him. I called out to Alfred: 'Grab your wife and get out over the backyard! I will cover your retreat!'

They had pulled the sub-machine guns out of their bags, and I prepared my grenades. The sound of their sub-machine guns came from upstairs, alerting the Russians squatting beside their fires, who started going across. They did not notice the dirty Gipsy going behind the third truck and throwing a grenade inside, and again into the last-but-one truck, before heading for the street corner. Not that it mattered, for their time was up.

The blast of the explosion blew me to the end of the street and I blacked out. When I recovered consciousness, all I could see was a sea of rubble. The explosion had destroyed the convoy, knocked down the boundary wall and pushed in all the windows and their frames on the other side of the street. My guardian angel had taken care of me again. I had only suffered bruises, but the Russians had been spattered against the walls. Whether Alfred had managed to escape, I could not stay to find out. I limped away.

TO THE LAST MAN

It was now really dark and I had to find somewhere for the night and get off the streets, which were still alive with looters.

I overtook an old woman pulling a fully loaded handcart and offered to help her take it home. She looked at me sideways: 'I know, you are looking for a place to stay. Unfortunately, not with me. I have two daughters at home and there is coming and going day and night. The Russians just open the door. You know how it is.'

So I had to keep on looking. Eventually I came across an old man coming out of a shop cellar unsuccessfully trying to carry two large boxes on his shoulders. I offered to help. He too saw straight away what I was after. 'I only have two rooms,' he said, 'but my wife is away, so take a box and come along.'

He passed me over a box and we went off like two loaded donkeys. The Russians did not look at us, for people running away do not carry boxes, as those naive lads knew. On our way I discovered what we were carrying. The boxes contained cans of green beans.

'I'll prepare something to eat when we get home,' the old man said, and he did. 'It would be best if you lay down on the bed with a wet cloth on your head and pretend to be ill. The Russians are bound to look in soon and see who I have brought with me.'

This seemed a good idea, and when the Russians looked in shortly afterwards I groaned in Russian that my head hurt and that I thought I had cholera, which sent them off in a hurry. Then we had our meal of green beans and burnt potatoes.

The night was full of the screams of women being raped.

Next morning I had a real Russian cat wash, which went as follows. I rinsed my mouth with the precious water, then put my head back and sprayed it into the air so that it fell over my face, which I then wiped with a cloth. The old man commented that I was still dirty, so I repeated the process.

Again we had green beans and baked potatoes. Clearly that would be the old man's diet for the foreseeable future.

Now I needed to scout out the ground. I asked the old man if he could spare me a couple of buckets. As I did not know if I would be returning, I bade him a provisional farewell and thanked him for his support. He said: 'I have a couple of grandchildren in the same situation as yourself, so it was only natural.'

I went along the street with my buckets looking for a street pump. I found one and stood in the queue for water, as there were quite a few people ahead of me. I half filled the buckets and set off, not back to the old man, but first to Alfred's apartment to find out what had happened. With my buckets no one would suspect me of being on the run. There were many posters ordering all soldiers, Volkssturm, Party members, officials and others to report to the nearest Soviet post or be shot immediately.

When I got to Alfred's street an old Russian soldier was shovelling the remains of his former comrades into ammunition boxes to bury them. When I asked him what had happened, he said that there had been an accident.

Below Alfred's window lay three dead bodies that had been

thrown out of the window. They were my comrades and Alfred's wife. When the Russian saw me looking at them he commented: 'Fascists with no sense of fun!'

I went off with my half filled buckets. The nearer I got to the city centre, the more and stronger the checkpoints I came across. I noticed that they seemed more interested in those leaving the city centre than those entering, which was understandable as fighting had been taking place only the previous day. There was a checkpoint ahead of me where papers were being examined. I stopped and put down my buckets as if taking a rest.

Then a Russian one-and-a-half tonner, one of their own primitive construction that had no battery and whose windscreen wipers were hand operated, drew up and stopped near me. Inside were three men packed close together on the narrow seat, the driver and two officers, with a German civilian standing beside them on the running board. The officer on the outside hit the civilian in the face with his fist, swore at him and threw him off.

This, I thought, is my chance. I quickly went up to the vehicle and asked the Russians if I could help. They were happy to have found someone who could speak Russian and show them the way to the Reichstag. I said: 'I am a Pole and so not at home here, but I do know the way to the Reichstag and can take you there. But there is nothing there for you to take.'

'We just want to scratch our names on the pillars of the Reichstag. Every Russian soldier with legs is making his way to this central point to scratch his name, and if he has a photograph of it he will be a hero back in Russia. Anyone can say he did it, but he needs evidence that he was there. Now stop talking and come!'

This I did as quickly as possible and told the driver to set off. We came to the checkpoint and went through without stopping. When we reached the Reichstag I jumped off the running board, A female supervisor grabbed me and wanted me help clear the rubble. I swore at her in Russian. Then one of the Russians came up to me and asked if I could use a Leica. He had acquired it somehow but did not know how to use it. I checked the camera to see if it had a film in it, then they stood in front of the Reichstag and I took several pictures of them. Then I had to give the camera to the driver for him to take a photograph of me with the two officers.

They were anxious to scratch their names, so I left them without saying goodbye. I wanted to make my way across to Friedrichstrasse to say farewell to my dead comrades if they were still lying there. I thought that the wounded would already have been taken to hospital. Close by was the Charité where during the fighting a point had been made of not taking in military casualties in order to preserve its civilian status, but that probably did not apply any longer.

The Friedrichstrasse was still full of dead and some German prisoners of war were clearing those away on the Weidendammer Bridge. Bulldozer tanks were pushing the burnt out wrecks into the ruins to clear the street.

I still had no papers to identify me, not even the usual Waffen-SS blood group tattoo under the armpit, as I had missed having it done through having been on guard duty when the company was tattooed.

As I passed up Friedrichstrasse into Chausseestrasse I passed a shot-up armoured personnel carrier, a picture of which was later featured in many books. To avoid walking over the dead soldiers lying there, I passed the vehicle on the right side in which there was a small entry hole from a captured Panzerfaust. Several of the occupants had managed to bale out but had then been mown down by machine gun fire. When I reached the place where our way out had ended, I found my comrades lying entangled in death with soldiers of other units. No infantry had been able to get any further, only some armoured vehicles that had been shot up later.

I then looked into the ruins where we had pulled our wounded comrades. They still lay there, not as wounded but dead. The Russians had murdered them with shots at close range, that was obvious. They had been plundered, their pockets opened and their watches taken. Naturally this hit me hard. I stood there and could have howled like a young dog that has lost its master, but I sensed that I was being watched and crept away through the side streets, drawn like a magnet back to the Reichs Chancellery.

I do not know what impelled me, but I made my way through the Tiergarten and over Potsdamer Platz to come to Hermann-Göring-Strasse. There I saw that the boundary wall to the Reichs Chancellery plot had been demolished and one could see over

234

into the garden, where many dead were lying around. (I later learned that the Russians had tasked an engineer battalion to blow down the wall, expecting strong resistance, and that they called it 'The Suicides' Garden' after the many suicides to be found there.) The dead were especially thick around the former fountains in the centre.

I walked around the whole complex like a bored stroller. The Wilhelmstrasse entrance was also open. On a post that had been set up I saw a badly charred corpse that, when I got close, I recognised as Goebbels. Russian soldiers and foreign workers were standing around making comments and making a mockery of his corpse.

I decided to make my way to Lichterfelde and tell Frau Mundt what had happened to her husband, but as I approached the Potsdamer Bridge a new obstacle confronted me. Bulldozers and engineers were making the bridge passable again, but impassable for me. A checkpoint was demanding to see the papers of anyone not a Russian soldier. I was wondering what to do next when the one-and-a-half-tonner came to my rescue once more. They spotted me leaning against a pillar and beckoned me over. Now they wanted to go to Steglitz and asked me if I could help them find it. 'I have more to do than just drive around with you, but since no one else can help you, I will. Only, that is not on!' I said, pointing at the checkpoint.

'Oh, we will soon see about that!' said one of the officers. 'Climb aboard!'

He drew his pistol and, when one of the sentries asked for my papers, he showed him the drawn pistol. 'That's OK then,' said the sentry and let us through.

When we reached Steglitz the Russians were about to thank me and disappear into a house. 'What now?' I asked. 'I have had no breakfast and am terribly hungry and now have a long way to go back into the city!' So they gave me a hunk of bread and a large piece of bacon, and I said goodbye.

In similar cheeky manner Rogmann was finally able to make his way home through Russian occupied territory, cross the Elbe at Magdeburg and get home to his wife in the still American-occupied part of the designated Soviet Zone at Eilsleben. Here, his luck ran out. His jubilant wife told a neighbour in confidence of his return, the word spread and someone betrayed him to the Americans, who captured him still in bed the very next morning.

After the war Rogmann was banished by the East German government to a remote hamlet in the Erzgebirge Mountains, close to the Czechoslovakian border, where he resumed his original trade as a builder.

1 This would have been the Sten Gun, a cheaply manufactured weapon produced in vast quantities.
2 The MG 42 was commonly known as the 'Spandau' from its original place of manufacture.
3 The major tank battle of the Second World War fought at Kursk-Orel in July and August 1943.
4 'Sippenhaft' was the system whereby the whole family of a criminal were arrested and imprisoned.
5 11th SS Panzergrenadier Division 'Nordland'.
6 In the German Army and Waffen-SS potential officers were selected from the ranks and ultimately sent to Officer School before commissioning. In this case a potential officer serving in the ranks with the equivalent of sergeant's rank (Oberjunker).
7 The Iron Cross was awarded for bravery in the ascending order: Second Class, First Class, Knight's Cross, Knight's Cross with Oak Leaves, with Oak Leaves & Swords, and with Oak Leaves, Diamonds & Swords.
8 The Thor mortar was of 600mm calibre with a 5.07m barrel, weighed 120 tons, and could fire 12 shots per hour up to a range of 6,800m. According to General Bokov, writing about General Bezarin's 5th Shock Army, elements of which stormed the Schlesischer station, they also had 2,000 guns and mortars of 80mm calibre and over with orders not to spare the ammunition, for they had just received 2,000 railway wagonloads. The Schlesischer station is now the Ostbahnhof.
9 The senior garrison engineer.
10 The Waffen-SS belt buckle bore the motto 'Meine Ehre heisst Treue' (Loyalty is my Honour).
11 SS-Colonel Peiper of the 1st SS-Panzer Division 'Leibstandarte Adolf Hitler' was accused of slaughtering American prisoners during the Battle of the Bulge offensive.
12 The obsolete machine gun that had been replaced by the MG 42 in general service.
13 The theme of the statue at the Soviet War Cemetery at Treptow Park.
14 Schweizer's breakout from the Zoo Flak-bunker had occurred sometime after midnight and his group managed to get away unscathed during a lull in the fighting, but these conditions did not apply either earlier or later up to the surrender at dawn on 2 May.

Appendix

How believable is Rogmann's account? Though much of it reads like the script of the latest Indiana Jones adventure, there is no doubt of Rogmann's military exploits as the following citation obtained from the former Berlin Documentation Center shows.

CITATION

1st SS Panzer Division
'Leibstandarte Adolf Hitler'
SS-Panzer-Grenadier-Regiment 2

Commendation No: 87
For the Award of the
German Cross in Gold

AWARDED 8 FEB 45

Regtl HQ, 15 Dec 44
(signed)
SS-Obersturmbannführer
and Commanding Officer

Short basis and recommendation of the nominee's superior officer:

SS-Sergeant Major Rogmann, as a member of the Leibstandarte has taken part in all the engagements of the Regiment in the East and in Italy.

In the battle for Rostock in 1941 he was awarded the Iron Cross First Class for his personal courage.

237

In the winter battle for Charkov in February–March 1943 he distinguished himself as a section leader in the 6th Company, SS-Panzer-Grenadier-Regiment 2, by his personal bravery and courage.

Despite being wounded, he always remained with his men until the situation allowed him to seek medical attention. In all, R. was wounded eight times.

On 9 Nov 43 his company, which was under strong enemy pressure, received the order to move to new defensive positions that were already occupied by the bulk of the battalion. On his own initiative, R. attacked the head of the attacking enemy forces with his section and drove them back in close-quarter fighting. As a result of this counterattack the company was able to occupy the positions it had been ordered to.

On 19 Dec 43 the battalion had the task of breaking through the enemy positions in the bushy and woodland area of Korosten, and roll them up. At 0430 hours R. received the order to reconnoitre and find a weak point in the enemy positions. R. carried out his task, returning with prisoners. The attack on these positions at 1000 hours was a complete success, the successful breakthrough bringing the Malin-Korosten airstrip into the battalion's possession. During the attack R. especially distinguished himself by his personal drive.

During the night of 21/22 Dec 43 the enemy attacked our weakly held positions in front of Melini four times with strong forces. R., who was lying in front of the company position with his machine gun, through his exemplary handling and steadfastness with this machine gun and his men, mowed them down, so that the enemy were driven back each time. At 1100 hours the battalion launched an attack on Melini, but the attack was stopped short through the enemy outflanking. Again it was R. with his machine gun that prevented an enemy breakthrough on the flank.

The company moved to new defensive positions in front of Bobrick on 2 Jan 44. Several enemy attacks were successfully beaten back but, after a renewed attack, the enemy were able to break through on either side of the company and surround it, thus cutting it off from the battalion. At 1630 hours the company commander gave the order to break through the enemy lines and re-establish contact with the battalion. Charging forward with his men, R. destroyed three enemy machine gun nests, thus effecting a breach in the enemy line, and took over the protection of the right flank. Once the company was through, R. attacked an enemy position and rejoined the company with six prisoners.

On 5 Jan 44 SS-Sergeant Major Rogmann was occupying an advanced position with his section when the enemy launched an attack on the positions near Katchkian during the morning hours. R. let his position be overrun by tanks and then engaged the charging enemy. Through his cool thinking and his determination he was able to maintain complete control of the situation, the main mass of the enemy being brought down by rifle and machine gun fire. He then engaged those of the Bolsheviks that had got through to this position in close-quarter fighting until the area was cleared. R.'s courageous behaviour was decisive here and prevented a sudden enemy breakthrough.

On 6 Jan 44 R. and his section were the first to break back into our own positions that had been occupied by the enemy near Pietki, and then pinned down enemy resistance with fire until it was possible to reoccupy the whole of the position once more. R. destroyed three enemy machine gun nests during this engagement.

In the hard defensive fighting southwest of Proskuroff, the enemy attacked the battalion's positions on the northwestern edge of Andreievka with armoured support during the evening. The enemy cut through our weakly occupied lines and established themselves on the northern edge of Andreievka. Eight enemy tanks tried to force their way into the village, four of them being destroyed by our own self-propelled guns. R. received the task of establishing the strength of the enemy on the northern edge of Andreievka. At 2000 hours he attacked the enemy with a storm troop, using the enemy's surprise to split up the enemy combat teams. The enemy fled, leaving 20 dead and two prisoners behind. This decisive act enabled the battalion to establish a new security line on this position.

At 2000 hours on 2 Apr 44, R. received the task of launching an attack on two enemy occupied farms near Losiacz. R. was the first to commence clearing the farms, which were taken after some hard close-quarter fighting, the enemy having to leave

several dead behind them in the farms. Several enemy counterattacks that followed shortly afterwards were beaten back successfully by R. until he received the order to redeploy to the edge of a wood nearby. R. covered the redeployment and inflicted such heavy casualties on the enemy spearheads that the new positions could be occupied unhindered by the enemy.

In all his engagements with the enemy, SS-Sergeant Major Rogmann has proved himself to be exemplary, and was awarded the Close Combat Clasp in Gold on 1 Sep 44. In view of his exceptional personal courage and his ever determined drive, I consider him worthy of the award of the

'German Cross in Gold'

and request that it be awarded to him.

Comments of the Divisional Commander:

SS-Sergeant Major Rogmann has shown himself to be a manifestly brave NCO in all the engagements of the 1st SS-Panzer-Division 'LSSAH'.

I request that he be awarded the German Cross in Gold for his exceptional bravery.

> (*signed*)
> SS-Oberführer and
> Divisional Commander

Comments of the 1st SS-Panzer-Corps:

I approve this commendation

> (*signed*)
> The Commanding General
> SS-Gruppenführer and
> Lieutenant General of the Waffen-SS

Comments of HQ 6th SS-Panzer Army:

The proposal is approved

> J. Dietrich
> SS-Oberstgruppenführer and
> Colonel General of Armour
> of the Waffen-SS

This citation is also notable for omitting an important incident involving Rogmann in late March 1944. The 'Leibstandarte' had been encircled with the rest of the 1st Panzer Army near Kamenets-Podolski on the western edge of the Ukraine, when their officers were all flown out on orders from above in order to reform the division in Flanders. Rogmann, then a sergeant, was left commanding the remains of his battalion, and eventually broke out with only six men. When he reported back to the division in Flanders, his reappearance was totally unexpected.

Index

Index

Index

Index